THE GOOD FRIDAY AGREEMENT

THE GOOD FRIDAY
AGREEMENT

SIOBHÁN FENTON

Biteback Publishing

First published in Great Britain in 2018 by
Biteback Publishing Ltd
Westminster Tower
3 Albert Embankment
London SE1 7SP
Copyright © Siobhán Fenton 2018

ISBN 978-1-78590-373-1

10 9 8 7 6 5 4 3 2

A CIP catalogue record for this book is available from the British Library.

Set in Adobe Caslon Pro and Trade Gothic

Printed and bound in Great Britain by
CPI Group (UK) Ltd, Croydon CR0 4YY

CONTENTS

INTRODUCTION

In April 1998, the seemingly impossible happened. Northern Ireland's political parties agreed on a peace treaty bringing an end to the bloody conflict that had engulfed the region for the past thirty years. Some 3,700 people had died in the bloodshed, which had become known by the grimly understated euphemism 'the Troubles'.

I was five years old when the Good Friday Agreement was signed. My parents recall with great distress going out to vote in the referendum held in May that year on whether or not to approve the political parties signing it. They later remembered the intense anxiety and trepidation that followed the referendum as they waited to see if this thing, this new 'Good Friday Agreement' experiment really was the end or merely another false start only to be followed by the bitter backlash of more bloodshed. After a botched and short-lived ceasefire just a few years before, we were all too aware of how false hope could add to the sense of despair and helplessness amid the otherwise continuous dreary horror that had come to characterise much of Northern Irish existence. Across the region, people waited anxiously to see if or how power-sharing would work, desperate that this would be the means through which peace would finally take hold and Northern Ireland's nightmare would finally end after decades of unimaginable and inexcusable horror. There was a growing sense that Northern Ireland had long since reached its limits and there was only so much trauma left to take before we would all lose our minds collectively.

The Good Friday Agreement was a significant event, we all knew. But we did not know if it would usher in peace, or merely give enough progress to spark a major backlash of violence in the form of a huge atrocity or killing spree. My mother would switch on our thick '90s box television set every evening while she attempted to distract herself making dinner, yet always watching the news out of the corner of her eye for another mass murder, another massacre and another sign that the Good Friday Agreement had failed like all the measures before it.

It's a period that I was too young to understand at the time, something restricted to 'big people' talk between adults from which us children were excluded. In many ways such a period of trepidation is simply unfathomable for my generation precisely because of those efforts our parents made towards peace, which mean we simply lack the horrific memories capable of framing such events adequately.

After the referendum passed and power-sharing was established, a whole nation's hopes were pinned on the Stormont Parliament. As the rusty doors creaked open for the first time in decades, a weary population held its breath. As the first elected politicians walked through those doors and into the parliamentary chamber, there was a palpable sense that this was it – Northern Ireland, long out of last chances and final warnings, had its last chance at normality.

Mercifully, the anxiety that surrounded the Good Friday Agreement experiment in 1998 soon turned out to be unfounded. While not without its hiccups and problems in its initial years, power-sharing at Stormont succeeded in finally beginning to heal our deeply divided society. After decades of bloodshed and division, it seemed Northern Ireland was finally on the path to peace. The Agreement was celebrated the world over and heads of state around the globe urged the parties to work together and ensure the region did not slip once again into the dark days that had gone before. The moment is still cited by many politicians and international relations experts around the world as an example of an iconic peace process to which other divided societies should aspire.

Yet, twenty years on, it's a rosy image that few in contemporary Northern Ireland might recognise.

Once the world's media packed up, the cameras stopped rolling and global heads of state flew home, Northern Ireland has ceased to be much discussed or understood. Indeed, one could get the impression that Northern Ireland has been suspended in time since the Good Friday Agreement was signed, the region and its people entirely frozen at the moment the parties put their pens to the document, like an odd fairy tale whereby a nation of one million people slipped into slumber like post-conflict sleeping beauties.

Northern Ireland's story did not end in 1998. Arguably, it only entered a different phase of complexity. While the society is no longer engulfed in violent conflict, hopes that a normalised society would emerge have yet to be realised. Instead, Northern Ireland continues to be home to a deeply unsettled and divided region still split along the Protestant–Catholic axis. It is a society in which armed paramilitary gangs, although no longer the overt scourge they once were, continue to carry out 'punishment' shootings, plant bombs and threaten security forces on an almost weekly basis. It is a society still struggling with questions over how or even if it should acknowledge its dark past. It is a society still grappling with whether or not to accept modern social changes and which continues to define LGBT people as lesser in law and to arrest women for having abortions.

To further complicate matters, it is also a society which now faces particular and entirely unexpected challenges on a national and an international stage due to the UK voting to leave the European Union in 2016, as Northern Ireland is the only part of the UK that shares a land border with another EU country, in the form of the Republic of Ireland. Similarly, stability in the region was further destabilised when the Westminster government entered into a pact with one of Northern Ireland's parties in 2017 after the general election failed to grant any of the English parties a majority government.

Particularly troublingly, most recently Northern Ireland has been left without any government at all following a power-sharing collapse in January 2017, when the main nationalist and unionist parties could no longer agree to share power and govern together.

This book does not seek to underplay or ignore the major role the Good Friday Agreement played in Northern Ireland's peace process. However, it asserts that on the twentieth anniversary year of the Good Friday Agreement, we owe it to ourselves and each other to question what peace we have and on what it is based.

It seeks to do this for three reasons. Firstly, at a local level: because Northern Ireland deserves better. It is hoped that this can contribute to greater understanding of and reignite debate over the many aspects of life in Northern Ireland that have slipped into being the status quo but ought to be challenged and contested.

Secondly, at a national level: because the UK's own failure to understand or often even acknowledge Northern Ireland's existence holds the nation as a whole back. This tendency has most recently been thrown into sharp relief as events such as Brexit, when it was only after the UK voted to leave the European Union that many people (both politicians and voters) realised they shared a land border with the EU in the form of Northern Ireland and this resulted in them scrambling to swot up on their unfamiliar cousin in time for Brexit negotiations – often unsuccessfully so. Similarly, when the UK government entered a pact with Northern Ireland's Democratic Unionist Party following the 2017 general election, it once again became clear that many voters and even political experts were unaware of Northern Ireland as online searches of 'What is the DUP' jumped to vertiginous heights, becoming the eighth most googled question in the UK in 2017 (slotting in just below 'What is waterboarding' and above 'What is Pink's real name'). Simply put, it is in Great Britain's best interests to have at least a basic awareness of this part of the UK, which for decades has been marginalised and misunderstood.

Thirdly, at an international level: within the context of wider discussions about Great Britain's global legacy of colonialism and imperialism. Northern Ireland is merely one example of the ways in which Great Britain has colonised other countries throughout history for its own economic and strategic interests before withdrawing once they cease to be of use (though in Northern Ireland's case, this withdrawal has arguably been merely psychological). This has been most brutally observed in countries such as India and Uganda. Britain's Plantation in Northern Ireland has fortunately never been as brutal or violent as its oppression of some other nations, largely due to the white privilege enjoyed by the overwhelming majority of Northern Irish people, and so the limits of comparison to other colonised nations must not be overstretched. However, it is important to consider the ways in which Britain interacts with countries with which it has had a colonial relationship and to look at the issue of colonial legacy, memory, trauma, responsibility, reparations and other recourses to justice.

WRITING THIS BOOK

Like many young people growing up in Northern Ireland, I was filled with an urgent desire to leave as soon as I could. Northern Ireland, it was often said, was an interesting place to have come from but a much less interesting place to be in. When I was nineteen and went to university in England, I latched on to my way out with a deep sense of relief. Northern Irishness was something odd, awkward and imbued with a kind of pain that could make English people feel uncomfortable just from hearing your voice. It was something I was keen to shrug off during my time in England, although it was almost invariably betrayed by my gruff accent and gobbledygook name.

I began my career as a journalist based in London, mainly reporting on British politics and social affairs. In March 2017, I was sent on assignment by my editors at *The Independent* to cover the snap election in Northern Ireland, which had been called to try to save power-sharing. Uncertain of how long negotiations might take, I booked a one-way flight from London to Belfast, thinking it would take a week or perhaps two for a deal to be reached. One year on, the Parliament at Stormont lies vacant as negotiations continue, and that return flight has yet to be booked. This book has been the product of my reporting and researching during that year. It was written primarily over the course of 2017 when the main nationalist and unionist parties refused to share power together. During this period, I was based in Stormont (Northern Ireland's Parliament building) while negotiations were taking place between the parties to see if the government could be salvaged. During this time, I also attended inquests of 'cold-case' murders from the Troubles which are only now coming before the courts. I also interviewed people from across different communities and perspectives and invited them to discuss the issues that they felt most urgently needed addressing twenty years on from the Good Friday Agreement.

Like almost everyone from this place, my feelings towards my home country are complex. If growing up in Northern Ireland has taught me one thing, it is to be wary of blind national pride, as it has the potential to be a harmful and toxic thing with an unnerving capacity to dehumanise those who are considered to run outside of our national identity. Therefore, I will not describe my feelings towards the place as a sense of love or *duty* per se, but perhaps a complex mix of responsibility, affection and tenderness towards this extremely abnormal place which has been the site of so much suffering. This book does not seek to be party political in advancing the views or agenda of any one party or any one 'side'. But it will of course be deeply political due the nature of life in Northern Ireland, which has a relentless way of politicising the quotidian quite unlike anywhere else in the world. The only political stance I wish to advance is that Northern Ireland's peace process is far from resolved and that the progress in the region has been hampered by an unwillingness both locally and internationally to look squarely at the kind of peace we have, on what it is based and where it is going. I seek only to share the experiences and stories of people here in the hope that better awareness of this place may result in better understanding of it. Beyond that, the political solutions will be for the individual reader to contemplate and question.

I am conscious that I do not wish this book to appear to be dismissive of the efforts that the generation above made. Their work in ensuring that elusive concept of peace finally took hold should never be underestimated or downplayed. However, I am also aware that so many of those efforts were made in my generation's name – the refrain often uttered was that this had to be done 'for the sake of the wee ones'. Now the 'wee ones' are grown up and being arrested for having abortions, treated as lesser if they are LGBT, go to solely 'Protestant' or 'Catholic' schools, live on solely

'Protestant' or 'Catholic' streets and suffer from intergenerational trauma. It is in this context, therefore, that I feel it is important for the post-peace generation to take up this ethos of those who brought us peace, not to erase their efforts, but to continue their ethos in pushing for Northern Ireland to do better for the most vulnerable people for whom it is home.

This book seeks to shine a light on some of the main issues in contemporary Northern Irish society by sharing the stories of some of the people most affected by these issues, as well as explaining the challenges that different groups both face and represent. It is by no means an exhaustive exploration. Twenty years of any society is far too rich and complex to be distilled into one book. However, it seeks to arm readers with an awareness of some of the main issues in the hope that it will increase their awareness and understanding of many of the core issues facing Northern Ireland at this time. I hope it can be of use in some small way in informing discussions both locally and internationally as we mark this milestone of the Good Friday Agreement's twentieth anniversary.

At this critical junction of two decades, it is not enough to merely say that Northern Ireland is at peace. Instead, we must look critically at what kind of peace has emerged, at what cost it came and whether it is something we can continue to take for granted. Through this exploration, we can best understand how this peace can be protected in the present day and further secured in the future.

This book is also inevitably shaped by my experiences as a Northern Irish person. One of the questions I am most frequently asked by editors, producers and fellow journalists from elsewhere in the UK about my reporting is this: am I Protestant or am I Catholic? It is a question asked apparently on the assumption that my writing is written either from a Catholic perspective or a Protestant one and that knowing clearly which 'side' I am on will alert them to the biases and prejudices in my work, or what in academia tends to be referred to with the euphemism of 'positionality'. I can understand why it is a question that people unfamiliar with Northern Ireland ask. Nonetheless, it is a question to which I do not have a clear or simple answer.

It is a question I have had considerable reservations about addressing, as it is a deeply personal one. But, knowing it is one that might otherwise be in the reader's mind throughout this book, I will try to address it as fully as I can now. The true answer, which will no doubt be a disappointment anyone hoping for a straightforward one, is that I am not quite either. I was born to an English father and a Northern Irish Catholic mother at the tail end of the conflict. At the time of their marriage in 1985, relationships such as theirs were known as 'mixed marriages' and were taboo in Northern Ireland. In Republican communities especially, there was strict policing of relationships across what were considered to be 'enemy lines'. In particular, Catholic women in relationships with Protestant men or Englishmen suspected of having connections to the army or MI5 were considered the most objectionable. During the conflict, such women were often subjected to a horrific process known as 'tarring and feathering', whereby they would be dragged from their homes by the Irish Republican Army (IRA), shaved bald, tied to a lamppost, covered in hot tar and then doused in feathers in a sadistic act of humiliation to punish their perceived 'disloyalty'.

Belfast at that time was a dangerous place to have an English accent, as was shown most horrifyingly when two Englishmen were effectively lynched as they drove past an IRA funeral in the west of the city in 1988. After locals became suspicious of the strangers and heard their English accents, they formed a mob around their car, dragged the men from the vehicle and viciously beat them, before driving them to a secluded area where they were ruthlessly executed. It later emerged that the men were off-duty soldiers. Many people, particularly in Catholic communities, were deeply mistrustful of anyone with an English accent.

As a result, after they married, my parents moved to England to start our family, as far as possible from the IRA, from the threat of being tarred and feathered and from lynch mobs sparked by English accents. My siblings and I were born in Southampton and lived there until the IRA declared their 1994 ceasefire, after which my parents hoped it would now be safe to return and moved back to Northern Ireland. I was three years old when we made the move. I am therefore part of a generation known in Northern Ireland as the 'peace babies' or the 'ceasefire babies', as my peers and I largely have few memories of the conflict itself and instead have mostly encountered it through its shadow. For me, this was true bar one traumatic incident, and I have known more of Northern Ireland's peace process than its violent days. Following our return after the IRA ceasefire, my family was raised in a little village in a rural stretch just outside Belfast, which was mostly composed of recently married young Catholic couples from West Belfast who moved there specifically to raise their children away from violence and Republicanism. My upbringing was therefore primarily Catholic, as almost all of our neighbours, classmates and friends were Catholic. However, as my father was English and had had a very brief stint training in the British Army (though he was never involved in any combat), he fell within the Northern Irish context of being 'Protestant' due to being associated with England and Britishness. This meant that many in our community considered our family a 'mixed family' which was not quite Protestant or Catholic, inhabiting something of a grey area.

When with my father, I would be assumed to be a Protestant child due to his accent. Conversely, when with my mother, I would be read or perceived as being a Catholic child. This resulted in very different experiences of police or the British Army, who would naturally relax when they encountered my father, who was considered 'one of them', in ways that they would not around my mother. Similarly, Catholics or Republicans would speak with an ease around my mother while stiffening upon hearing my father's accent. One of the key ways in which people in Northern Ireland work out which 'side' someone is on is through their name. In that regard, my name has also often proved confusing for people due to my first name being in the Irish language, and therefore read as being Catholic or nationalist, while my surname, in its stiff Englishness, would not be out of place on an English MP or a character in a Jane Austen novel. My positioning in the Northern Irish context was therefore somewhat fluid while I was growing up, being at various times within or without, considered at once both and neither. Whether this has given me a useful perspective through which to view Northern Irish society from multiple sides, or is so odd an experience as to entirely invalidate my ability to understand either, will be for the reader to decide.

LANGUAGE AND TERMINOLOGY

As we will see, language and terminology are highly politicised and fiercely contested in Northern Ireland. Throughout this book, I have used the standard terms generally used by mainstream media outlets and the legal or official terms for places and regions, as they are generally deemed the most neutral terms used in reporting. For instance, I have referred to the region as Northern Ireland, as that is its official name and is generally considered the most neutral term, though I acknowledge that some in the Protestant/unionist community prefer the term 'Ulster' or 'the province', while some in the Catholic/nationalist community prefer the term 'North of Ireland' or 'the six counties'. Similarly, the name of the region's second city is deeply controversial: unionists prefer to refer to it as 'Londonderry', while nationalists call it 'Derry'. As a result, the term 'Derry-Londonderry' is used by many media outlets and government bodies in Northern Ireland as a means of acknowledging this tension while not passing a judgement on the validity of either perspective. For the same reasons, the term 'Derry-Londonderry' is used throughout this book.

CHAPTER ONE

A BRIEF HISTORY OF THE TROUBLES

Full disclosure: what follows is not a definitive, objective, exhaustive history of the Troubles conflict. Nor could it be. There can be no one, sole, definitive, objective history of the Troubles.

Any writer of history who claims to offer a definitive document on an event or community is trading in snake oil – at worst wilfully misleading and at best self-delusional. This is true of any portrayal of the past, which cannot be viewed through one lens alone but is best approached by considering different accounts, perspectives and versions.

This limitation is particularly acute when writing a history of a conflict which pivots on 'two sides', each having vastly varied understandings and interpretations of historical events. Indeed, much of the conflict in Northern Ireland itself stems from the different communities fiercely contesting historical events.

Nor is it merely the case that there is a 'Protestant history of the Troubles' or a 'Catholic history of the Troubles', although of course many conflicting accounts do differ along these ethno-religious lines. Rather, a reading of events centred on working-class people's experiences might yield different results from one which prioritises the middle-class experience. Similarly so with a history centred on the experiences of women, LGBT people, ethnic minorities or people with disabilities.

Therefore, what follows is a history of events which I consider important in giving a framework to understand the main issues involved in causing and constituting the Troubles conflict as well as the parallel peace process climaxing in the Good Friday Agreement. Of course, it is not exhaustive. While it seeks to present a history as free from ideological bent and bias as possible, there are no doubt other events that other authors would include or prioritise.

For the reader who is unfamiliar with Northern Irish history, therefore, reading other histories and accounts in addition to this is encouraged as providing further context and an awareness of some of the contested histories of the region.

THE ULSTER PLANTATION

Although the Troubles itself largely took place between the late 1960s and late 1990s, the roots of the conflict stretch back some 400 years, to the sixteenth century.

Prior to this time, the English had had some considerable presence in neighbouring Ireland but never succeeded in subsuming the island totally under their power. During his reign, Henry VIII was keen to neutralise the threat of having a Catholic enclave just off his shores. The newly Protestant monarch feared a Papist attack could be launched as relations between him and Rome further soured. In 1541, he was declared King of Ireland.

The Ulster Plantation began in earnest in the early seventeenth century under James I, as the British forcibly confiscated land and property from the native Irish and gave it to thousands of trusted Protestants from England and Scotland instead. The scheme benefited Britain as it stripped potentially rebellious Irish Catholics of their land and prominence and transferred it to loyal British Protestants who could be counted on to support the crown. In turn, it benefited the planters financially and socially, as through the scheme they received not only valuable property and land but also considerable social influence and power as they were installed as the new ruling class.

However, a further dynamic also affected how many of the planters perceived themselves – a crucial dynamic that helps explain some of the mindset of hardline loyalists to this day. Many planters considered themselves to be doing God's work in setting up home in Ulster, a region they considered to be a promised land which they had a divine right to own and to rule. Following the intense religious tensions of the Reformation, they considered themselves to be righteously subduing errant and damned Catholics by instilling the correct and true religion.

Under the Plantation, a number of discriminatory practices were enacted against the native Irish communities. The two communities seldom mixed. Many present-day Protestants are direct descendants of the Protestant planters, while many present-day

Catholics are direct descendants of the native Irish Catholic communities.

Therefore, it is important to note at this stage the terminology that emerged when describing the two communities in Northern Ireland. When discussing the Troubles, the common terms used for the conflicting 'sides' are 'Protestants' and 'Catholics'. This stems from long-held terminology dating back to the Plantation era. The terms are, however, somewhat misleading and risk giving the unfortunate and over-simplistic impression that the conflict is a religious war. There can be no doubt that religion plays a part in both groups' identities; however, the terms 'Protestant' and 'Catholic' are convenient linguistic signifiers for much more complex identities and conceal as much as they convey about the real causes of division. When people in Northern Ireland speak of 'Protestants' in the context of the Troubles, they refer to the culture and identity of these English and Scottish planters who identified strongly with the Protestant faith but also with English and Scottish culture, who consider themselves to be British and have a reverence for and loyalty to the British monarchy. Similarly, when we speak of 'Catholics' in the context of the Troubles, this tends to indicate not only people of the Roman Catholic faith but also the culture of the native Irish communities, for instance a desire to see Ireland self-determined rather than ruled by Britain or the British, and an affinity for Irish cultural pursuits such as Gaelic sports or the language.

Thus, when we speak of Protestant and Catholic communities in conflict, we are not speaking of an ecclesiastical war. The unfortunate terms wrongly give the impression that people in Northern

Ireland are rioting on the streets over theological issues such as whether Christ truly transubstantiates in the Eucharist, or the authority of the Pope, which is not the case. Rather, the terms Protestant and Catholic are long-standing labels which reflect ethno-nationalist divisions dating back to the Ulster Plantation – of which religion is an aspect of community division but not the defining characteristic.

This distinction is particularly worth noting as Northern Ireland, like so many other parts of the Western world, is becoming increasingly secular as the social role of Christianity wanes. As the old joke in Northern Ireland goes, you may be an atheist, but are you a Catholic atheist, or a Protestant atheist? Regardless of personal religious belief, Northern Ireland people are still largely pigeonholed as Catholic or Protestant depending on their links to Irish native or British planter culture.

As the planters settled in the region, a status quo was soon established. The Protestant community held political power and continued to wield most influence, while Catholics were discriminated against, with laws limiting their rights to own land, vote or participate in business.

In the southern two thirds of the island of Ireland, rebellion against British rule was particularly strong and escalated throughout the nineteenth century. The Easter Rising of 1916, centred in Dublin, was the breakthrough which finally gathered enough momentum for the south to gain independence.

However, when the south declared itself independent of Britain, the north did not. The unionist majority continued to consider itself British and did not seek independence, instead preferring to stay in the UK. Therefore, when the southern part of the island was given independence, the island was partitioned in two. Six counties in the north would remain in the UK, while the other twenty-six would become the Irish Free State and later the Republic of Ireland.

THE BIRTH OF NORTHERN IRELAND

Northern Ireland came into being on 3 May 1921.

To unionists, the new state represented victory as they had succeeded in staving off the threat that they would be a Protestant minority in a new Irish state. For now, at least, Northern Ireland was still British.

However, the relief felt by unionists was momentary. From Northern Ireland's inception, many unionists were subsumed by paranoia and uncertainty.

When their ancestors had first set foot in the region 400 years earlier as founding fathers in the Ulster Plantation, they had quickly acquired a siege mentality, perceiving themselves as a frontier community fighting off dangerous rebels. This mindset was evidenced in attitudes towards locals, who were often perceived as unpredictable troublemakers who were determined to force the planters out. At times, this siege mentality lingers linguistically in much of the language used by loyalists, such as the maxims 'no surrender' and 'not an inch'.

Fear that they too could lose their Britishness persisted, along with profound suspicion of the state they considered their sworn enemy, just across the border. Closer to home, they also perceived similar threats from the nationalist or Catholic community within Northern Ireland. Many Catholics were deeply bitter at partition and continued to aspire towards a united Irish state, free from British control or influence. Many were hostile towards or unaccepting of the new Northern Irish state, which they saw as having no legitimacy, representing a mere unfortunate stage on the road to ultimate reunification.

From the start, the Northern Irish state was one in which Catholics were not treated as equal to the Protestant community and viewed variously as odd aberrations outside mainstream Protestant culture or as a ticking time bomb for rebellion, determined to undermine the whole state.

Many among the Protestant ruling class therefore regarded Catholics with suspicion and fear. As Ulster Unionist Party leader David Trimble said in a 1998 speech: 'Ulster Unionists, fearful of being isolated on the island, built a solid house, but it was a cold house for Catholics. And Northern nationalists, although they had a roof over their heads, seemed to us as if they meant to burn the house down.'

In this state of paranoia, a number of steps were taken to marginalise the Catholic population and secure Protestant supremacy. Those who did so acted in good faith, as they considered themselves to be reducing the risk of unreliable and disloyal Catholics wreaking havoc on the fledgling state. However, it established a system of discrimination and oppression which was to sow the seeds of long-term alienation and division which eventually sparked the conflict.

The first council elections in Northern Ireland saw unionists win control in some two thirds of councils. However, some with nationalist majorities immediately began unsettling the state through symbolic votes to secede from Northern Ireland and join the Irish Free State. Fearing this could represent the beginnings of nationalist attempts to undermine the new Northern Ireland, reforms were introduced in 1922 to infringe upon Catholic voting rights. Proportional representation was abolished and instead replaced by the first-past-the-post system, which would return more unionist politicians. As a result, nationalists lost their majorities in thirteen of the twenty-four councils that they controlled.

This was further compounded through redrawing of electoral boundaries to artificially create unionist majorities in nationalist areas. The most overt instance of this practice occurred in the city of Derry-Londonderry, where 10,000 nationalist voters returned eight political representatives, while 7,500 unionist voters returned twelve.

Furthermore, the Northern Irish state did not operate on modern democratic principles of one vote per person, instead using a number of conditions on votes in order to further disenfranchise Catholics. Voting in local governments was open only to ratepayers and their spouses. Therefore, only homeowners and their wives could vote. The homeless and those living with their families or as lodgers could not vote. Subsequently, unionist politicians sought to limit Catholics' access to housing in order to ensure the 'correct' people received homes and the democratic rights that came with them.

Local politicians sitting on council housing committees had

the power to allocate new homes. As new houses were built, they ensured that they went to the Protestant community. In 1963, the chairman of Enniskillen housing committee spoke candidly of the practice, saying:

> The council will decide what wards the houses are to be built in. We are not going to build houses in the South Ward and cut a rod to beat ourselves later on. We are going to see that the right people are put in these houses and we are not going to apologise for it.

In 1968, a senior unionist politician wrote of his unease at the way in which Catholics had been systematically disenfranchised, in private correspondence to the Northern Ireland Cabinet. He said:

> If ever a community had a right to demonstrate against a denial of civil rights, Derry is the finest example. A Roman Catholic and nationalist city has for three or four decades been administered (and none too fairly administered) by a Protestant and Unionist majority and secured by a manipulation of the ward boundaries for the sole purpose of retaining Unionist control.
>
> I was consulted by [then Northern Ireland Prime Minister] Sir James Craig at the time it was done. Craig thought that the fate of our constitution was on a knife edge at the time and that, in the circumstances, it was defensible on the basis that the safety of the State is the supreme law. It was most clearly understood that the arrangement was to be a temporary measure – five years was mentioned.

Any projections that such measures were to be temporary faded as they continued to be the status quo. Many Catholics boycotted what they considered to be a rigged system and ceased to vote or run as electoral candidates. In many cases, elections became mere formalities as unionist candidates ran unopposed and were returned with landslides.

Elsewhere in public life, alienation of and discrimination against Catholics was rife. A 1943 survey found the civil service to be overwhelmingly Protestant. Among the lower ranks, 10 per cent of jobs were held by Catholics. Among the middle ranks, this dropped to 6 per cent. At the top rank, not a single Catholic was employed among the fifty-five posts.

Similar discrimination existed among the police force, which recruited almost exclusively from the Protestant/unionist community. Many Catholics also perceived the name given to the police force to be another deliberate slight to deter their participation further. It was called the Royal Ulster Constabulary (RUC), using both the unionist name for Northern Ireland, 'Ulster', and also invoking the royal family, whom many Catholics considered a foreign colonial presence.

Other key resources such as universities and the creation of towns were also deliberately put in Protestant areas, despite Catholic areas often having greater need, adding further to many Catholics' sense of grievance.

One government minister in the Northern Ireland Parliament, Basil Brooke, who later went on to become Prime Minister of the region, said in one speech: 'Many in the audience employ Catholics, but I have not one about my place. Catholics are out to destroy

Ulster with all their might and power. They want to nullify the Protestant vote and take all they can out of Ulster, then see it go to hell.'

When Northern Ireland Prime Minister James Craig was asked if he stood by his minister's strongly worded remarks, he gave his approval, saying: 'He spoke entirely on his own when he gave the speech, but there is not one of my colleagues who does not entirely agree with him, and I would not ask him to withdraw one word he said.'

The London government was aware of how the Catholic community was being treated but adopted a policy of not interfering, judging that it was a matter for the Northern Irish Parliament to determine themselves. In 1928, a delegation appealed to the Conservative Home Secretary to act against Catholic voter suppression. However, he told them it was a matter for the Northern Irish Parliament and subsequently wrote to Prime Minister Craig: 'I don't know whether you would care at any time to discuss the matter with me; of course I am always at your disposal. But beyond that, "I know my place", and don't propose to interfere.'

His remarks echo generations later, as they remain the UK government's official position to this day when lobbied on human rights and equality issues, such as abortion access and same-sex marriage in Northern Ireland.

James Craig summarised the reality of the established order as he told his Parliament: 'All I boast of is that we are a Protestant Parliament and a Protestant state.' His words were designed to reassure Protestants that they were standing strong to protect their culture against the much-feared threat of Irish reunification. To

Catholic ears, however, it was an admission of a discriminatory system in which they were cast as outsiders.

THE CIVIL RIGHTS MOVEMENT

The 1960s was a decade of social revolution throughout the world, be it massive social changes in Britain, the black civil rights movement in the US or student protests in Paris. Even Northern Ireland, a place not known for its progressive politics, could not resist the wider social revolutions around it, and the revolutionary era gave the civil rights movement even greater energy and inspiration.

The Northern Ireland Civil Rights Association (NICRA) was founded in 1967 by members of the Catholic/nationalist community in a bid to push for equality. UK-wide post-war educational reforms had created a Catholic middle class which was better positioned to mount a coordinated campaign highlighting discriminatory practices under the unionist government.

Hope for reform had increased as new Northern Ireland Prime Minister Terence O'Neill entered office in 1963. The moderate unionist was vocally more sympathetic to the Catholic population. In an oft-quoted speech, he tried to explain to his unionist colleagues that ending Catholic alienation could actually increase stability in Northern Ireland:

It is frightfully hard to explain to Protestants that if you give Roman Catholics a good job and a good house they will live like Protestants because they will see neighbours with cars and television sets; they will refuse to have eighteen children. But if a Roman Catholic is jobless and lives in the most ghastly hovel, he will rear eighteen children on National Assistance.

O'Neill sought to achieve this vision of an integrated Catholic community by making a number of symbolic gestures towards them, including meeting with his counterpart in the Irish Free State, Seán Lemass, as well as visiting Catholic schools. His approach horrified the more extreme elements of hardline unionism, some of whom took to throwing stones, flour and eggs at him during official visits.

Across the Irish Sea, agitation against anti-Catholic discrimination had also begun to gain momentum. In 1965, the Campaign for Democracy in Ulster was formed in Westminster by a group of Labour MPs in order to lobby for change.

NICRA self-consciously modelled its work and style on the black civil rights movement in the US, replicating practices such as singing the civil rights song 'We will overcome' during protests and other events. The group's key demands were: one vote per person (thereby ending rules which meant only ratepayers and their spouses could vote); redrawing of electoral boundaries; a transparent system for housing allocation; and anti-discrimination laws to prohibit the marginalisation of minority groups.

The group's first major action came in 1968, when nationalist MP Austin Currie squatted in a house in County Tyrone. Two Catholic families squatting in the area had applied to live in the home but had their applications rejected. Instead, the house had been allocated by a local unionist politician to a nineteen-year-old Protestant woman who was secretary to the politician's solicitor, who was himself a unionist parliamentary candidate. The same politician who allocated the home to the young woman rather than either of the two Catholic families had also allegedly opposed the building of homes for Catholics elsewhere in the area. For many Catholics, the case was one of clear discrimination and an embodiment of the oppression they faced under unionism.

Currie had raised the matter repeatedly in the local council, Stormont and the House of Commons. After his appeals fell on deaf ears, he decided to take matters into his own hands and squatted in the house. The RUC removed him but the stunt highlighted the issue and inspired collective action by nationalists around Northern Ireland.

A march was organised to call for housing reform, to be held in the city of Derry-Londonderry. The unionist government banned the event. Activists insisted on marching regardless. Video footage from news teams reporting on the event captured the RUC using violence against the demonstrators. RUC officers were seen beating peaceful protesters with batons, as well as using water cannon to disperse crowds. Mayhem ensued, resulting in multiple injuries. The video footage, a recent development in reporting due to the advent of television, was shown throughout the world and stunned many viewers who had previously known little about life in Northern Ireland or the treatment of Catholics there.

O'Neill was curtly summoned to London by Prime Minister Harold Wilson and ordered to explain himself and produce a plan for reforms. Unionists in Northern Ireland refused to contemplate any concessions to the civil rights activists. Many were suspicious that they were not sincerely activists but IRA members using the pretence of voting rights as a ruse to undermine the unionist government.

As Wilson threatened to cut financial subsidies to Northern Ireland, the unionist government proposed a package of measures, including limited reforms to housing allocation and voting rights and a commission to run Derry-Londonderry. O'Neill made a passionate television appeal explaining the proposals and their significance. Describing Northern Ireland as having reached a crossroads, he told nationalists that their concerns had been heard and would be addressed. He urged unionists to back the reforms, saying: 'Unionism armed with justice will be a stronger cause than unionism armed merely with strength.'

His plea was not heard, or at least not heeded by either the nationalist or unionist communities. For many unionists, any reform put the Northern Irish state at risk of being toppled by nationalists; for many nationalists, the reforms were far too little and far, far too late. Within weeks, scenes of violent clashes on Northern Ireland's streets were to be beamed yet again into homes around the world. The violent chaos that would become the Troubles had begun.

NORMALITY DISINTEGRATES

The following month, a radical group of civil rights activists known as the People's Democracy set out on a march from Belfast to

Derry-Londonderry. The planned route was to pass through a number of loyalist (hardline unionist) areas, with chances of a violent confrontation high. The event was banned by authorities, but the marchers insisted on continuing regardless. As they passed Burntollet Bridge on 4 January 1969, the march was ambushed by hundreds of loyalists, many of whom attacked the marchers. The RUC was accused of standing by as the loyalists did so and a number of off-duty officers were even accused of being among the angry mob. News bulletins once again carried dramatic and disturbing footage of brutalised and bleeding civil rights protesters. What little sympathy had existed for the unionist government shrank considerably, while attention turned to the role of the RUC and allegations of bias.

In the following weeks, further marches and counter-protests took place throughout Northern Ireland. A number of bombs were planted at electricity and water facilities. The bombings were attributed by the RUC to the IRA, although much later it was revealed that they had been the work of loyalists in an attempt to undermine O'Neill's government further.

In March, the untimely death of a unionist MP caused a by-election which was promptly won by civil rights activist Bernadette Devlin. Her maiden speech in the House of Commons was used to bring further publicity to the ongoing chaos in the region.

O'Neill managed to pass legislation finally securing one man, one vote. But it was too late for him to save his own career. Swallowed up by the chaos which he had long ceased to have any control over, he resigned in April 1969.

The summer marching season was looming, further exasperating a situation already on a knife edge. Marching season in Northern

Ireland has occurred for centuries and often proves a lightning rod for violence between the two communities. It sees loyalists march through various areas with large, loud marching bands decked in loyalist symbols such as images of the Queen or of other Protestant figureheads. The marchers will also often sing songs celebrating triumphs of Protestants over Catholics in various historic battles. It was common for the marches not only to go through Protestant areas but to specifically detour through Catholic areas. Perhaps unsurprisingly, this is often perceived by members of the Catholic community as a deliberate attempt to humiliate or provoke them. Therefore, some loyalist marches were met with Catholic protesters who argued that marches should only occur on the marchers' own 'territory' and not include Catholic streets.

In 1969, when a controversial loyalist parade embarked on its annual march through the majority Catholic city of Derry-Londonderry, it was met with violent clashes as some Catholic residents threw petrol bombs and bricks. When the RUC was dispatched to the area, locals created makeshift barricades and used force to refuse them entry. The RUC used tear gas in return. As the RUC finally gained entry, loyalists followed behind them, attacking Catholics and their homes. Parts of the city soon became no-go areas for authorities, sealed off by barricades which were to remain in place until 1972.

The violence spread to Belfast, where hundreds of homes were set alight, barricades were strewn across streets and the crackle of gunfire punctured the air in otherwise deserted communities. Evidence submitted to a subsequent inquiry into the events gave this evocative description of the chaos:

The street lights in Hooker Street had been deliberately extinguished during earlier disturbances and the street was plunged in darkness, relieved only by fires burning in houses and other adjacent premises. In the Crumlin Road and the side streets were to be found, and stumbled over, all the clutter of urban rioting – barricades, debris, flame and liquid petrol. Normal traffic movement had stopped: the noise of hostile, jeering crowds, the crackle and explosions of burning buildings, and the shattering of glass had enveloped the area. But, save where the fighting was in progress, the streets were empty.

Any semblance of a functioning society had long since departed. The police force tried but failed to quell the violence, which by now was far exceeding their number and resources. Prime Minister Chichester-Clark admitted defeat and called on London to send in the army.

The army's presence was initially welcomed by the Catholic community, who were optimistic that soldiers would be more even-handed than the sectarian RUC. However, this sentiment soon soured after the army sealed off many Catholic areas and conducted searches of residents' homes. In the process, three people were shot dead and a fourth was crushed to death by a military vehicle, while major damage was done to homes and their contents as soldiers ransacked them in pursuit of weapons.

The IRA, which had been involved in conflict during the fight for independence in the early twentieth century, was reformed in a new guise in Northern Ireland. In this context, it was initially created under the auspices of defending Catholic communities during the violence, but it soon became a highly structured and ruthless terrorist group. In response, a number of loyalist paramilitary groups were formed, including the Ulster Volunteer Force (UVF) and Ulster Defence Association (UDA), with a view to protecting loyalist and unionist communities from IRA violence.

In March 1971, three Scottish soldiers were ruthlessly murdered by the IRA after they befriended local women who brought them to a property in North Belfast, in what appears to have been a 'honey trap' set up to lure them to a vulnerable position. The men were executed by the IRA, before their bodies were dumped on a rural road and eventually found by children.

In August 1971, the government introduced internment, a process whereby suspected terrorists could be held by authorities without charge for long periods. The practice was criticised as having the potential to wrongly imprison innocent people, but was defended by others as being a necessary evil to ensure order. The new Northern Ireland Prime Minister, Brian Faulkner, said: 'You can no more deal with such deep-rooted terror without toughness and determination than you can excise a deep-seated tumour without cutting the flesh. It is not a pleasant business. Sometimes innocent people will suffer.'

In reality, however, the policy of internment meant that many innocent Catholics were arrested and held for long periods without any evidence of wrongdoing. Furthermore, the practice was a nakedly sectarian one, with few unionists or loyalists interned. The British ambassador to Dublin, Sir John Peck, later wrote: 'What was worse, it was directed solely against the Catholics, although there were many Protestants who provided just as strong grounds for internment.' Faulkner also recorded British Home Secretary Reginald Maudling urging him: 'Lift some Protestants if you can.'

Internment therefore led to the radicalisation of many young nationalists who had previously had no connections to armed Republicanism but now joined the IRA's ranks. It increased many Catholics' sense that they were victims of an authoritarian state which was determined to alienate them and deprive them of their liberty. Rather than decreasing terrorist activity, internment did the very opposite.

BLOODY SUNDAY

In what came to be known as one of the most infamous events of the Troubles, a civil rights march set out through Derry-Londonderry on 30 January 1972. The march had been banned by authorities but proceeded nonetheless.

Soldiers in the army's Parachute Regiment opened fire on the protesters, killing thirteen people and fatally injuring another who died later.

Ted Heath ordered Brian Faulkner to London for a meeting on Northern Ireland's future. The discussions were by all accounts terse. Heath ordered internment to be phased out, control of Northern Ireland security issues to be transferred to London, and the unionist government to share power with the nationalist/Catholic community.

When Faulkner returned to Belfast to inform his Cabinet of the demands, they all promptly resigned. The Parliament at Northern

Ireland adjourned for the last time on 28 March at 4 p.m. The chamber was to remain vacant for many decades to come.

Direct rule was now in place. Responsibility for running the region transferred to a new department of the British government: the Northern Ireland Office, which was to be run by the Secretary of State for Northern Ireland (more often referred to locally as the Northern Ireland Secretary). The first person appointed to the role was William Whitelaw.

Keen to improve relationships with the Catholic/nationalist community in a bid to quell violence, Whitelaw released a number of internees. He also conceded 'special category' status for paramilitary prisoners, meaning that they would receive different treatment to 'ordinary' criminals, in a move which was to later have serious and far-reaching consequences during the 1981 hunger strikes. He also arranged for a number of senior Republicans to be secretly flown to London in July 1972 for talks with the British government. The delegation included Gerry Adams and Martin McGuinness, who later went on to become leading politicians, heading up Sinn Féin. The discussions were not productive at the time, with Republicans demanding a united Ireland immediately and the British government refusing to concede. Whitelaw later wrote in his memoirs: 'The meeting was a non-event. The IRA leaders simply made impossible demands which I told them the British government would never concede. They were in fact still in a mood of defiance and determination to carry on until their absurd ultimatums were met.' However, the fact that a meeting had taken place at all was hugely significant, particularly for Republicans; many came to believe it showed a willingness within the British government to negotiate with them. The meeting was the beginning of what would prove intermittent behind-the-scenes talks between the British government and Republicans. At the same time as his first meeting with Republicans, Whitelaw also met with loyalist paramilitaries, holding a meeting at Stormont Castle in which senior loyalist figures attended, concealing their identities under masks and dark sunglasses.

The summer of 1972 saw more bloodshed in Northern Ireland. On 11 July, a gang of loyalists broke into the home of a Catholic family, where they killed a young man with learning disabilities and raped his mother. In the subsequent murder trial, a lawyer commented: 'The restraints of civilisation on evil human passions are in this case totally non-existent. You may well think that in this case we have reached the lowest level of human depravity.'

On 21 July, the IRA detonated twenty bombs in Belfast city centre in just over an hour. Nine people were killed and a further 130 people were injured in the carnage. The day came to be known as Bloody Friday. One police officer who attended the scene later gave this harrowing account:

> You could hear people screaming and crying and moaning. The first thing that caught my eye was a torso of a human being lying in the middle of the street. It was recognisable as a torso because the clothes had been blown off and you could actually see parts of the human anatomy.

The pace of violence proved relentless. A week later, the IRA detonated a car bomb in the village of Claudy, in County Derry-Londonderry, claiming another nine lives.

In November, Whitelaw published a discussion document titled 'The Future of Northern Ireland', which outlined the general principle and priorities of Britain's approach to the spiralling crisis. The document highlighted that Northern Ireland being part of the UK brought with it an obligation to uphold British values of democracy, stating that a place in the UK 'carries with it the obligations of membership including acceptance of the sovereignty of Parliament as representing the people as a whole'. It also stated that the Republic of Ireland had a legitimate interest in Northern Ireland's affairs: 'Any new arrangements should, whilst meeting the wishes of Northern Ireland and Great Britain, be so far as possible acceptable to and accepted by the Republic of Ireland.' The concession amounted to a considerable break in the status quo and infuriated many unionists, who continued to maintain that the Republic was a foreign country which could have no say on what they considered to be internal UK matters. In his memoirs, Ted Heath explained his reasoning:

> It was no good just pretending that nationalist aspirations did not exist and that Irish nationalism in Northern Ireland would either be contained or burn itself out. The strength of feeling in the Catholic community had to be addressed, and that meant finding some way of involving the government of the Republic directly in the affairs of the province.

Most controversially, the document also raised the prospect of a united Ireland, although it made clear that this would only come about if a majority in Northern Ireland backed it: 'No UK

government for many years has had any wish to impede the re-
alisation of Irish unity, if it were to come about by genuine and
freely given mutual agreement and on conditions acceptable to the
distinctive communities.'

Unionist politicians began to take even more hardline positions
in response to the ongoing violence and fears within the community that the British government was conceding too much ground
to the Catholic/nationalist community. William Craig, a leading
unionist who formed the Vanguard movement, told a meeting in
London:

> I am prepared to come out and shoot and kill. Let us put the
> bluff aside. I am prepared to kill and those behind me will have
> my full support. When we say force we mean force. We will only
> assassinate our enemies as a last desperate resort when we are
> denied our democratic rights.

In 1973, some of the first loyalists were interned. In response, loyalists and unionists carried out a one-day strike which saw greater
loyalist violence and five deaths. In March, IRA bombs detonated
in London, killing one person and injuring almost 200 others. The
attack marked a new approach by the IRA which would see a
greater number of attacks in England.

The same month, a border poll on Irish reunification was
held. Whitelaw hoped such a poll would reassure unionists, as it
would inevitably see majority support for the union with Britain.
In response, however, nationalists boycotted the poll in a bid to
undermine its validity. When the votes were tallied, 99 per cent of

ballots cast were for Northern Ireland remaining in the UK, on a turnout of 59 per cent. The unionist community took little comfort from the exercise.

THE SUNNINGDALE AGREEMENT

Soon after the border poll, the British government published a White Paper titled 'Northern Ireland Constitutional Proposals' suggesting a new cross-community Parliament at Stormont, elected via proportional representation to ensure a coalition comprised a cross-section of nationalists and unionists. The proposals included new North–South links, while a number of sensitive issues would remain under the control of the British government, including elections, the legal system and security. The proposals were met with little enthusiasm among both communities. Nationalists were disappointed not to secure the end of internment, while unionism was split between moderates willing to begrudgingly accept the cross-community nature of the new Parliament and hardline unionists who refused to share power with nationalists. Elections to the new government were held in June 1973. The results showed support for the proposals within the population overall, but not within unionism. Pro-Agreement members of the moderate unionist grouping the Ulster Unionist Party (UUP) received 25 per cent of the vote share. However, anti-Agreement members of the UUP received 10 per cent of votes cast, bolstered by the hardline loyalist and anti-Agreement Democratic Unionist Party (DUP) receiving 11 per cent. Republicans boycotted the election and nationalists resoundingly backed the Social Democratic and Labour Party (SDLP), a centre-left nationalist party committed to achieving a united Ireland through peaceful and democratic means, which had roots in the civil rights movement. The Alliance Party – a centre-ground, liberal party with an anti-sectarian ethos – took a further 9 per cent of votes. A smattering of other smaller parties also received a small proportion of votes, including the Labour Party and loyalist groups.

Following the election, the fledgling Parliament's future looked uncertain due to the high representation of anti-Agreement unionists at its heart. The UUP insisted that they be allowed to have a majority in the executive (the ministerial board with a similar function to the Cabinet in Westminster). However, other parties opposed this as the UUP did not have a majority in the new Parliament.

The problem proved intractable until a compromise was struck on a technicality, in order to placate both sides. The UUP would have a majority of ministers in the eleven-man executive; however, an additional four ministers without voting rights would be appointed from the other parties, giving them an overall majority of seats. This meant that the SDLP and Alliance could also claim they had succeeded in breaking unionist dominance in the executive, while the UUP could reassure its voters that they had succeeded in retaining a majority among ministers with full voting rights. It was a sleight of hand which enabled both sides to claim victory and which was replicated in myriad ways throughout the peace process over the ensuing decades.

The UUP, SDLP and Alliance Party then met at a civil service training centre at Sunningdale in Berkshire to thrash out what came to be known as the Sunningdale Agreement. It was agreed that a Council of Ireland would also exist, composed of seven Northern and seven Southern ministers. This solution placated nationalists who wanted to see the Republic have some say in the new government, while unionists were assured their role would only be advisory and the Parliament would still have to approve any of their suggestions before they could be enacted.

In a gesture towards unionists, the Republic of Ireland would roll back on their constitutional claim to the island of Ireland and re-lease a statement declaring their support for the people of Northern Ireland's right to self-determination. Due to the nature of the Republic's constitution, any change to the principles within it requires approval in a nationwide referendum. It was agreed that no such referendum would be held (amid concerns the Republic's population might not accept such a move and a 'No' vote could badly damage North–South relations) but that the government would make the announcement instead as a gesture of goodwill towards Northern Ireland's unionist population.

The power-sharing executive took office on 1 January 1974. The UUP's Brian Faulkner took the position of 'chief minister', with the SDLP's Gerry Fitt as his deputy. The executive they led together included ministers from the UUP, SDLP and Alliance. Within days, its future was in doubt.

Three days after the executive was formed, the Ulster Unionist Council called a meeting to discuss the new Parliament. The body was linked to the UUP but also encompassed a number of more hardline unionists and loyalists, including affiliated delegates from the Orange Order. The Ulster Unionist Council condemned the newly negotiated Council of Ireland, which they saw as a ruse to undermine Northern Ireland's Britishness. Pro-Agreement politicians were defeated by anti-Agreement unionists. In response, Faulkner resigned as party leader, to be replaced by the hardline anti-Agreement unionist Harry West. His resignation severely damaged Faulkner's position as chief minister of the executive, as he clearly could not command majority support within his own political party. Across Northern Ireland, loyalist killings increased as hardline unionists sought to demonstrate a show of strength.

Faulkner's authority was further undermined when, soon after, a legal challenge was mounted in Dublin arguing that the Republic of Ireland government's promises to him were unconstitutional, as the government could not agree to reduce the nation's constitutional claim to Northern Ireland without the backing of a referendum.

When the Assembly met for the first time later that month, open violence broke out among the elected representatives. Police were deployed to physically break apart fighting politicians, in scenes which dismayed many in Northern Ireland and beyond. One newspaper account recorded:

> The loyalists entered at 2.30 in the afternoon, prayed, and rushed forward to seize the seats designated for the executive. There were shouts and howls. Some climbed up and danced on desks. Other loyalists leaped upon the table beside the dispatch box, removed the mace, and began a parade about the chamber. One danced upon the speaker's table and shouted, 'We have driven

the money-changers from the temple.' He then chained and padlocked himself to a bench.

Five RUC officers were injured in the disturbances. For many people, the scenes embodied their worst fears: that Northern Ireland's political landscape was dysfunctional beyond repair and anti-Agreement politicians would be able to bring it down from within by engaging in sabotage.

In the event, the final blow bringing down the Sunningdale executive came not from within but without. Amid British Prime Minister Heath's battle with the trade unions, a UK-wide general election was called for February. The elections were deeply destabilising and divisive at a time when Northern Ireland needed continuity in order for the new power-sharing experiment to find its feet. On the day of the election, eleven of the twelve Northern Irish Westminster seats were won by anti-Agreement unionists. The Belfast Parliament's claims to legitimacy were gravely undermined. Seizing on this result, a coalition of loyalists and unionists working in trade unions came together as the Ulster Workers Council (UWC) and announced a strike to protest the Sunningdale Agreement. The strike began on 15 May. To begin with, the strike did not receive majority backing within Northern Ireland; however, its supporters employed heavy-handed and often violent tactics to ensure it was still able to bring the region to a standstill. Due to anti-Catholic discrimination, most of the key industries in Northern Ireland had a predominantly Protestant workforce, including ship building, electricity production and engineering. On the first day of the strike, large-scale intimidation of workers occurred as masked loyalist men visited key industries, blocking their entrance with barricades and issuing threats. These tactics ensured many workers stayed at home for their own safety and were participating in the strike whether they liked it or not. The RUC did little to intervene, as many of its members sympathised with the loyalists undertaking the intimidation. The army also refused to get involved, arguing that the loyalists' actions did not constitute terrorism and so it was not within their remit to act.

It did not take long for the effects of the forced strike to be felt across Northern Ireland. Soon, electricity output was slashed to 60 per cent. Another loyalist show of strength occurred three days in, as they detonated bombs in the Republic of Ireland. Explosions in Dublin and Monaghan killed thirty-three people. The UVF later claimed responsibility for the attack. The army warned that loyalists could begin sabotaging generators, plunging Northern Ireland into greater chaos as hospitals would lose power and sewage could begin to flow in the streets.

In a bid to quell loyalist anger, the executive backed down and announced the Council of Ireland would not be implemented until after the next Assembly election. However, this concession had no effect and the stranglehold continued, bringing local industry to its knees and causing deep uncertainty and fear within Northern Ireland's population.

Prime Minister Harold Wilson sought to shame the loyalists into ending the strike through a short-tempered television broadcast that came to be known as the 'spongers speech', in which he called them 'people who spend their lives sponging on Westminster and British democracy and then systematically assault democratic methods'. Far from causing the loyalists to experience a change of heart, many defiantly wore scraps of sponge on their lapels. Two weeks into the strike, Faulkner lost all hope for the power-sharing executive and resigned, bringing an end to the Assembly. The power-sharing experiment had failed and now lay in tatters. It had been in operation for a mere five months.

Once again, Northern Ireland was at a crossroads and its future lay in doubt. However, the debacle had made one thing abundantly clear: hardline loyalists had the ability, strength and determination to pull down initiatives they opposed. For now, at least, a Council of Ireland or any similar measures to give the Republic a say on Northern Ireland (symbolic or otherwise) would not be countenanced.

Talks continued between local parties, facilitated by the British government, but relationships between them were fractured following the dramatic collapse of the Sunningdale executive and hope was faint.

In the meantime, violence continued. Autumn 1974 saw a series of IRA atrocities in England. A blast at a pub in Birmingham killed twenty-one people and injured 200 others, while bombings in pubs in Guildford and Woolwich claimed another seven lives.

Contacts between the IRA and the British government continued through a number of back channels throughout this time. The links were controversial, as many feared that such talks could embolden the IRA by giving them a sense of legitimacy which they did not deserve, while many unionists and loyalists argued it was immoral to negotiate with terrorists. As a result of talks, the IRA announced a short ceasefire over Christmas 1974 and in response the British government promised security forces activity would be reduced and no new internment orders would be signed for the near future. The ceasefire continued into the New Year, whereupon Northern Ireland Secretary Merlyn Rees released a number of detainees and ordered a reduced army presence in nationalist areas. The ceasefire lasted for much of 1975, but was breached regularly, with IRA attacks on security forces and Protestant civilians still occurring (although at a reduced rate from previous years). However, as the months went on, it became clear that the IRA and the British government could not reach an agreement. The IRA continued to insist on a united Ireland, which the UK could not agree to. The Republican movement became bitterly divided between those who believed they could convince the British government to 'withdraw' from Northern Ireland, and those who believed they were being strung along and manipulated. Morale in the IRA ebbed and infighting threatened authority among its leaders. By November, violence had returned to normal levels and the ceasefire had all but dissolved.

In December, the British government announced internment would end and the remaining internees would be released. This was welcomed by the nationalist community, including by the SDLP, who had long argued it was an abuse of power and resulted in innocent Catholics being wrongly imprisoned. However, the process coincided with a clampdown on suspected terrorists, with another 1,100 people being charged that year. Many still feared security services were being unnecessarily heavy-handed but now in a different way.

1976 brought more bloodshed as the IRA continued its attacks.

In January, the terror group slaughtered ten innocent Protestant men in what came to be one of the most notorious attacks of the Troubles. Twelve men were travelling home from work near the Kingsmill village close to the Irish border in the evening when their vehicle was pulled over at the side of the road. They were ordered to line up and the only Catholic among them was ordered to leave. The remaining eleven Protestant men were then repeatedly shot at close range, with just one man surviving the massacre.

In July, the IRA assassinated the British ambassador to the Republic of Ireland, Christopher Ewart-Biggs, just twelve days after he had taken up the post. The murder occurred while he was in Dublin and on his way to a meeting with the Republic of Ireland's Foreign Minister Garret FitzGerald. FitzGerald spoke of his shock at the murder and his shame that the Irish government had not succeeded in protecting an ambassador.

Loyalist killings also continued throughout this period. A collection of UVF members committed a number of disturbing and sadistic murders throughout 1975–77. The group would drive around Catholic areas at night, selecting random Catholics to drag off before torturing and killing them. The group often slit their victims' throats with butchers' knives and cleavers, earning them the disturbing nickname 'the Shankill Butchers'.

In August 1976, a tragedy sent shockwaves through both of Northern Ireland's communities. An IRA member was shot dead by soldiers while at the wheel of a car during a car chase in Belfast. The car spun out of control, mounting a pavement and crushing a Catholic woman who was out walking with her three young children. The children, an eight-year-old, a two-year-old and a six-week-old baby in a pram, were killed. Their mother, Anne Maguire, was badly injured and woke up in hospital two weeks later to be told of her children's deaths. The horrific incident was denounced across Northern Ireland and gave fresh impetus for peace. A new movement called Women For Peace was set up by the children's aunt, Mairead Corrigan, and local resident Betty Williams. The group, which later went on to be known as the Peace People, held large rallies denouncing violence and imploring both communities to embrace peace. They were awarded the Nobel Peace Prize that year. However, the group's success was short-lived, gradually losing momentum and fading from public consciousness. Anne Maguire never recovered from the psychological impact of the tragedy and took her own life three years later. Her sister Mairead later explained:

> Anne never saw her children buried. In her own mind she refused to accept their deaths. She would often talk about seeing them playing in the garden. Their deaths and the brain bruising she suffered resulted in psychotic depression. Anne became a troubled soul, knowing no peace of mind. She seemed to lock herself in a private world with her dead babies.

Margaret Thatcher's election as Prime Minister in May 1979 proved a watershed moment for relations between the British government and Northern Ireland and much of her reputation as the 'Iron Lady' stemmed from her perceived steeliness with the IRA. Shortly after she took office, the IRA assassinated the Queen's cousin, Lord Mountbatten, while he was holidaying in County

Sligo in the Republic. On the same day, eighteen soldiers were slaughtered by the IRA at Warrenpoint in Northern Ireland. The ruthless killings showed no sign of abating.

THE HUNGER STRIKE

Throughout this period, tensions were growing inside prisons among inmates who were unhappy with their treatment and conditions. Paramilitary groups had first gained 'special category' status in 1972, following a concession from William Whitelaw which he later said he regretted. The special category label given to paramilitary convicts separated them from 'ordinary' criminals and recognised that their crimes were connected to the ongoing conflict. The men, who were known as 'special cats', wore their own clothes while in prison, were allowed extra visits and additional parcels. Most controversially, they were allowed to divide into separate compounds based on the Republican or loyalist group they were affiliated with, and the compounds were largely left to self-govern, rather than obeying the prison wardens. Whitelaw's decision had proven deeply contentious, as many argued it amounted to approval of the IRA's narrative that they were engaged in a war, rather than terrorism. In 1975, it was announced that special status would be phased out from the following year for any newly convicted prisoners. As part of this change in approach, new prisoners would not be sent into the existing compounds, but were sent to specially built cell blocks. The blocks came to be known as 'H-blocks' due to their shape.

Loyalists had objected to the changes and staged protests in a bid to retain the status. However, when this proved ineffective, they begrudgingly accepted the policy change. By contrast, Republicans were outraged at the thought of being treated as 'common criminals', which ran in direct opposition to their belief that they were soldiers in a legitimate army. Over the following years, they staged a number of protests including 'dirty protests', which saw some inmates refuse to wash and smear their own excrement on the walls of their cells. Such protests received little attention or public support.

In 1980, a new tactic was employed. Republican prisoners decided to engage in a hunger strike in a bid to force the British government's hand. The decision did not have the backing of Republican leadership or the wider nationalist community, many of whom considered the debate around special category status to be a side show distracting from the wider 'struggle'. Gerry Adams later explained that he wrote to the inmates at the time, telling them that he was 'tactically, strategically, physically and morally opposed to a hunger strike'. Nevertheless, the strike began in October, and a second followed from 1 March 1981. The men planned a phased strike, which would see the first prisoner refuse food, followed by a second two weeks later and then another each week after that, with a view to putting constant mounting pressure on Thatcher. The men had five demands:

- To be allowed to wear their own clothes rather than prison uniforms;
- To be exempt from prison work;
- To be allowed to associate freely with each other;

- To be allowed extra parcels and visits;
- For all remission that they had lost due to previous protests to be restored.

The first hunger striker was a 26-year-old man named Bobby Sands, a commander in the Maze prison who had been sentenced to fourteen years' imprisonment in 1977 for possession of a firearm while on an IRA operation. Five days after he began his strike, one of Northern Ireland's Westminster seats was left vacant following the sudden death of an MP. Sands's name was put forward for candidacy in the ensuing by-election. In a considerable propaganda coup for Republicans, he was duly elected. Thatcher continued to insist her government would not back down and allow special category status for the prisoners, stating: 'If Mr Sands persisted in his wish to commit suicide, that was his choice.' The case garnered publicity around the world. Thatcher's response allowed Republicans to frame the strike as a battle of the harsh British state against an individual martyr, tapping into traditional Republican mythology.

After sixty-six days on hunger strike, Sands died in the early hours of 5 May. He was twenty-seven years old. Thatcher's cold approach continued after his death, as she stated: 'Mr Sands was a convicted criminal. He chose to take his own life. It was a choice his organisation did not allow to many of its victims.' Locally, however, his death had a profound impact. Some 100,000 people attended his funeral. Most significantly, the experience was the genesis of Republicans eventually coming to embrace electoral politics as they realised the potency and publicity that could come from engaging in elections. Although Sinn Féin had existed throughout the conflict as the IRA's political wing, it had yet to develop into a sophisticated electoral force. The public response to Sands's election opened many Republicans' eyes to the benefits of running for elections they had previously boycotted.

To this day, Sands is considered one of the Republican movement's most glorious martyrs, and a large mural celebrating him continues to adorn the gable wall of Sinn Féin's main Belfast offices.

Following his death and amid Thatcher's refusal to give in to Republican demands for special category status, the hunger strike continued. As the months wore on, a slow drip of deaths occurred, as had been designed through the staggered approach to the strike. Eventually, the British government agreed to some but not all of the men's five demands. As time progressed, an increasing number of the strikers' families intervened once they had lapsed into the coma which preceded death, allowing authorities to revive them medically. Sensing the British government would not agree to all their demands and aware that their own families were thwarting their tactics, the men called an end to the strike in October. In total, it had lasted 271 days, with ten men dying. By this time, Republicanism had irrevocably changed and now stood poised to be an electoral force. Three weeks after the hunger strike ended, Danny Morrison, an aide for Gerry Adams, told a Sinn Féin conference: 'Who here really believes we can win the war through the ballot box? But will anyone here object if, with a ballot box in one hand and the Armalite [rifle] in the other, we take power in Ireland?' Sinn Féin began to contest elections as a serious tactic to advance Republicanism. Between 1982 and 1985, Sinn Féin averaged 12 per cent in the four elections they contested. This amounted to 40 per cent of the nationalist vote, placing them behind the moderate SDLP but giving them a considerable foothold. Gerry Adams was among the Sinn Féin figures elected, becoming MP for West Belfast in 1983.

In parallel, shifts were occurring within moderate nationalism. Within the SDLP, politician John Hume evolved his theory that the barrier to a united Ireland was not Britain wanting Northern Ireland to remain in the UK, but rather Northern Ireland's unionist population wanting to remain in the UK. This approach reframed the debate, casting Britain not as anti-nationalism but as a neutral arbiter between the two sides. According to this line of thought, the key to reunification lay in nationalists convincing their unionist counterparts of the merits of a united Ireland and reassuring them their religion and traditions would be respected within it.

At the same time, Republican violence continued unabated. On 12 October 1984, the IRA conducted one of its boldest attacks as it came close to killing Margaret Thatcher. A bomb exploded in the early hours of the morning at the Grand Hotel in Brighton, where the Conservative Party conference was taking place. Five people including an MP were killed, while Thatcher survived. The devastation the IRA had managed to wreak on the heart of the political establishment shocked and repulsed politicians across Britain.

THE ANGLO-IRISH AGREEMENT

In November 1985, the Anglo-Irish Agreement was formally signed following months of careful negotiations and close contact between the British and Irish governments. The Agreement opened with a joint statement from both countries that Northern Ireland's place in the UK could only change if that was the wish of a majority of its people. It also pledged a new 'intergovernmental conference' to facilitate UK–Irish cooperation, which would be jointly chaired by London and Dublin ministers. As with previous agreements, the Republic would have no formal powers to govern Northern Ireland but the conference gave the Republican an official consultative role in Northern Ireland, and both the UK and the Republic pledged to use the conference as a means of resolving their differences and involving each other in issues of mutual interest. Thatcher's decision to sign the accord shocked many people in Britain and in Northern Ireland's unionist community, as they considered it to contain surprising concessions for a woman known for her hardline approach to the Northern Ireland question. Unlike her predecessors, many people had believed Thatcher had held a genuine desire and personal commitment for Northern Ireland to remain in the UK. However, for Thatcher the Agreement did not amount to undue concessions to the Republic; she viewed it as less a political accord than a security one, amid ongoing bloodshed. She later explained in her autobiography, 'I started from the need for greater security, which was imperative. If that meant making limited political concession to the South, much as I disliked this kind of bargaining, I had to contemplate it.' Unionists had refused to engage in the talks at an early stage, assuming Thatcher would not agree to an accord from which they had excluded themselves. However, this proved to be a politically costly miscalculation.

Following the announcement, unionists and loyalists mirrored their previous obstructionist responses to agreements they disapproved of. They held an enormous rally outside Belfast City Hall, where more than 100,000 denounced the accord. DUP politician Peter Robinson hinted at violent unrest to come as he demanded of the Prime Minister: 'What is Mrs Thatcher going to do after she has shot the first thousand unionists in the streets of Belfast?' There was an increase in killings by loyalist paramilitaries, as well as a campaign of violence against RUC officers which saw some loyalists petrol-bomb police officers' homes. Robinson staged a dramatic event in which he, along with a group of loyalists, mounted an 'invasion' of sorts across the border into the Republic of Ireland. He was arrested for the act. Northern Ireland's fifteen unionist MPs resigned their seats in order to trigger by-elections. They had intended to use the fresh elections as a show of strength by being re-elected on anti-accord platforms. However, the ploy backfired when one of the seats was lost to the SDLP. Despite the many ways in which the unionists illustrated their opposition, the Anglo-Irish Agreement remained. For the first time, unionists were on the receiving end of Thatcher's firm resolve and she refused to give in to their protests. The approach marked a considerable break from the traditional dynamic between the British government and unionists, much to the latter's surprise.

1987 brought fresh horror and condemnation of IRA violence as the group detonated a bomb at a Remembrance Sunday memorial ceremony in the quiet Fermanagh village of Enniskillen. Families and elderly people were among those gathered when the blast exploded, killing eleven people. The atrocity was condemned around the world, as many denounced the IRA as reaching a new low in murdering innocent people while they were at a memorial commemorating their war dead.

THE FUNERAL MURDERS

The following year, a series of events occurred in quick succession which prompted fears that Northern Ireland's conflict was spiralling into new depths of depravity. In March 1988, three IRA members were shot dead by the SAS in Gibraltar, a British territory within a corner of Spain. The manner of their deaths is still deeply contested. It is generally accepted that the trio, who became known as the Gibraltar Three, had gone to the territory in order to plant a bomb. However, it is disputed whether they posed a threat at the time of their deaths. Some witnesses claimed they had been unarmed and were surrendering to authorities when they were repeatedly shot dead, despite posing no active threat. When their bodies were returned to Belfast, thousands attended highly publicised funerals for them. In Milltown cemetery, while mourners were gathered, pandemonium broke out as a lone loyalist attacker lobbed hand grenades into the graveyard and shot at the bereaved. He killed three people before attempting to flee. A mob of mourners pursued him and beat him unconscious, before he was eventually rescued by police.

When one of those killed in the funeral attack was laid to rest in West Belfast, a car carrying two Englishmen inexplicably entered the funeral cortège. Fearing the men might be loyalists about to mount another attack, the mourners besieged the car. One of the men fired a warning shot in a bid to disperse the crowd. However, the mob soon dragged them both from the car and carried out a frenzied attack which resembled a lynching. They were brought to a sports ground, where they were badly beaten and stripped, before being taken to a patch of waste ground, where they were shot dead. It later emerged that the men were British soldiers. The army has never been able to explain why they were present that day, in what was deemed a 'no-go' area for soldiers, particularly on a day such as a Republican funeral, when community tensions were running particularly high.

To many both within and beyond Northern Ireland, the double funeral killings appeared to illustrate how the country had become trapped in an endless cycle of retaliatory killings and senseless violence.

In November 1990, the British government made a statement which was the cause for much optimism within Republican and nationalist communities. The Northern Ireland Secretary Peter Brooke said in a speech: 'The British government has no selfish strategic or economic interest in Northern Ireland: our role is to help, enable and encourage. Britain's purpose, as I have sought to describe it, is not to occupy, oppress or exploit, but to ensure democratic debate and free democratic choice. That is our way.' Such a sentiment may have appeared obvious to most, as Northern Ireland had long been a financial burden on the rest of the UK rather than adding to Britain's finances. However, for Republicans this was a clear rejection of what they considered Britain's colonial stake in Northern Ireland. Many studied the statement carefully and debated whether this was a departure from what they considered to be Britain's imperialist role. Similarly, among moderate nationalists, the comments were seen as backing John Hume's theoretical shift towards seeing Britain as a neutral arbiter rather than a necessarily pro-union force.

Violence continued in 1992 with the Teebane Crossroads attack, in which an IRA bomb was planted at the side of a road in rural Tyrone. It detonated as a van of Protestant workers drove past on their way back from carrying out building work at an army site. Eight men were killed. The tremendous force of the blast scattered body parts across the surrounding landscape in a nightmarish scene. Emergency services took some time to establish how many people had perished due to the manner in which severed limbs and torsos were strewn across roads and fields. A few weeks later a retaliatory attack occurred as an off-duty RUC officer arrived at Sinn Féin's Belfast office in plain clothes, posing as a journalist. Once he was allowed entry to the building, he pulled out a shotgun he had been concealing and proceeded to shoot dead three men in the office. He then drove to a secluded area and killed himself. A day later, yet more retaliations occurred as two members of the UDA entered a betting shop frequented by Catholic men on South Belfast's Ormeau Road. They opened fire and shot five dead within a matter of minutes.

In April, the IRA carried out a major attack in London by setting off two bombs in the city's financial district. Three people died, including a teenage girl, while more than £700 million of damage was caused to buildings and the surrounding area. It was the first time Republicans had sought to target the financial markets, which many had considered to be immune from such attacks as they were perceived as separate to British political structures and therefore not viewed as a 'legitimate' target.

In October 1993, an IRA bomb was planted in a fish shop on the loyalist Shankill Road. The target of the attack was a room above the shop, where loyalist paramilitaries were said to meet. However, the attack was botched. While an IRA member was attempting to place the explosive device, it detonated early. The blast occurred at lunchtime on a Saturday, when the street was busy with weekend shoppers, including families milling around. Nine Protestants, including two children, died. The IRA man who was fitting the device, Thomas Begley, also died in the explosion. No loyalist paramilitaries were among those killed. A police officer described the scene:

I was one of the first in. I remember an old man being recovered. His head was the first thing to appear from the rubble, and that was quite a frightening experience. I knew he was still alive because his eyes were blinking. An ambulanceman put an oxygen mask over his mouth but by the time he left the rubble he had died. After he was moved we continued to remove rubble from where we standing, but unknown to anybody we were standing on other bodies. As the rubble was being removed – and it will stay with me until I die – I saw a young girl's foot. I knew it was a young girl's foot because her shoe size was about three or four. It poked through the rubble, and I wanted to stop digging then, because I knew I was going to see quite a horrendous sight; and in fact I did.

Gerry Adams was among those who carried the coffin of the IRA man responsible for the attack. His decision to do so was condemned by unionists and British politicians alike. Prime Minister John Major was said to be furious and openly questioned whether it was possible to reach any agreement with Republicans, given Adams's apparent support for the Shankill Road bomber.

A number of loyalist revenge attacks followed the fish shop killings. Two gunmen entered a bar in Greysteel, near Derry-Londonderry, opening fire on the 200 revellers within. Eight people died, of whom seven were Catholics. The killings were followed by further disturbing scenes as one of the men charged with the attack was filmed on his way into court, apparently laughing manically at the victims' families. The scenes were televised in Northern Ireland and shocked many due to the apparent glee the man felt. Further loyalist killings saw another six people shot dead.

Then, in November 1993, local journalist Eamonn Mallie revealed that despite the British government's official stance of not talking to terrorists, they had indeed been in contact with the IRA at various points for several decades. The British government admitted that contacts had occurred but said they had only begun that year and insisted that senior politicians in Britain had not authorised it. Sinn Féin disputed the British government's version of events and published correspondence which appeared to disprove the claims. The British government then announced they had accidentally made a number of mistakes in their initial response due to transcription errors and typos. The incident caused a considerable blow to the British government's credibility. It spooked many unionists, who feared they could not trust London as they were creating side deals with their enemies behind their backs. The revelations also caused bad blood between London and Dublin, as the Republic's government also felt they had been left in the dark. In December 1993, John Major met with then Taoiseach (Irish Prime Minister) Albert Reynolds for tense talks. However, despite the controversy, the talks were productive and resulted in another joint declaration between the two governments which was to prove a major moment in the peace process.

THE DOWNING STREET DECLARATION

The document stated: 'The British government agree that it is for the people of the island of Ireland alone, by the agreement between the two parts respectively, to exercise their right of self-determination on the basis of consent, freely and concurrently given, North and South, to bring about a united Ireland, if that is their wish.' In and of itself, the document was not a major break with the British government's previous position, which had long advocated that Northern Ireland's place in the UK was dependent on majority support for the status quo. However, the language of the declaration was much more overt in referring to 'a united Ireland'. Previous British Prime Ministers had learnt to their detriment how such declarations could prompt unionist uprisings in Northern Ireland. Major, therefore, was strategic and spent considerable time before the announcement talking to unionist leaders in order to prepare them and encourage them to respond calmly. Mainstream unionists complied. Republicans and nationalists were content with the text's language, which appeared to be more sympathetic to their aims than previous statements from the British government. For the first time in decades, both communities appeared to be able to tolerate the declaration. Unionists' acceptance of the text was crucial to its overall reception and appears to have been due to prolonged work by Major to maintain respectful relationships with key unionist figures in order to keep them on board. The recent horrors of that year had renewed a hunger for peace within both communities, which may have also helped explain the measured response. As Major later recorded in his memoirs, 'The process was on a knife-edge. I think it would have broken down had not the Shankill and Greysteel tragedies intervened.'

In the US, President Bill Clinton also took a number of steps to try to bolster the apparent progress. His administration dropped the existing ban on Adams entering the US. Adams duly visited the country, where he was given a warm reception and received as a major political figure, meeting key politicians and appearing on prestigious television programmes. The trip provided further impetus for Republicans to engage in political life, giving Adams another glimpse of mainstream political engagement.

THE CEASEFIRES

In 1994, the number of killings dropped amid improved relationships. In particular, IRA violence appeared to wane. In March, a bizarre incident occurred when the IRA appeared to lob mortar bombs onto the runway at Heathrow Airport. However, the devices did not detonate and it later emerged that they had been altered in such a way so that they would not explode. The attack appeared to have been designed to scare rather than kill, a chilling calling card to remind Britain what the IRA was capable of. Speculation grew that the IRA could be on the cusp of announcing a fresh ceasefire.

In June 1994, horror returned afresh to Northern Ireland as loyalists slaughtered a group of Catholic men at a pub one evening who were gathered to watch Ireland play in the World Cup. The attack occurred in quiet village of Loughinisland in rural County Down, which many felt was a safe haven far from the traditional flashpoints for violence in Belfast or Derry-Londonderry. The UVF entered the Heights Bar, spraying bullets into the backs of the men as they faced the television screen showing the match on the opposite wall. Six men were killed.

On 31 August, the IRA announced that it was entering into a ceasefire from midnight that night. Once again, people across Northern Ireland anxiously held their breath to see if the violence had finally come to an end. Jaded by past false hope, many viewed the development with suspicion as they waited to see whether the ceasefire would last.

In a bid to consolidate the progress, Taoiseach Albert Reynolds met with Gerry Adams and John Hume the following week and publicly shook hands with them both.

As the weeks passed and the IRA stayed true to their word, optimism grew. In October, loyalist paramilitaries followed suit and declared their own ceasefire. A number of loyalist paramilitaries began to engage seriously in democratic politics, most notably the UVF, which grew a political wing called the Progressive Unionist Party and developed an electoral focus beyond their previous violence. Similar to the internal revolution Sinn Féin had undergone following the hunger strike, when they realised the potential of electoral politics, many loyalists began to develop a considerable enthusiasm for politics, as many felt their violent campaigns were becoming futile and greater opportunities lay in electioneering.

However, the ceasefire soon appeared unsettled. The IRA continued to carry out so-called punishment attacks whereby they would 'discipline' members of their own community for perceived wrongdoing such as drug dealing. The ceasefire was further destabilised when, in November, a man was shot dead during an IRA robbery in Newry. The IRA's senior ranks quickly issued a statement saying the killing had not been officially sanctioned, and the ceasefire held.

In response to the decrease in loyalist and Republican violence, army presence decreased on the streets of Northern Ireland and something almost resembling normality re-emerged for the first time in decades. Army patrols still occurred but were less frequent in number. Roads crossing the border between Northern Ireland and the Republic which had been closed for decades by soldiers were once more reopened. The police also became less heavily militarised, in a move which reassured locals, with some conducting patrols without their usual heavy flak jackets and rifles, and in cars rather than heavily armoured vehicles.

As the ceasefire continued, attention turned to what should

happen to existing weapons within the paramilitary groups. John Major urged the IRA to relinquish its weapons and put them beyond use, in a process known as decommissioning. However, Republicans were reluctant to do so as many feared the optics of such a process would make it seem that they were surrendering to the British. In March 1995, the British government stated that in order for Sinn Féin to be allowed to attend negotiations with the other political parties they would have to demonstrate a willingness to disarm; reach an agreement on the practicalities of decommissioning; and decommission a number of arms as a gesture to illustrate their commitment to the peace process.

In November 1995, the British and Irish governments both agreed that an international body would be set up to deal with the issue of decommissioning, as it was hoped this may be perceived by the paramilitaries as being more neutral than an organisation chaired by either or both governments. This new body would be chaired by senior US politician George Mitchell. In a bid to further capitalise on the momentum of the fledgling peace, US President Bill Clinton visited Northern Ireland in a highly publicised trip which celebrated the recent reduction in violence and outlined an optimistic vision for a conflict-free future.

A few weeks after his visit, the ceasefire appeared uncertain once more as a number of men were executed in Belfast in suspected IRA attacks. A new group calling itself Direct Action Against Drugs took responsibility for the attacks, arguing that they were Republicans killing local drug dealers and this therefore did not constitute a ceasefire breach. Few doubted the new group was a mere fig leaf for the IRA, but the explanation was enough for the ceasefire to remain intact.

Amid the ceasefires, 1995 saw the lowest murder toll for a generation, totalling nine killings. This figure was down from sixty-nine killings the previous year and a far cry from chaotic years at the peak of the Troubles, which often saw hundreds of deaths occur.

In January 1996, the decommissioning body chaired by George Mitchell released its report, stating that decommissioning should not be required of groups before they could be involved in negotiations but instead should happen in parallel with talks. The following month, an IRA bomb detonated in London near the city's Docklands, killing two people. The ceasefire and much of the peace process now appeared in doubt.

In May, an election was held in Northern Ireland for locals to vote on which groups could provide delegations to inter-party talks. Sinn Féin performed surprisingly well in the poll, receiving 15 per cent of the vote as many Republicans who had never voted before did so for the first time. Many saw this as Republicans moving away from violence and giving credibility to political processes instead. However, despite their strong performance at the polls, Sinn Féin was excluded from talks due to the ongoing IRA violence and told they could not attend unless a new ceasefire was called. In June of that year, a major bomb was detonated in Manchester. The IRA denied the attack had been sanctioned, but later admitted that individual IRA members had been behind it. Many began to fear that the IRA lacked the discipline within its own ranks necessary to fully end violence. Sinn Féin's exclusion from talks continued.

THE NORTHERN IRELAND
WOMEN'S COALITION

In 1996, amid ongoing frustration at male-dominated politics, the Northern Ireland Women's Coalition was established. It was a cross-community group with equal numbers of Protestant and Catholic members and delegates. It advocated for the rights of women and girls to be a consideration in the peace process and for a gender-based approach to be applied to the negotiations. The group noted that much of the violence and the subsequent posturing by politicians was embedded in toxic masculinity and male aggression. Nearly all violence was committed by men, as most paramilitary organisations and the army had almost exclusively male membership. By contrast, women were disproportionately affected by the violence – often performing unrecognised and underappreciated 'emotional labour' to keep communities and families together amid the chaos of the war. Women and girls performed the bulk of 'caring duties' incurred by the violence, such as visiting relatives in prison to provide emotional support, caring for injured relatives, or advocating for peace in their local communities. The Women's Coalition was established as a non-sectarian grouping with no stance on the constitutional question but instead aimed at advocating for women on both sides of the divide. It was headed by Monica McWilliams, an academic from the Catholic community, and Pearl Sagar, a social worker from the Protestant community, who led a mixed group of candidates that began contesting elections and lobbying for inclusion in peace talks.

DRUMCREE

Throughout the Troubles, the July marching season proved a lightning rod for loyalist violence, and many feared that the marches in 1996 could catastrophically undermine the still-delicate peace process. Their worst fears were realised in a suburb called Drumcree. As had become the annual custom, loyalists insisted on marching through Catholic streets in the area, while Catholics fiercely opposed them. The loyalists argued it was their right as the majority community in Northern Ireland to march where they pleased, while Catholic residents argued that the marches were a sectarian act which loyalists engaged in to intimidate them. Fearing violent clashes if the march proceeded, the RUC banned the event. When Orangemen attempted to enter, they were met by police officers in full riot gear, backed up by barbed wire and armoured vehicles. Loyalists were outraged and sought to reassert their dominance by staging numerous roadblocks and barricades across Northern Ireland. Rioting ensued, with loyalists intimidating officers and their families, setting properties alight and looting. More than a hundred people were injured and one Catholic man was shot dead by loyalists. The crisis came to a climax when loyalists arrived with a bulldozer to physically drive through the police's barricades. Unable to contain them any longer, the RUC backed down and allowed the marchers to conduct their parade. Riot police instead set about physically moving the Catholic residents so the Orangemen could march through. This time, nationalist communities rioted, causing disorder and violence. Once again, Northern Ireland's instability was exposed.

Talks between the main parties continued throughout the year but were ultimately unproductive.

TONY BLAIR'S PREMIERSHIP

1997 began with a number of loyalist killings which were widely condemned. In Portadown, a Catholic man was kicked to death by a mob in controversial circumstances, as it was alleged that a nearby RUC patrol had failed to intervene and save his life. A police officer was also kicked to death by loyalists in a similar murder in County Antrim soon after. A Catholic teenage girl was shot in the head by a loyalist as she slept in her Protestant boy-friend's home.

May brought a new Prime Minister in the form of Tony Blair, bringing fresh enthusiasm for talks between the parties. The election was also notable for a considerable increase in the nationalist vote. Since the foundation of the Northern Ireland state, unionists had commanded a considerable majority and, indeed, this had been a deliberate design of the new jurisdiction. However, with each generation the unionist majority was in decline, as Catholic families tended to have higher birth rates than their Protestant counterparts. In the May election, this trend was evidenced as unionists lost control of four councils they had previously governed, including Belfast. The rise of the nationalist electorate strengthened nationalists' political bargaining power and made the case against the return of unionist majority rule much stronger.

In his first weeks in office, Blair illustrated his personal commitment to the peace process, as one of his first acts as Prime Minister was to visit Belfast. He also appointed Mo Mowlam to be his Northern Ireland Secretary, the first woman to hold the position. She was known for her unconventional charisma and informal nature, often swearing and speaking in blunt language. This was a considerable break from the stiff and remote figures who were more often tasked with the position. While her different approach shocked many local politicians, it also helped establish rapport with others.

Soon after, the British and Irish government announced that political talks would begin in September. They would not make IRA decommissioning a pre-requisite for Sinn Féin to enter the all-party talks. Instead, the party's participation was dependent on the IRA embarking on a new ceasefire for six weeks prior to entering the talks.

This new ceasefire duly began in July. One newspaper recorded at the time:

Nobody in Northern Ireland was indifferent to the IRA cessation of violence, but nearly everybody pretended to be. Most people simply stayed home, lounged in the garden or visited the pub or the supermarket: no cheers went up, no champagne popped, no church bells rang. It was a most understated ceasefire.

If few emotions were expressed, it was not because they did not exist: rather it was that there were too many of them, and that they went too deep. There is hope for the future, relief and a deep desire for peace; but there is also bitterness, suspicion, fear and even rejection.

The focus was now on unionist politicians to see if they would accept Sinn Féin's presence in the talks. The DUP, who said they would not engage in a process alongside people they considered to be IRA terrorists, refused to take part. After some deliberation, the UUP remained but voiced their deep reservations about Sinn Féin's inclusion.

In a further bid to bolster unionist appetite for the talks, Mowlam took the controversial step of visiting loyalist paramilitaries in prison in order to secure their support for the process. Within hours of her trip, they agreed to give the talks their backing.

Following their foundation in 1996, the Northern Ireland Women's Coalition had achieved moderate success, gaining enough support to be entitled to two seats at the negotiation table. Their focus was on advocating for the peace process to be viewed as a feminist issue and for resolutions to be gender-aware in noting the particular issues faced by women and girls as a result of the conflict. One of the coalition's candidates, Annie Campbell, explained to the *New York Times* in a 1997 interview that she had joined the party

to bring issues to the political agenda that have been absent. We straddle the Catholic–Protestant line. What we say is quite different. We've opened a space, an opportunity for people who want to put human rights at the centre and have no political agenda. Women have really kept families together, kept things from debilitating into a Bosnia situation. The political arena has been a reflection of the war on the streets. The more huffing and puffing you can do, the less you're prepared to listen, the higher you'll rise in politics in Northern Ireland. We want to dispel that macho myth.

Their ethos, and indeed their presence, shocked the almost all-male delegations present at the negotiating table and many of the men were openly and unapologetically hostile towards them during talks. Unionist male delegates heckled them to interrupt their speeches, shouting 'Stupid women' and 'Traitors' and urging that their time would be better spent if they went home and 'stood by the men of Ulster' from the fireside instead. DUP politician Ian Paisley Jr, who is still an MP twenty years on, was among the most openly hostile and would make loud mooing noises in order to drown the women's voices out when they made speeches, making their contributions impossible to hear over the din. Monica McWilliams, one of the party's leaders and one of their two delegates, was also physically attacked as she attended a silent vigil in support of cross-community relations in 1997. An angry crowd gathered at the event and a brick was thrown at her face, leaving her bruised. McWilliams later described the treatment she and her colleagues faced at the negotiating table as 'ritual humiliation' but asserted it was worth toughing in order to continue to raise their agenda. She told the *New York Times*: 'Women are the ones who've had to pick up the pieces after relatives and friends are murdered, blown up. We're the ones who recognise we have to rise above it – not to let it cripple us.'

In February 1998, Sinn Féin was excluded from the talks process following a number of IRA killings. The other parties, primarily led by the UUP on the unionist side and the SDLP on the nationalist side, continued negotiations in earnest. Talks continued to be tense, but both communities seemed determined to grasp the opportunity for peace. A series of all-night meetings took place. On 10 April, which happened to fall on Good Friday that year, an agreement was announced.

THE GOOD FRIDAY AGREEMENT

The text produced was officially called the Belfast Agreement but went on to be known as the Good Friday Agreement due to the date of the announcement. The biblical analogy was not lost on Northern Ireland's highly religious population, as Good Friday in the Bible marked a moment of death and despair followed by resurrection and salvation. The document was an ambitious and ingenious document based on a bold reworking of Northern Ireland's constitutional status. Its language and provisions were finely balanced to carefully reassure both communities and secure their support for an agreed way forward.

The Agreement was that Northern Ireland would remain in the UK until such time as a vote was held in which a majority of the people of both Northern Ireland and the Republic of Ireland expressed a wish to bring about a united Ireland. The Republic would drop its long-standing constitutional claim to the entire island of Ireland. Following the signature of the Agreement, Stormont would once again sit, but not in the same manner as some decades before, when unionists exercised majority rule unchecked. Now, mandatory power-sharing would be in place, which would mean that the largest nationalist party and the largest unionist party would exercise power together. Rather than having a Prime Minister for Northern Ireland, as previously, the region would now have a First Minister and a Deputy First Minister, one a nationalist and the other a unionist, both holding equal powers, who would govern together. Power to govern in a number of key areas would be devolved from Westminster to Stormont, including health, education and agriculture. However, the British government would retain control of a number of key controversial areas, including security and justice, while pledging to also devolve these areas in the future if Northern Ireland had stabilised to a point where this would be practical.

Other safeguards to prevent discriminatory majority rule included a mechanism called a Petition of Concern, which would allow members of the Stormont Parliament to block or veto certain pieces of legislation. All members would be required to register as a nationalist politician, a unionist politician or neither. If faced with a piece of legislation they considered discriminatory to their community, they could trigger the Petition of Concern, upon which the legislation would no longer require a simple majority to pass but a majority of support among both nationalist and unionist communities. This would ensure that no one side could introduce legislation which would cause discrimination or oppression for the other side.

The Parliament would also be very large, with 108 politicians elected – a huge number for a region with just over a million inhabitants. Politicians would be elected using a system of proportional representation, rather than the first-past-the-post system used in Westminster. This system meant a greater number of minority views would be represented. The logic behind this was that all people in Northern Ireland could feel they had a say in the government, rather than only the mainstream views.

Other mechanisms in the Good Friday Agreement related to Northern Ireland's relationships with the rest of the UK and Ireland. Vertically speaking, a North–South ministerial council would be set up to allow cooperation and the exchange of ideas between Northern Ireland and the Republic of Ireland. Horizontally speaking, a British–Irish council would facilitate cooperation and the exchange of ideas between the UK and Ireland.

On the thorny issue of decommissioning, all parties were required to agree that they would use their influence to ensure paramilitaries gave up their weapons within two years.

The Agreement acknowledged that policing was a deeply contentious issue in Northern Ireland and provided for a review to be carried out into how the RUC force could be improved. Although Catholics comprised 40 per cent of Northern Ireland's population, they amounted to just 7 per cent of the police force, amid claims of sectarian policing. It was agreed that a body would be set up to review the RUC's policies and practices to see how this situation could be improved.

In recognition of the human rights abuses which were alleged to have occurred throughout the conflict, often at the hands of the British or Northern Irish states, a new emphasis on human rights and equality would be key to the new government. Bodies tasked with this safeguarding focus were set up, including the Equality Commission for Northern Ireland and the Northern Ireland Human Rights Commission.

Prisoners who were jailed as a result of violence related to the conflict would be eligible for early release if the paramilitary groups they were associated with stuck to their ceasefires.

People born in Northern Ireland would be entitled to have British citizenship, Irish citizenship, both or neither, and would have the right to identify as they saw fit.

Much of what was agreed in the Good Friday Agreement echoed the Sunningdale Agreement of 1973. Indeed, the SDLP's deputy leader Seamus Mallon is often quoted as having described the Agreement as 'Sunningdale for slow learners'. However, what made this treaty different was the atmosphere in which it was crafted and received. By now, Northern Ireland was exhausted by violence. Republicans were becoming increasingly aware that a united Ireland would not be achieved through physical force and that the British government had the power to match their military might indefinitely. Similarly, Republicans had got a taste of the power they could wield at the ballot box, and the increasing nationalist vote strengthened the potential to achieve a united Ireland through peaceful means. Many in the unionist community were also weary and exhausted by the violence and were desperate for peace to be achieved. The changing demographics illustrated to many unionists that a majority government which only reflected the needs of their community was no longer defensible and some form of power-sharing with nationalists was inevitable. In addition, the Agreement cleverly delegated the issue of police reform to an external review, perceiving that any reform proposals could prove too controversial to unionists (who supported the status quo for policing). For now, unionists merely agreed to a set of non-objectionable principles, and the specific, inevitably controversial, policies necessary to bring change about were delayed. Furthermore, what distinguished this Agreement was the smart strategic decision to immediately put it to the popular vote, to bolster its standing through a referendum.

After being agreed upon by Northern Ireland's politicians, the Agreement was put to the people in a referendum. An effective PR campaign was run to urge Northern Ireland's people to vote 'Yes'. The charismatic and highly popular Prime Minister Blair proved an effective and enthusiastic salesman for the accord. In one memorable moment leading up to polling day, the Irish rock band U2 held a concert in favour of a 'Yes' vote, with UUP leader David Trimble and SDLP leader John Hume making an appearance on stage during the event. In parallel, a less effective but passionate campaign against the Agreement was run, joined by the DUP, who considered it to be morally objectionable as it represented concessions to Republicans they considered to be terrorists.

When polling day came, turnout was a record 81 per cent and returned landslide support for the deal, with 71 per cent voting yes. A parallel referendum was held in the Republic of Ireland to approve the decision to drop their constitutional claim to Northern Ireland and proved even more resounding, with 94 per cent voting yes. The agreement was co-signed by the UK government and the Republic of Ireland government, who were identified as the co-guarantors of the document. It was then lodged with the United Nations.

In June 1998, elections were held for the new Parliament. A solidly pro-Agreement majority of politicians was elected. Dust was wiped off the parliamentary benches, the light bulbs switched on and Stormont's now rusty doors were once again opened. A new era had begun.

THE OMAGH BOMBING

Despite the tectonic shift in the political landscape, peace was by no means instantaneous. A number of rogue paramilitary elements continued to operate, despite the Agreement. As July marching season approached, traditional tensions were once again exposed. In the early hours of 12 July 1998, loyalists threw a petrol bomb into the County Antrim home of a 'mixed marriage' family headed by a Catholic mother and a Protestant father. Their three small boys were burnt to death.

In August, Republicans detonated a bomb in the County Tyrone town of Omagh. Those responsible telephoned a warning to the police in advance but an unclear message meant that members of the public were directed towards the blast rather than away from it. Twenty-nine people were killed, one of the highest death tolls of any attack in the entire conflict. One witness later described the horror at the scene, as a burst water pipe carried fragments of bodies down the street in a flow of water: 'There were people, or actually pieces of people, bodies being washed in, which is something that you never forget. They were just basically piling up at the corner where the gully was. Bits and pieces of legs, arms, whatever, were floating down that street.' Another recalled: 'There were limbs hanging off, bodies being carried on doors, everything was chaotic. Then just as the bus was ready to leave [to transport people to the hospital], the door opened and someone handed a severed arm in. I think that was just too much for the driver. I think he cried all the way to the hospital.' Many feared the horrific attack marked the end of the peace process. In a bid to calm people and prevent chaos or bloody retaliations, the British and Irish governments both recalled their parliaments from summer recess to pass security measures. US President Bill Clinton also flew to Omagh to meet with victims' families and the injured. It emerged that those behind the attack were not the 'mainstream' IRA but so-called dissident Republicans who rejected the peace process and were continuing to engage in violence.

THE DECOMMISSIONING HURDLE

As decommissioning had not yet taken place, power was not yet devolved to the new legislature at Stormont. Debate about decommissioning continued, amid concerns the IRA was not serious about giving up arms, and division over when it should happen. In September 1999, George Mitchell returned to Belfast for more intensive talks on the subject which finally yielded progress. Trimble relented on his previously held position that he would not agree to Sinn Féin entering government without prior decommissioning. As a result of his compromise, it was announced that the new Stormont government could finally form an executive. Ministries were appointed using an allocation system known as the D'Hondt method to give the various perspectives a presence at the executive table. Of the ten ministerial positions, three were allocated to the UUP, three to the SDLP, two to Sinn Féin and the final two to the DUP. Due to their ongoing rejection of the Good Friday Agreement, the DUP took ministries but would not attend meetings. In December 1999, the powers pledged to the new Assembly under the Agreement were finally devolved from London.

THE POWER-SHARING GOVERNMENT

The new power-sharing experiment began in earnest, with previously sworn enemies now taking up seats alongside each other as colleagues. Politicians whose work was usually limited to dramatic speeches and electioneering were now required for the first time to govern, and set about acclimatising themselves to more 'normal' politics, including having policies on issues beyond the constitutional question. Instead, they began to engage in more mundane issues, such as the technicalities of health policies or the education system. After decades of bloodshed and despair, a daring experiment was underway to try to seize peace.

CHAPTER TWO

DIVIDED SOCIETY

Late one night as the clock edged towards midnight, a young Belfast chef heard a knock at his door. The 23-year-old had recently moved into the area, a new neighbourhood nestled in the outskirts of the city, along with his pregnant fiancée, twenty years old, and their young child. The young couple were looking forward to setting up their new home for their expanding family, as they prepared to welcome their second child into the world.

The knock at the door, however, shattered that.

On the doorstep that Tuesday evening were two police officers who had come to deliver a message on behalf of the loyalist terrorist group Ulster Volunteer Force (UVF). The couple, both Catholics, were not welcome in the area, the Protestant group had decreed. 'We believe there is a threat on your life if you're not out of your property by Friday,' the officers informed him.

The family were gone by the morning. Soon after, other Catholics living in the street also fled.

Perhaps the most jarring aspect of the events of that night was that they happened not in the dark days of Northern Ireland's troubled past, but in autumn 2017.

Twenty years on from the signing of the Good Friday Agreement, Northern Ireland continues to be a deeply divided society. Perhaps the most overt sign of this division lies in how few people in the region will live alongside people from the 'other side', instead preferring to live largely segregated lives.

It's something few in polite society will admit to. Most people in Belfast, if questioned, don't want to talk about it on record, or if pushed simply utter magnanimous statements that of course they don't have a problem with people from 'the other community' living next door.

Nevertheless, the data is damning. According to the Northern Ireland Federation of Housing Associations, '90 per cent of social housing estates are still single-identity', i.e. home only to either Catholics or Protestants. In Belfast, that figure rises to 94 per cent.

Walking around Belfast, the division is not subtle but jarring and overt. Around the suburbs of the city, the streets snake and slip through Catholic areas and Protestant areas within a few miles, or sometimes over the course of a few hundred yards.

Of course, as has been previously discussed, it is worth remembering that although the terms 'Catholic' and 'Protestant' are used to describe the two communities in Northern Ireland, in reality religion has very little to do with it. Rather, the terms are linguistic shorthand for nationalism and unionism. Therefore, a 'Catholic' home is not identifiable by rosary beads pegged on the front door, nor Protestant ones by bibles propped up in the porch. Instead, the streets are most often marked by the kerbstones at the side of the pavement, daubed orange, green and white to represent the Republic of Ireland flag in Catholic areas, or red, white and blue to represent the Union Jack in Protestant areas. Flags representing the respective nations fly on lamp-posts and from individual homes. In Catholic areas, an increasing number of streets have road signs in the Irish language or using font evocative of old Irish scrolls. Newsagents in Catholic West Belfast will stock newspapers with a nationalist viewpoint, including newspapers from the Republic of Ireland, while their counterparts in Protestant East Belfast will stock newspapers penned with a unionist slant and shoppers will be unlikely to find on the shelves newspapers from the south of the island. Murals at the end of terraced houses also provide a canvas on which the stories of the respective communities are told. In Catholic areas, tributes might be paid to Republican prisoners who took part in hunger strikes. In Protestant areas, homage is paid to British soldiers in the world wars or local loyalist paramilitary groups.

More often than not, this segregation happens not as a result of anything so dramatic or disturbing as the UVF death threat delivered that evening on the chef's family. Instead, most people segregate themselves often without being conscious that they are doing so. Sectarianism's often imperceptible but nevertheless irresistible gravitational pull has a peculiar way of exerting influence on people's everyday lives without them noticing. Few would admit to not wanting to live next to the 'other side' but instead want to live near family and friends, the school they want their children to attend, or near their work. As social circles, education and work are still deeply segregated environments, this can on a secondary level make neighbourhoods even more segregated.

Such overtly visual tribalism is most pronounced in working-class areas, which bore the brunt of most of the violence in the Troubles. In more middle-class areas, such overt symbols of politics are considered uncouth, and areas like South Belfast's affluent Malone Road suburbs are decorated only with leafy trees lining walkways or the occasional feature fountain in an immaculately landscaped garden. That is not to say that sectarianism is solely limited to working-class areas, but rather that overt visual symbols are more often found there, as middle-class communities perform sectarianism in more subtle or socially sanctioned ways. For instance, many middle-class Catholics will show their political allegiances by owning a holiday home in the Republic of Ireland, often in Donegal. Among middle-class Protestants, some will support sports such as rugby or cricket as a way of showing British allegiance.

Many in Northern Ireland had assumed or perhaps hoped that segregated living would simply fade away. Many simply believed that as peace took hold and society normalised as a result, fear of living next door to Catholics or Protestants would become an irrelevant relic of the conflict and the two communities would naturally begin to blend and mesh, house move by house move. Conscious that after twenty years of peace, this integration had not occurred, Northern Ireland's Housing Executive faced an awkward dilemma. On its housing lists, people waiting for homes would often still refuse to take a home in the 'wrong area' and instead hold out for somewhere in the 'right area'. By tolerating these preferences, the executive ran the risk of being accused of condoning sectarian living. It would not be allowed in another part of the UK for someone to refuse a council house on the basis of their neighbours' religion. If, say, a council in England had been found to be allowing tenants to refuse to live next door to a Muslim, there would have been outrage. So – both legally and morally speaking – how could council houses in Northern Ireland continue to be dealt out like this?

In the early 2000s, moves began towards integrated social housing. The Shared Neighbourhood Programme was set up to encourage and promote Catholics and Protestants living alongside each other. Within new houses built in the scheme, no more than 70 per cent of houses could go to members of one community or the other.

The programme, while admirable in intent, raised a number of issues. Firstly, it placed the onus on working-class people, who were more likely to require social housing than the middle classes, while doing little to address the sectarianism that also exists in the upper echelons of society. Secondly, it raised concerning ethical issues over whether it would be right to refuse social housing to people who would refuse to live with 'the other side'. While such a refusal was often sectarian, such strongly held views were more common among those who had suffered the most in the conflict and had experienced the most trauma as a result. If a Protestant family had previously been attacked by Republicans, for example, then their continued fear of living next to Catholics was, on a human level, harder to condemn outright. Perhaps, critics said, it would have been better to engage in wider community work aimed at dismantling prejudice than to ignore such tensions for years and then use those untreated biases to refuse housing to people in need.

Nevertheless, the scheme began in earnest and ten areas were earmarked to be new Shared Neighbourhoods. One of the flagship programmes, however, was in Cantrell Close, the street on which the young chef and his family lived. The future of the scheme is now uncertain. Of course, the UVF members issuing death threats represent a small portion of Northern Irish society. Indeed, in the days and weeks after news of the young family's ordeal became known, it was condemned by politicians from both sides, who voiced horror and surprise that such malice could exist.

Regrettably, however, the threat was frightening enough to cause an exodus of the Catholics in the area and many more may now be deterred from moving in there. This is, no doubt, exactly the desired effect that the UVF sought when they informed the police of their message.

Unfortunately, it appears that twenty years on from the Good Friday Agreement, for some in Northern Ireland it is still far too much and far too soon to have Protestants and Catholics living side by side.

Hopes of the two communities being able to live alongside each other have been further stunted by the presence of the so-called peace walls in Belfast and Derry-Londonderry. The large metal walls lie strewn across the cities at the areas where the two communities meet. They were erected in 1971 as a temporary measure at 'interface' areas which were proving flashpoints for violence as the conflict escalated.

Almost fifty years on, these temporary fixtures remain as seemingly permanent features. Multiple generations of children have now grown up in their shadow, feeling or hearing but never seeing the presence of the 'other side' as they go about their business just a few yards away.

The walls are perhaps the most overt sign of Northern Ireland's division, as they are a means to physically separate the two communities at a most literal and primitive level through mammoth sheets of steel and iron. Some hundred or so still exist in the two main cities. They make for bleak architectural features, forming scars on the city's landscape. Some are as tall as 18ft and are topped with an ominous garnish of barbed wire.

At the time of the Good Friday Agreement, many hoped that as peace took hold the peace walls would slowly be stripped away, allowing Protestants and Catholics who had lived next door without ever seeing each other to finally be able to mix and interact freely. Politicians at Stormont have pledged to remove them all by 2023.

However, such a moment has still not come. In fact, it appears further away than ever. A study commissioned by the Northern Irish government's Department of Justice and undertaken by Ulster University in 2015 found that an increasing number of people living next to peace walls want them to stay. One thousand people living next to or near the structures were surveyed and 30 per cent wanted the walls to stay, up from 22 per cent who felt that way in 2012. In particular, Protestant residents were more likely to want the walls to remain, backing them by 44 per cent compared to 23 per cent of Catholics.

One resident told researchers:

I love my house, but if the peace wall wasn't here I wouldn't be here. I feel secure with the peace wall – the peace wall, to me, has to remain. There's no way that I would be here [without it], I know my neighbour next door wouldn't be here as well, because we still get bricks and bottles and golf balls coming over the wall, maybe not every week, but every two weeks or three weeks. Without that wall they'd be in at my back door, there's no two ways about it.

It is clear that serious anxiety remains among people living alongside the peace walls. It is hard to know whether these concerns are justified or are imbued with the understandable fear of the unknown, as so many people are so used to the walls that they no longer seem a symbol of dysfunction but merely the status quo. However, research shows these fears are deep-rooted and appear to be deepening further.

While the walls remain, Northern Ireland's claims to be a normalised society appear somewhat hollow. If people in interface communities feel that they are able to evade violent attacks from their neighbours only because their neighbours are physically unable to reach them, then the peace that exists in Northern Ireland cannot be said to be a truly settled peace but rather one where sectarian attacks are prevented not by a change in attitude but purely by a lack of opportunity.

DIVIDED SOCIETY

It is not only housing that remains divided on sectarian lines within Northern Ireland. Schools, hospitals, GP surgeries, parks and public swimming pools are often used almost exclusively by either Protestants or Catholics in Northern Ireland. Indeed, even buses are affected, as many bus routes are effectively Catholic routes or Protestant routes due to stopping off beside the homes or schools of one community or the other.

Further to the social cost of having a divided society, it also means the region is haemorrhaging money as the price of public services vastly outstrips other parts of the UK and the Republic of Ireland.

Research by Ulster University estimates that the cost of running duplicate services for 'both sides' costs around an additional £800 million annually, a considerable sum for a region with just over 1 million inhabitants.*

EDUCATION

Education in Northern Ireland is deeply segregated. More than 90 per cent of school children in Northern Ireland are educated in either a Protestant school or a Catholic school. As most children make their first friends and have their first experiences of developing a social circle while they are at school, this often means they have little or no experiences with children from 'the other side'.

The religious nature of such schools can be apparent in the prayers said in school assemblies or the school calendar observed,

---

* 'Cost of Division: A benchmark of performance and expenditure' (Ulster University Economic Policy Centre, January 2016), accessed at https://www.ulster.ac.uk/__data/assets/pdf_file/0006/86523/Cost-of-Division-Detailed-Paper.pdf

as Catholic schools in particular will give pupils holidays on particular feast days or saints days in line with the Roman Catholic church. In some Catholic schools in Northern Ireland, nuns or priests will continue to have a presence as teachers, head teachers or members of the school board. However, this practice is declining due to the waning influence of the Catholic church, thanks to increased secularisation and lower attendance rates at Mass among younger generations.

Beyond strictly religious influence, school segregation manifests itself in other differences between children's education. For instance, Catholic schools are more likely to offer the Irish language as a course option, while Protestant schools tend not to.

When pupils are applying for universities, Catholic schools will often offer coaching in how to apply to universities in the Republic of Ireland (which uses a separate application system from that of UK universities), while Protestant schools are less likely to do so.

Even sports lessons are often divided on sectarian lines. In Protestant schools, British sports such as cricket, rugby or hockey will be taught and played, while in Catholic schools, traditional Irish football, Irish hurling or the Irish traditional sport camogie are more likely to be offered.

The segregated schooling system means that children often go through their childhood and adolescence only having meaningful interaction with or exposure to people who are in their 'side'. They are brought up with different cultural frameworks far beyond merely theology or religion, as they often practise different sports, speak different languages and are encouraged to apply to different universities.

Parents who send their children to segregated schools (which amounts to nine out of ten parents in Northern Ireland) insist that they are not sectarian. Instead, they argue that they are merely bringing their own children up within their own culture and this must be allowed as a form of both parental choice and freedom of expression.

However, it is undeniable that Northern Ireland's segregated education system is continuing to hold back the region's community relations. Few would have thought that twenty years after the Good Friday Agreement, children (or at least their parents) would still be unable or unwilling to share classrooms together.

LOVE

One of the clearest metrics of the remaining divisions in Northern Irish society twenty years after the Agreement is how few people fall in love across the divide. Research published in the *Journal of Religion and Health* in 2014 shows that just 10 per cent of relationships in Northern Ireland are 'mixed', i.e. involving a Protestant and a Catholic.

It is likely that this situation is largely fuelled by segregation elsewhere in Northern Irish life which means many people's workplaces, social circles or local area will be primarily or solely made up of members of their own community, reducing their opportunities to meet or date people from the other side.

However, in some sections of society, considerable stigma remains over dating or marrying across the divide. Research conducted in 2016 by the Northern Ireland Life and Times Survey found that throughout Northern Irish society as a whole, just 10 per cent of people are opposed to a member of their family marrying someone from another religion. However, among hardline Protestants this appears to be much more of an issue. Research conducted by the University of Liverpool on members of the dominant unionist political party, the DUP, found that 75 per cent would either 'mind a little' or 'mind a lot' if a relative were to marry someone from a different religion.

PARAMILITARY PRESENCE IN NORTHERN IRELAND

One of the most disturbing and dangerous threats to the peace process in modern-day Northern Ireland is the ongoing presence of paramilitary terrorist organisations. Officially, the major groups agreed to disband as part of the Good Friday Agreement, which committed all of its signatories to 'total and absolute commitment to exclusively democratic and peaceful means of resolving differences on political issues, and … opposition to any use or threat of force by others for any political purpose, whether in regard to this agreement or otherwise'. Despite this pledge, paramilitary groups continue to have a considerable presence in Northern Ireland, often meting out 'punishments' to those in their communities who disobey them, whether with beatings, strategic shootings or even murder.

In 2015, two murders shocked Northern Ireland amid concerns that they were related to an internal feud between Republicans.

A 47-year-old man, Gerard 'Jock' Davison, was gunned down in broad daylight on a May morning in a residential area of Belfast as he walked to work. A few months later, one of the suspects in his killing, Kevin McGuigan, was also shot dead. Both men had been former IRA members and founding members of Direct Action Against Drugs, a Republican dissident group which the IRA sometimes called themselves when committing murders during ceasefires. Following the men's deaths, a report was commissioned to examine the extent to which paramilitaries still exist in Northern Ireland almost two decades on from the signing of the Good Friday Agreement. It was jointly drafted by the PSNI and MI5 and found: 'All the main paramilitary groups operating during the period of the Troubles remain in existence.' The groups, called 'dissident' paramilitaries due to their decision to dissent from the peace process, were not only still operating with old members but actively recruiting new members. It found key differences within the 'two sides'. Dissident Republicans, many of whom call themselves 'the Continuity IRA', were found to pose a considerable terrorist threat, carrying out an average of fifteen to forty terrorist attacks of varying seriousness and success each year, e.g. attacking police officers. Dissident loyalists were less likely to be engaged in terrorism-related activity and instead were found to be more focused on having control in their communities through 'petty crime', e.g. attacking drug dealers or car thieves. Many were involved in smuggling goods, dealing drugs and demanding 'protection money' from local businesses, which amounts to cash in exchange for not attacking the premises. Republican paramilitaries were also found to engage in much of the same kind of petty crime. The groups were found to still have stocks of guns and other weapons, but on a much smaller scale to the arms caches held during the Troubles. They were also found to continue to organise themselves in the same traditional paramilitary structures that had been operational during the conflict, such as 'army councils' or 'brigades'.

In 2017, concerns over the possible ongoing presence of loyalist paramilitaries erupted again following a public execution in a supermarket car park. On a May bank holiday weekend, a man was gunned down in a Sainsbury's car park as he was putting his three-year-old child into his car. In a subsequent murder trial, a detective told the court: 'We believe the murder was part of ongoing mounting tensions within [loyalist paramilitary group] East Antrim UDA.'

Unlike during the Troubles, when violence was deliberately focused outwards towards the 'other side', twenty years on from the Good Friday Agreement the focus of such attacks tends to be directed inwards, to the culprits' own communities. Instead of strangers, the victims of paramilitary groups are now people known to them. Deaths occur as a result of infighting among group members, or members 'policing' drug dealers or petty crime in their own neighbourhoods. As a result, such crime largely remains out of sight of mainstream society in Northern Ireland. The groups operate in the most socially and economically deprived areas, where residents already tend to be among the most marginalised in society and have poor relations with the police, making reporting harder for victims.

One of the most disturbing aspects of modern-day paramilitary presence in Northern Ireland has been the ongoing use of so-called punishment shootings. In 2017, a PSNI police officer explained to me the disturbingly precise honour code within which such attacks are carried out. The shootings happen when a paramilitary group decide that someone within their own social circle or community has transgressed in some way and needs to be 'punished'. This most commonly occurs when someone has been buying drugs from the group and failed to pay on time, or is a rival drug dealer who represents business competition, but it can also include people who have engaged in petty theft or anti-social behaviour. A member of the group will inform the person that they are going to be punished and agree a time and a meeting place for the punishment to be carried out. At the agreed time and place, the paramilitary members will meet the person they are punishing and then 'kneecap' them – shoot them through their knees. The groups are precise shooters and will shoot just above or just below the kneecaps, so as to cause pain but not permanent damage. If the person being punished does not cooperate when they are approached and agree to attend their punishment, the group will carry it out anyway but may choose to shoot them in part of their knee which will cause more damage. On some occasions, if the person is considered to be particularly uncooperative, the group will shoot them multiple times in a 'six-pack': a bullet in each elbow, ankle and knee. The police officer told me that because the victims know the shootings are happening in advance, they will prepare by taking drugs or alcohol to numb themselves to the pain, and will often wear tracksuit bottoms rather than denim jeans as the fabric is less likely to complicate a wound. Some will wear shorts, or take their trousers off when they reach the location and neatly fold them in a spot far enough away to avoid blood splatters. Some will inform a friend or family member in advance of what is happening, so that they can help the victim make their way to the local hospital for surgery to remove the bullets. When they turn up at hospitals, doctors will give them medical treatment but the victims will refuse to disclose the details of how they came to have bullet wounds in their bodies or who is responsible. On the rare occasions the police are called, the victims will more often than not refuse to press charges, either because they respect the paramilitary system or because they fear retaliation.

In 2017, one teenage victim of 'kneecapping' explained his experience to the BBC:

My mummy visited me and said, 'Listen, I've been talking to someone to try and sort it out to get someone to give you an easy shooting.' I put my shoes on straight away and said, 'Yes, let's get it over and done with.' On the night it happened I was told to walk up the street and I looked behind me and two men were there. I turned around and said to them, 'There are ten times as many people out there doing worse [crimes] than me.' He just said, 'Listen, kid, I'll look after you.' How's that looking after you? I know people in the organisation who were stealing cars and selling drugs, still selling drugs. They're scumbags. The first time they shot me I only moved a bit but the second time they shot me I was screaming. It went right through and hit my main artery. It busted my whole knee bone. I've actually lost count of how many times I've tried to kill myself [since].

Another explained:

> They got in contact with someone in my family. They told me
> that I had to go and meet them. I changed my trousers, went
> out of my house and went to the pub. I had two pints and then
> I got the text message that I had to go, so I walked over on my
> own. And that was it. I walked to the place they told me to go
> and they were standing there. They showed me the gun and told
> me to lie down on the floor. It's a burning sensation for like two
> minutes straight and then it stopped for thirty seconds – then it
> started again. It was burning and burning.

It is perhaps the precise and premeditated nature of 'kneecapping'
that is most disturbing, as it verges on having its own etiquette
and honour code. The victims' own complicity in agreeing to such
attacks is chilling. The reason such processes can still exist in
Northern Ireland lies in how the Troubles caused a fundamental breakdown in law and order in many communities and how
its legacy continues to be felt today. As many areas, particularly Republican ones, felt during the conflict that they could not
trust the police system, many began to believe they had no option
but to police and protect themselves. For some, there is lingering
stigma about contacting the police or inviting them into particular
neighbourhoods to investigate crimes, as they are still perceived
to be the enemy. As a result, if a car is stolen or local youths are
tormenting neighbours with anti-social behaviour, many will not
think to contact the local authorities but will instead phone their
local paramilitaries. The groups that conduct the attacks have a

financial incentive to do so as they can often control considerable drug money through such punishments, as well as enjoying social power and control in their local areas. Those who make use of paramilitary punishment shootings are a small and extreme minority in Northern Ireland. However, their presence cannot be overlooked, as the attacks continue on a regular basis and even appear to be increasing with time. Figures obtained by the BBC found ninety-four such attacks were reported in 2016/17, an average of two per week. Most worryingly, this was an increase of 30 per cent on the previous year.

DIVIDED SOCIETY AFTER
THE GOOD FRIDAY AGREEMENT

Twenty years after the Good Friday Agreement, the intense sectarian hatred that came to characterise parts of society has thankfully quelled. Where once hardly a day went by without a sectarian murder being committed, peace now exists.

It is important not to be dismissive of the enormous progress this represents. Nevertheless, as we have seen in this chapter, sectarianism has far from ended. As has been illustrated, Northern Ireland remains a deeply divided society in which most people live, work, study or fall in love on the basis of the side they were born into. It would be unfair to characterise this as being the result of intense sectarian hatred, yet is also too pronounced to ignore.

While Northern Ireland is now at peace, it is a deeply fractured peace. The fear and violent anger that once existed has now largely gone, but what has replaced it cannot be considered true cohesion or harmony. In many ways, Northern Ireland continues to be characterised by two almost completely separate communities living quietly and peacefully alongside each other but also not integrating. Although this division is more subtle than rioting on the streets, it is in many ways just as sinister and just as damaging for Northern Irish society.

A society in which Catholic and Protestant children cannot be educated in the same classrooms, or their parents cannot live in the same streets, in which peace walls are increasingly clung to, and dating across the divide remains taboo, is not a society in which sectarianism has ceased. Rather, the violence may have been drained from it, and it may have been spruced up to look benign and innocuous, but sectarianism has not truly ended. It has been refashioned for a post-conflict generation, but it continues to divide just as much as ever.

CHAPTER THREE

COLD-CASE MURDERS

In a quiet pocket of rural Northern Ireland, there's a town whose name has come to be synonymous with grief. It was once an unremarkable set of streets and shops that was the centre of the world for local farmers and families but little known beyond the small community it cradles. During the conflict, however, its name was one of infamy after it became home to one of the Troubles' deadliest and most gruesome mass murders.

Decades on, the streets on which the massacre occurred have been dismantled and reconfigured, along with, to a lesser extent, the communities around it. Marking the atrocity is a small but dignified memorial in the town, erected by well-wishers determined not to forget those who were killed in the massacre while life in the town moves on around the site where it happened.

Locals walking past will often pause as a sign of respect as they go by the memorial, while visitors, or 'blow-ins' in local parlance, stop for a moment in its shadow while reading the inscriptions and a brief account of the horrors that occurred.

Recently, however, a curious thing has happened. Someone has taken to vandalising the memorial. Locals scratch their heads and purse their lips, confused as to who could do something so callous.

It's a low-level mystery that has been the subject of gossip and whispered conversations in the town in recent months. Few expect to ever unmask the culprit and instead the speculation continues with tattle by the counter in the post office and in line at the bank.

I'm taken aback, then, when a relative of one of the victims makes an unexpected confession to me on a visit to the town. It has been them – the victims' families – vandalising the memorial to their own relatives.

She tells me: 'We don't want anyone to know. But this way, we can all see it as our secret; it's a bit of empowerment.'

She explains that the victims' families have felt increasingly helpless about the murders. No one has ever been held to account for their loved ones' deaths. A special police team charged with investigating cold cases from the Troubles reopened the case a few years ago and gave them hope for the first time in decades. However, nothing ever came of it and that hope faded again as the inquiry was once more wound down. There are persistent rumours that the killers live in the town and walk the same streets as the victims' relatives every day. Throughout this ordeal, the relatives have begun to feel that, due to the infamy of the murders, the memories of their loved ones have become hijacked by politicians wishing to make points about the wider conflict despite knowing little about the lives they are ostensibly commemorating.

For these relatives, vandalising the memorial is an outlet for their anger at the botched grieving process to which they have been subjected. The woman tells me: 'Isn't it awful to have to do something like that to feel a bit of empowerment? But it's other people who have done this to us.'

I find myself speechless – at once bewildered by the logic and loath to disagree or tell them how they should or should not grieve.

I agree to keep the secret, mindful of the judgement and likely ostracism the relatives would face from their neighbours if the truth were revealed. As I leave the town and in the weeks and months afterwards, I remain struck by what a jarring act of desperation it is to desecrate a memorial to one's own loved ones and what it says about the ongoing distress of these families who feel they have no option but this to feel control. Left lingering in limbo by a lack of convictions for their relatives' deaths and feeling strung along aimlessly by a botched legacy inquiry, they are just some of the thousands of people across Northern Ireland aching for closure as those responsible walk free.

* * *

Over the course of the Troubles, some 3,637 people were murdered in ways deemed to be a direct result of the conflict, whether at the hands of terrorist organisations, the police or the army.* Few resulted in prosecutions or convictions at the time, and twenty years after the Good Friday Agreement thousands remain unsolved.

It is perhaps one of the most serious failings of the Agreement that it did not put in place any mechanism for dealing with these

---

* David McKittrick et al., *Lost Lives: The Stories of the Men, Women and Children Who Died as a Result of the Northern Ireland Troubles* (Mainstream, 1999)

thousands of cold-case murders. In other post-conflict societies globally, inventive measures have been engaged to deal with pasts in which large-scale murders have gone unsolved. For instance, in post-apartheid South Africa, a Truth and Reconciliation Commission was established whereby those who confessed to 'politically motivated crimes' could be granted pardon in exchange for revealing their actions, thereby, it was hoped, allowing victims' families to gain closure and the nation to fully understand and learn from the past. Similarly, in post-genocide Rwanda, a community resolution was set up through 'Gacaca courts' whereby communities could discuss atrocities and confront perpetrators.

Notably, no mechanism was put in place by the Good Friday Agreement. The omission is perhaps understandable given that it is likely that any suggestions would have been rejected by one or other faction and the Agreement's authors therefore opted to remain silent on the matter in the interest of getting any measure of consensus. Perhaps it was hoped that once peace came, Northern Ireland's politicians would eventually reach such a point of maturity and mutual understanding that they would be able to agree on a collective way of addressing the unsolved murders. This has not come to pass.

Twenty years on, there is no agreed means to investigate unsolved murders in the Troubles. Far from relatives' agitations fading with time, the matter is only becoming more and more pressing with each passing day. Thirty or forty years on from when most Troubles deaths occurred, many of those accused, witnesses and relatives are slowly dying of old age. Others are now finding their memories clouded by time or conditions such as dementia. Evidence is rotting, decaying or vanishing.

In one of the most infamous cases of the conflict, the death of Jean McConville, time risks becoming an insurmountable barrier to bringing her killers to account. McConville was kidnapped by the IRA from her home in West Belfast after the group were said to have become suspicious that the mother of ten may have been informing the British Army about IRA activity. Her remains were found by a member of the public on a beach in the Republic of Ireland in 2003. With the help of information contained in the Boston College tapes, a history project conducted by the US university, charges were brought against an elderly Republican man almost half a century after McConville's disappearance on two counts of soliciting her murder. In 2017, the suspect's lawyers told the court that their client, who was by now eighty years old, had dementia and that to subject him to a trial now would be 'oppressive'. The case was by no means unique.

The same year, I was in court reporting on the reopening of an inquest into the death of Joseph Parker, a 25-year-old Catholic man who was shot dead by soldiers while he was attending a Christmas disco in North Belfast with his sister in 1971. He had an eighteen-month-old daughter and his wife was pregnant with their second child. The circumstances of his death have been disputed by witnesses inside the dance hall and by the soldiers. Fellow dancers said they saw a number of soldiers enter the hall suddenly, where they were met by a hostile and unwelcoming crowd of around 100 attendees of the dance, some of whom shouted at the soldiers to leave and threw bottles at them. A skirmish was said to have occurred, before a soldier began firing shots indiscriminately into the crowd. Panic broke out, with dancers ducking to the ground to shield themselves from bullets. When the chaos had calmed and they got to their feet, Parker (known to his family as Joe-Joe) lay wounded on the ground and later died in hospital. By contrast, the soldiers' account was that they had been on patrol in the area as part of the Queen's Lancashire Regiment that evening and had seen a suspicious man, possibly carrying a gun, appear to slip into the hall. They say they entered the hall to see if it was an IRA man on the loose and did not expect to find a packed dance hall of people who were hostile to their presence. They said any shots fired were not deliberately aimed at anyone or intended to injure a civilian. An inquest had been held shortly after the death and recorded an open verdict in 1972. Since then, Parker's family had insisted the inquest had not been balanced or thorough, and pushed for the case to be reopened. In 2017, forty-five years later, the inquest was reopened at Laganside Court in Belfast.

Parker's sister, Teresa Watt, was the first witness to address the inquest. Now seventy-one, her body was clearly frail and she appeared to be struggling to stand. Leaning on a relative for support, she was slowly deposited in the witness box, where she was then asked various questions by a lawyer for the coroner and a lawyer for the soldiers about what had occurred forty years earlier. Reliving the moment her brother was shot dead in front of her, Watt did her best to answer the questions but soon became confused and distressed. Initially she could remember the events, then she could only remember the aftermath, then she couldn't remember giving a statement to the coroner a few months ago, then she couldn't remember things she had said mere minutes ago. After a while, she merely looked at the coroner and said in an emotional voice, 'Please, are you finished with me yet?' The exchange was agonising to watch. Watching it unfurl minute by minute, I was shocked that such a scene could occur in a UK court. Watt was clearly distressed and appeared to be in too vulnerable a position to be subjected to a cross-examination from lawyers.

A pause was announced to allow Watt time to regather her thoughts. As she left the witness stand for her short breather out in the corridor, few in the court expected she would return to give evidence and indeed she did not. Outside the court, her lawyer explained that Watt had been uncertain of whether or not she'd be able to make it to court that day or be able to give evidence but she had been determined to do her bit for her brother. After waiting forty-six years for this to come to court, she didn't want to let him down.

Even more harrowing, this was not her first inquest of this type. Just months before she saw her brother shot dead, her husband Barney had also been shot dead by British soldiers. Her brother had taken her to the Christmas disco that evening in an attempt to cheer her up and coax her out of the house amid her grief. She had been through the same inquest process for her husband earlier in 2017 too.

Fading memories and confused witnesses were not the only aspects of the case that revealed the complexities of investigating events so long after they had occurred. By the time of the 2017 inquest into Joseph Parker's death, the dance hall in which the shooting had occurred had long been demolished, making it difficult to measure with minute precision exactly where the soldiers may have had a line of sight, or how long it might have taken for the dancers to flee. Instead of having a site to visit or modern-day architectural plans to scrutinise, the court viewed a number of grainy and low-resolution black-and-white photographs of what the hall had looked like. The coroner relied on a number of other sources in considering the evidence, including contemporary and fresher testimonies from civilians, testimonies from soldiers and post-mortem examination results.

When he announced his verdict in 2017, Coroner Joseph McCrisken found he did not agree with the previous inquests' findings of an open verdict and instead found the killing had been unjustified. McCrisken found that based on the evidence presented to the 2017 court, one of the soldiers had acted recklessly by shooting into the crowded dance hall while he was in a kneeling position, meaning the bullets shot Parker in both his thighs. The coroner's finding stated: 'At the inquest it was shown to my satisfaction that a soldier kneeling and aiming with a weapon in this position is the most likely to have fired the shot which struck Mr Parker.' He said that 'Mr Parker was not deliberately targeted' by the solider, but added: 'This soldier was acting recklessly when he fired shots at such a low level in a hall half full of civilians.' He concluded: 'I have not been presented with any evidence which suggests that Mr Parker posed any threat, either direct or indirect, to the military patrol. I am satisfied, therefore, that the force used against Joseph Parker was not justified since he posed no threat to members of the patrol.' The coroner was critical not only of the actions of the individual soldier but also of those of the wider patrol, finding that poor planning created a 'powder-keg' scenario whereby the soldiers burst into the hall without a plan on how to proceed or possibly diffuse the tense situation safely. The nature of an inquest is vastly different from a criminal trial, meaning that killings are found to be 'justified' or 'unjustified' rather than the accused being convicted of murder or any other criminal offence. Following a finding of an unlawful killing, therefore, the accused will not face prison time but many families find it a useful mechanism for making their loved ones' deaths a matter of public record, and the findings can also form the basis of possible civil proceedings against the Ministry of Defence.

Parker's daughters had been in court throughout, determined to see justice served for the father they had never had the chance to know. Asked how she felt hearing the coroner's findings, his daughter Charlene said her family had 'never once doubted the outcome' in the 46-year fight with the legal system, adding: 'It is devastating but we are elated. It's closure for us now.'

* * *

Numerous other cold cases presently being investigated within the criminal justice system are also facing complex legal and ethical issues due to the passage of time. Indeed, when it comes to many of the cold cases that are being reopened in the 2010s, an increasing number of relatives, victims and alleged culprits are also dying of old age.

In 2017, one of the key witnesses in the Guildford Four case died aged eighty-four. Former Metropolitan Police Commissioner Peter Imbert had been accused of failing to follow up an IRA confession in the 1974 Guildford bomb which killed five people and injured sixty-five others. A botched investigation at the time saw four people wrongly convicted for the crime and forced to serve fifteen years behind bars before being released. The real killers have never been caught. A fresh case was opened in the 2010s in a bid to finally find the truth. Lord Imbert died just weeks after lawyers submitted a request for a fresh inquest into the killings, and the future of that case is now uncertain.

The question of if and how these cold cases should continue to go before the courts raises a number of complex moral conundrums. On the one hand, many in Northern Ireland question the value of arresting and imprisoning people who are by now often very elderly and for whom imprisonment might be considered cruel or unfair due to their old age and often related ill health.

Similarly, many argue that one of the main principles of jailing people is to act as a deterrent and ensure a repeat occurrence cannot occur while the murderer is removed from mainstream society. While this may apply in normal policing environments, it is less applicable to a post-conflict society, as those responsible for deaths have largely stopped as they now consider the war 'over'. Can we accept that some people acted as they did purely in the context of the conflict and no longer pose a threat to society?

Conversely, many argue that, conflict or not, the fundamental rule of law must stand. It is hard to imagine any other part of the UK in which British citizens could shoot dead British subjects on British soil and face no repercussions. To let murderers walk free, this school of thought argues, is a negation of one of the most fundamental principles of a civilised society.

As has been outlined above, some families are not pushing for criminal proceedings against those responsible for their loved ones' deaths and are instead pushing for fresh inquests into killings. As these are not criminal trials, the role of inquests is not to deliver a criminal conviction for the accused but instead to determine whether a killing was justified or unjustified, and whether or not reasonable force was used. This means that where a killing is found to have been unjustified, those deemed responsible do not receive a criminal conviction or face prison time as a result of the inquest. Instead, the focus tends to be on correcting the public record of how someone died, which many families prioritise if they feel a biased or superficial inquest conducted at the time gave the wrong official account. Following a finding of unlawful killing, families can consider taking a separate criminal case or taking a civil case against a state organisation associated with the killing (e.g. the Ministry of Defence in cases where a soldier has been found responsible). Therefore, the inquest option can be useful for families who wish to see their loved one's name 'cleared', as they see it, but who do not necessarily wish to see someone go to jail or receive a criminal conviction for the death.

Regardless of what Northern Ireland decides to do about the cold-case murders, the region realistically has only a small window of the next few years to either investigate these murders or else accept that the truth will never come out. In recent years, some steps have been taken towards addressing this but have on each occasion been botched.

THE HISTORICAL ENQUIRIES TEAM

The Historical Enquiries Team (HET) was set up in 2005, and became operational in 2006, to re-examine 3,268 cold cases from the conflict. The unit was tasked with collecting information about the cases, reviewing evidence and trying to build a case that could be referred to the courts for prosecution. However, not long after it was set up, serious concerns were raised about the legal and ethical aspects of its work.

Research in 2009 by Ulster University academic Dr Patricia Lundy suggested fundamental flaws existed in the HET. She said the unit was giving preferential treatment to British soldiers accused of murdering people in the conflict, due to serious misinterpretation of the law.

As a result, a report was commissioned by Her Majesty's Inspectorate of Constabulary to look into the concerns Dr Lundy's research had raised. That report, published in 2013, found that British soldiers were indeed being probed 'less rigorously' than other alleged killers.

Furthermore, the HET was criticised for having insufficient legal powers to conduct full inquiries on the same level as police could. For instance, the HET had no power to compel witnesses or suspects to give evidence or respond to allegations.

The HET was finally disbanded in 2014. At the time, police cuts caused by austerity were blamed as part of the reason for its failure and ultimate closure, as it was a time- and resource-intensive undertaking and the police wished to use their officers in other areas.

Since its closure, the HET has been caught up in allegations which have undermined its credibility even more.

In 2016, an inquest into the Kingsmill massacre, in which ten Protestant workmen were gunned down by the IRA in South Armagh in 1976, had to be halted after it emerged that the HET's fingerprint expert had failed on two separate occasions to match fingerprints connecting a suspect to an alleged getaway vehicle used in the murders. It emerged that the HET had just one fingerprint expert working on all the cases it was examining.

After questions were raised in relation to the Kingsmill massacre, a quality assessment was carried out on his work whereby Northern Irish police, overseen by officers from London's Metropolitan Police, tested seventy of his cases, around a tenth of his overall 685-case workload. Of these seventy cases, a dozen were found to have flaws. Questions were raised as to whether the fingerprint expert had been overwhelmed by the workload, or suffering from ill health such as failing eyesight, but he was unable to explain how or why such errors had occurred. It has not been revealed which twelve cases were found to have flaws but it is now likely that a great many will be questioned for their veracity and validity, potentially causing greater confusion and distress to victims' families.

Amid the chaotic and botched implementation of the Historical Enquiries Team's work, a further stumbling block has arisen which as yet has proven insurmountable: the role of British soldiers and other state actors and whether they should be treated the same way as other killers.

BRITISH SOLDIERS

Precisely what happened on the day of John Pat Cunningham's death is disputed. However, this much is agreed: upon seeing two armed soldiers out on patrol near his home in County Armagh in 1974, he turned and ran. Five bullets rang out, three of which punctured his body. He died where he fell.

Cunningham was twenty-seven years old at the time of his death. He was someone who might in modern terminology be called a vulnerable adult, or someone with considerable learning difficulties.

Medical reports state he had the mental age of a child between six and ten years old. To his family, he was a kind and gentle son. A surviving black-and-white photograph of him, the surface of which is now yellowed and wrinkled by the intervening four decades, shows a man with a mop of dark curly hair and a bemused glint in his eye.

Those who knew him say he had a serious fear of men in uniform, who by this time were an increasing fixture in the lives of people in his village in Benburb, which borders the counties of Armagh and Tyrone, as armed officers were deployed to monitor the area for signs of possible IRA activity. They say that is why, when he was approached by two soldiers as he walked home from a day's work at a farm where he helped out, his response was to run.

The two soldiers, known only as Soldier A and Soldier B, were briefly interviewed about the incident by the RUC, the Northern Irish police at that time. The soldiers exercised their right to silence. No prosecution was brought against them. No documents from the RUC's investigation are available to shed any light on the reasoning behind the decision.

The case was one of those examined recently by the Historical Enquiries Team. By this stage the soldiers were now in their seventies. Again, they refused to speak or explain what happened.

The HET report stated of the RUC's original investigation: 'By not obtaining the soldier's [*sic*] account of what happened more vigorously, the investigation was not as thorough or effective as it could have been.'

The HET concluded of Cunningham's death: 'He was a vulnerable adult who was unarmed and shot as he was running away from soldiers. There is no evidence that he posed a threat to the soldiers or anyone else.'

However, as the two soldiers were still refusing to answer questions about his death and the HET had no power to compel them to do so, the HET report concluded: 'They have both chosen not to engage and there are no grounds to arrest and further interview them under caution. There are therefore no new lines of enquiry to progress the investigation into John Pat's death.'

In a statement, the Ministry of Defence apologised for the incident. However, the family were told that no more could be done. His death was something they would just have to make peace with.

Then, one Tuesday in April 2015, some forty-one years after Cunningham's death, one of the soldiers was arrested in England and taken to Northern Ireland for questioning. In 2017, Dennis Hutchings, then aged seventy-five, was formally charged with attempted murder and grievous bodily harm. The court was told that Hutchings was Soldier A at the scene and that the second soldier, known only as Soldier B, had since died.

The Director for Public Prosecutions had launched a fresh investigation in 2013 into the incident and deemed it had sufficient evidence to mount a prosecution.

Hutchings's legal team told the court he had seriously ill health due to his advanced years, including kidney failure. They said he and Soldier B were on alert that IRA men were armed and in the area, which was why they were on patrol. Hutchings asserts, therefore, that when he saw Cunningham run they had a right to assume there was a considerable risk he may have been an IRA man.

The case has become a lightning rod for much of the anger and discontentment over Troubles cold-case investigations. Those in favour of prosecution say it is fair and right that Mr Hutchings be put on trial, so that if he is indeed found guilty, someone can finally be held to account for Cunningham's death. However, those opposed say the trial amounts to unfair haranguing of a seriously ill ex-serviceman who was merely performing his duties to the best of his ability during an increasingly chaotic conflict.

In the autumn of 2017, I met Dennis Hutchings as he and ex-soldiers who had been based in Northern Ireland during the conflict held a rally outside Buckingham Palace in London, demanding an end to what they termed the 'witch-hunt' of ex-soldiers. Scores of former soldiers were present, most of whom were now in their sixties or seventies. Their march on Buckingham Palace was therefore more languorous in speed than the term 'march' might suggest, their movements soundtracked by intermittent chimes as the medals they proudly wore on their lapels clinked against each other with each slow stride.

Their number was swollen by scores more supporters marching alongside them, wearing T-shirts and badges with messages such as 'Support Our Soldiers'. Combined, they formed a block of around a hundred marchers who strode from Horse Guards Parade to the House of Commons, via Buckingham Palace.

Before the marchers set off on their journey, they gathered alongside the monuments to British soldiers from the world wars on Horse Guards Parade, in a positioning that is hard to see as anything other than a deliberate attempt to evoke 'great' war figures.

Alongside them, a small group of half a dozen or so counter-protesters emerged bearing placards bearing Cunningham's name. They held a silent protest, simply standing holding their signs. The soldiers' cohort was soon incensed and what followed was one of the most unsettling scenes I've reported on in my journalistic career.

Supporters of Hutchings, some of whom wore soldiers' uniforms and medals, squared up to the supporters of Cunningham and began jeering at them. They were told that they were 'scum' and were hounding brave British soldiers who had done nothing but good to the people of Northern Ireland. They were told that Northern Irish Catholics 'should be grateful' that the British Army were there in the first place: 'We were there to protect you lot and you turned against us!', shouted one man. Other insults shouted from Hutchings's supporters included that Cunningham's death was the fault of his family, who should not have let him out in public due to his learning disability. Others said the deceased probably 'would have joined the IRA anyway', had he lived, and his death therefore had saved the world from another terrorist.

The march continued, culminating in Hutchings gripping his war medals in his fists and throwing them through the gates of the Houses of Parliament to show his disgust at what he considers the British government's failure to protect men like him.

The rally ended and I spoke with Hutchings, who told me he was very pleased with the how the day had gone although somewhat disappointed with what he considered to be low turnout. He said he hoped the march would send a message to the British government over what he told me was an 'absolute travesty of justice'.

When I later wrote about what had happened, a man who identified himself as an organiser of the event took to social media to assert that it was untrue that anyone had called John Pat Cunningham's supporters 'scum' or jeered at them. He said that I was a Sinn Féin/IRA agent seeking to discredit the soldiers through my reporting on the event – an odd and unnerving echo of the argument the British Army often used in response to allegations during the Troubles.

The death of John Pat Cunningham is not the only cold case where British soldiers are accused of murdering innocent civilians. Indeed, figures show that of the cold cases being considered by authorities, scores feature soldiers as suspected perpetrators.

Although they represent a small proportion of the cases being investigated overall, the cases against British soldiers have opened up particular debate and controversy, coming to dominate and even distort discourse around Troubles legacy cases. The highest-profile investigation into alleged killings by soldiers was the Saville Inquiry into the 1972 Bloody Sunday atrocity, when troops from the Parachute Regiment opened fire on a civil rights march in Derry-Londonderry, killing fourteen civilians. At the time, the army had maintained that some of those killed were Republican terrorists who had shot first, prompting the soldiers to open fire in self-defence, a claim the victims' families fiercely denied. An inquest in 1972 had been rejected by nationalists as a 'whitewash'. In January 1998, three months before the signing of the Good Friday Agreement, Prime

Minister Tony Blair announced that a public and independent judicial inquiry would be conducted into the events. The inquiry became one of the longest and most expensive in British legal history. More than 1,000 witnesses were interviewed as part of the probe, which concluded twelve years later in 2010 and is estimated to have cost in the region of £200 million. The report found that:

> Firing by soldiers of 1 Para on Bloody Sunday caused the deaths of thirteen people and injury to a similar number, none of whom was posing a threat of causing death or serious injury. What happened on Bloody Sunday strengthened the Provisional IRA, increased nationalist resentment and hostility towards the army and exacerbated the violent conflict of the years that followed. Bloody Sunday was a tragedy for the bereaved and the wounded, and a catastrophe for the people of Northern Ireland.

Following the release of the report, then Prime Minister David Cameron made a statement to the House of Commons saying: 'What happened on Bloody Sunday was both unjustified and unjustifiable.' The inquiry has been welcomed by Northern Ireland's nationalist community, many of whom see it as vindicating their views that the army on occasion acted recklessly and attempted to smear innocent victims as terrorists in a bid to discredit them. However, many in the unionist community felt the inquiry to be an unnecessarily expensive and prolonged probe and questioned why the same scrutiny was not being applied to the actions of Republican terrorist actions, and why large-scale, well-funded investigations were not being launched into IRA attacks.

The scale and scope of the Bloody Sunday inquiry has not been replicated for any other contested deaths from the Troubles. The British government has maintained that while it was appropriate for that specific atrocity due to the notoriety and political significance of Bloody Sunday, it is not appropriate or manageable for similar exercises to be carried out into other Troubles deaths. Instead, the cases against British soldiers being brought before Northern Irish courts are primarily inquests to be considered by coroners' courts. Often, these involve reopening inquests that were undertaken at the time but which have been criticised as being biased or not thorough enough. These courts do not have the same resources or abilities as the large-scale Saville Inquiry, but are still tasked with tackling many of the same legal and ethical complexities involved in the hugely sensitive issue of investigating ex-soldiers.

In most circumstances in which a military is deployed to engage in conflict, war has usually been declared. However, no official war was ever declared in Northern Ireland, as the UK – perhaps wishing to avoid the legal possibility of the Republic of Ireland deploying troops, or perhaps for fear that such an announcement would cause serious panic and even further social unrest – instead always declared it an internal UK matter of civil disturbance.

Therefore, the usual rules of war did not apply. Those shot by the British Army in the Troubles have the same legal standing as if a soldier today shot dead a civilian on the streets of Tonbridge or Tottenham. In this context, ex-soldiers' indignation at being held to account for killings is perhaps understandable – they considered themselves at war; the law did not. There now exists an extremely fraught and legally complex situation which is without parallel in the armed forces' living memory.

The decision by the British government not to declare Northern Ireland an official war may have suited their interests at the time, but the legal ramifications which may not have occurred to them at the time are now considerable. In the minds of the ex-soldiers, it is grossly unfair that if there is a price to pay for this decision, it is they who will have to pay it, despite playing no part in high-level defence policy, which was agreed on in conference rooms and Cabinet meetings in which they had no say.

Indeed, many soldiers feel there was an understanding of sorts during the conflict that they would be granted immunity for any deaths they caused. An official UK government document emerged in 2010 dated 10 July 1972, some six months after the Bloody Sunday killings. It stated: 'The British Army should not be inhibited in its campaign by the threat of court proceedings and should therefore be suitably indemnified.' Many soldiers may have believed they were operating with an immunity which they later found had no legal standing.

Another disturbing case to go through Laganside Court in Belfast in 2017 further highlighted some of the complexities and nuances of investigating killings enacted by ex-soldiers. The case was an inquest into the death of eleven-year-old Francis Rowntree, who was shot dead by a rubber bullet close to a riot in West Belfast in April 1972. The boy, who was in his last year of primary school, was shot in the head and died two days later from skull fractures and lacerations to the brain. His death was deeply controversial at the time and he was the first person in the Troubles to die after being shot by a rubber bullet. Immediately following his death, some claims circulated that he had been involved in rioting or that he had not been struck directly but by the bullet hitting another surface and ricocheting into him. Following an investigation by the HET in 2010, a fresh inquest into his death was ordered. In his preliminary findings, coroner Brian Sherrard said he had found that Rowntree's killing had not been justified and that the soldier had used excessive force. He said that based on the evidence he had seen, it appeared that an army vehicle had stopped beside the Divis Flats, a Republican stronghold in the city. A crowd of locals gathered around the vehicle, some of whom were hostile and threw objects including stones at it. Rowntree was with a group of other children nearby who were curious to see what was happening and walked up to the crowd to see what they were doing. A number of soldiers were inside the vehicle, one of whom fired two rubber bullets out of the vehicle window to disperse the crowd. One of the bullets struck the child in the head. No warning had been given before the shots were fired. The soldier was given anonymity during the inquest and told the court he had no recollection of the day in question. In his preliminary findings, the coroner found that the British state would have known at that stage that rubber bullets were potentially lethal, due to tests they had conducted on the ammunition. However, the soldier in question had not been trained in how to use them and had not been warned of the threat to life they posed. He had not deliberately sought to target the child. The coroner said: 'The state provided [the soldier] with a lethal weapon without notifying him of its potential lethality or training him in its use. The absence of adequate training made it impossible for [the soldier] to assess whether to use lethal force.' Outside court following the preliminary findings, a small group of Rowntree's surviving relatives were gathered. His brother Jim, a shy and softly spoken man, was far from elated by the findings. Rather, he seemed dazed and sorrowful. With pain etched on his face, he explained that their mother had long held that Francis hadn't been rioting and was innocent. She had spent the past forty-five years campaigning for truth and against the use of rubber bullets, arguing they were too dangerous to be used by the army in residential areas. However, she had died earlier that year, just months before the coroner's verdict, and never lived to see justice for her son in court. Jim showed me a photo he had of her holding a picture of her lost son and said wistfully: 'It's just a shame she wasn't here to see it.' A solicitor for the family said they will reflect on the findings and consider taking a civil claim against the Ministry of Defence.

Francis Rowntree's death and the details that emerged at the 2017 inquest encapsulate some of the complex issues involved in killings by ex-soldiers. As the court found, the soldier had not deliberately sought to kill the child and seems to have had no way of knowing rubber bullets were potentially fatal, as he had not been trained by the army in how to use them or what the possible risks were. This can make responsibility for such deaths more complex. While the soldier in question was found to have fired the shot, Francis Rowntree's death was arguably due to failings happening far above the soldier's level in the Ministry of Defence. It could possibly be argued that those who failed to ensure soldiers were given correct training are more responsible than him.

As we have seen, inquests and investigations into killings by ex-soldiers are deeply controversial in Northern Ireland. In this context, many people, particularly in Northern Ireland's Protestant/unionist community, are strongly opposed to ex-soldiers being prosecuted for killings during the Troubles. However, rather than discussing the ethical and legal issues outlined above, their objections have largely been framed by arguments that cold-case investigations are unfairly skewed against ex-soldiers and they are disproportionately more likely to be investigated than terrorist killings. For instance, the DUP have denounced the investigations as 'one-sided', with their MP Jeffrey Donaldson saying in January 2017:

> The only structures which exist for investigating the past are focused on the activities of the state. There is no mechanism to bring the terrorists responsible for the vast majority of deaths to account. That is a one-sided process and it serves only to assist with the Republican aim of rewriting the history of what happened in Northern Ireland.

Similarly, UUP politician Doug Beattie said in March 2018, 'The systematic investigation of military personnel and not the numerous paramilitary killings in Northern Ireland gives the impression that the justice system is unbalanced in its treatment of legacy cases and is skewed towards the actions of the state.' He added:

> To pursue former soldiers forty-six years later simply will not be understood by many people, especially in the unionist community, who have looked on in bewilderment as terrorists have

been able to avail of royal pardons and on-the-run letters and see out their days in comfort, whilst former soldiers are hauled before the courts.

He warned that it is 'all too easy to review the events of 1972 from the comfort of an armchair in 2018'.

However, despite unionist concerns that probes into cold-case murders are disproportionately skewed against ex-soldiers, the data does not back up these suggestions. Figures show that of the 1,615 cases investigated by the HET into 2,051 deaths, 1,038 were against suspected Republican killers, 536 cases were against loyalists, thirty-two cases were against soldiers, nine against unknown culprits. This amounts to 1.98 per cent of cases probed so far being brought against ex-soldiers.

Nevertheless, the opinion that legacy inquests are an unfair 'witch-hunt' have persisted. In January 2017, Northern Ireland Secretary James Brokenshire told the House of Commons:

I am concerned that the existing mechanisms for investigating incidents which occurred during the Troubles are disproportionately focused on the actions of the Armed Forces and former police officers, rather than the terrorists who were responsible for 90 per cent of deaths. This is wrong and it has to change.

He followed his comments with a column in the *Daily Telegraph* the following week in which he expressed his concerns that an 'imbalance' existed in cold-case investigations, leading to a 'disproportionate' focus on killings by ex-soldiers. He wrote: 'I am clear the current system is not working and we are in danger of seeing the past rewritten.'

The following month, Prime Minister Theresa May told the House of Commons it was 'appalling' that, in her view, soldiers were being unfairly targeted. She said: 'The overwhelming majority of our armed forces serving in Northern Ireland served with great distinction and we owe them a huge debt of gratitude. The situation we have at the moment is that there are cases being pursued against officers who served in Northern Ireland.'

Subsequently, in April 2017, a report published by the House of Commons Defence Committee recommended a statute of limitations for soldiers who were stationed in Northern Ireland during the conflict. It stated:

> We recommend ... the enactment of a statute of limitations, covering all Troubles-related incidents, up to the signing of the 1998 Belfast [Good Friday] Agreement, which involved former members of the Armed Forces. This should be coupled with the continuation and development of a truth recovery mechanism which would provide the best possible prospect of bereaved families finding out the facts, once no-one needed to fear being prosecuted ... We believe that to subject former Service personnel to legal pursuit under the current arrangements is wholly oppressive and a denial of natural justice. It can be ended only by a statute of limitations. Our expert witnesses agreed that the UK Parliament has it entirely within its power to enact such a statute and we call upon the Government in the next Parliament to do so as a matter of urgency.

In 2016, it emerged that DUP leader and then First Minister Arlene Foster had used her power in office to block the release of funding for legacy inquests into Troubles deaths. She cited concerns that the investigations were skewed against ex-soldiers rather than terrorists. However, in refusing to release the funding, she blocked inquests across the board, regardless of the perpetrator. In 2017, it was announced that a legal challenge will be taken against Foster's decision, arguing that this is a breach of Article 2 of the European Convention on Human Rights (ECHR), which guarantees citizens the right to a full and fair investigation where a state actor has ended a citizen's life. In the meantime, many inquests cannot continue without the funds in place, causing more delays and anguish for victims' relatives as the fight to know how and why their loved ones died drags on.

Any hope that victims' relatives had that the British government might intervene and force Foster to release the funds appeared to be dashed by the DUP–Conservative Party pact forged after May lost her government majority and had to rely on DUP support to govern. The pact document stated that the Conservatives remain committed to legacy processes in Northern Ireland but added a jarring caveat on cold-case investigations:

> These are to be established so as to operate in ways that are fair, balanced and proportionate and which do not unfairly focus on former members of the armed forces or police. Both parties reiterate their admiration for the courage and sacrifice of the police and armed forces in upholding democracy and the rule of law and will never forget the debt of gratitude that we owe them.

The debate about cold cases from the Troubles, therefore, has largely been derailed by persistent assertions by right-wing politicians that the investigations focus unfairly on ex-soldiers, even though this conclusion is not supported by the data.

The former Director of Public Prosecutions for Northern Ireland, Barra McGrory QC, has described himself as 'mystified' by how this view has come to be established among politicians. He told the BBC in 2017: 'That is just not correct, that is inaccurate... The reality is that we have prosecuted more legacy cases connected with paramilitary cases than we have in respect of military cases... Mystified is about the mildest way I can put it.'

He added:

If they are not trying to influence me then they are certainly being personally insulting, and they are questioning my integrity. But what concerns me more about that is that it is insulting to this office and to the lawyers who work here and do their work day and daily with absolute integrity and to the best of their ability. So I am personally offended by the remarks, but I am more offended on behalf of the individuals who work for the public prosecution service and who do a fantastic job, so I think those who are making those comments ought to think a bit carefully before they speak in such a way.

Outside the framework of formal legal mechanisms, some are turning to unofficial ways of trying to get the truth. This often risks only complicating matters further.

BOSTON COLLEGE TAPES

In 2001, researchers at Boston College began a project in which they collected oral statements from different figures in the conflict, talking about their experiences. Participants were told that the audio files would only be released after their death, resulting in ex-terrorists giving open and frank statements which in some cases may have identified where, when or by whom people were killed. The aim of the project was to interview key figures while they were still alive, in order to give a historical record which could be released after their death and allow later generations to understand more about the conflict.

The recordings were held in the library of Boston College and thus became known as the Boston College tapes. The assumption was that the tapes would lie there gathering dust over the following decades.

However, the plan was thrown into disarray when one of the interviewees died young. Brendan Hughes passed away aged just fifty-nine, following a short illness. Upon release, his tapes proved nothing short of sensational. Hughes admitted to being behind the Bloody Friday bombs of 1972, when nineteen bombs exploded in Belfast city in the space of an hour, killing nine people. Even more shocking, his tapes revealed him stating that Gerry Adams, then Sinn Féin president, had ordered the killing of Jean McConville. Adams has always denied and continues to deny ever being a member of the IRA or being responsible for any killings. In 2014, Northern Irish police arrested Adams in connection with the murder but ultimately released him without any charges. The case shocked Northern Ireland and risked destabilising political relations in the region.

Furthermore, Northern Irish police took legal action against the academics in a bid to force them to hand over the tapes so they could use them in their work on cold cases. A US court backed the police and sided in favour of the tapes being released.

Boston College tapes later released to the police allegedly contained evidence of Ivor Bell admitting to involvement in McConville's murder, resulting in his subsequent arrest. As was previously outlined in this chapter, his legal team have sought for the case to be dismissed on the grounds that he has dementia and is unfit to stand trial.

In a preliminary trial for Bell, the librarian of Boston College accepted his defence lawyer's argument that the terrorists who took part had been misled into thinking they had full impunity to speak openly. The librarian conceded they should have added that the tapes were confidential only to the extent that US law allowed.

The Boston College tapes project may have been admirable in theory in seeking to allow the truth to eventually come out and to enrich historical understanding of the Troubles. However, as we have seen, the Northern Irish conflict inhabits a curious position as both historical and yet living. Although the civil war has ended, it cannot be said to be truly over. As relatives continue to grieve and cold cases continue to come before the courts, historical accounts cannot be neatly distinguished from confessions or admissible evidence.

The project highlighted that while legal mechanisms aimed at resolving cold cases are far from perfect, attempts at circumventing such processes can also be fraught with legal difficulties. Although the academics no doubt did not envisage anything like this occurring, their apparent misunderstanding over the levels of confidentiality they assure participants of is at best naive and at worst negligent. Rather than merely record history, the Boston College tapes have also altered its course.

COLLUSION

On 18 June 1994, as the Republic of Ireland's football team went head to head with Italy in the World Cup, groups of families and friends across the island of Ireland gathered around thick box television sets to cheer on the 'boys in green'. In the sleepy County Down hamlet of Loughinisland, the local pub was full that evening as men from the surrounding houses came together to watch the match while enjoying a pint. Their backs were to the pub's door as they faced the television set, when a gang of loyalist gunmen entered and opened fire. Within minutes, the pub's floor was sopped with blood and six men lay dead. The brutal murders shocked many in Northern Ireland, not only because the attack occurred in 1994, when hope for the peace process was gathering, but because the quiet rural hamlet was a world away from areas like Belfast or Derry-Londonderry and many had assumed it was a safe haven from such horror. In the immediate aftermath, the victims' families were assured that the RUC would 'leave no stone unturned' in their investigation to find those responsible and bring them to justice. The culprits were never apprehended, however.

The victims' families have been deeply critical of the investigation, arguing that key opportunities to find the killers were missed. The manner in which the investigation was conducted has since been at the centre of allegations that 'collusion' may have occurred – a process whereby the RUC are alleged to have turned a blind eye to certain murders which implicated their double agents within paramilitary groups. The British state and the RUC have always denied any wrongdoing or collusion. In 2016, a report by the police ombudsman stated that collusion had occurred. It found that the RUC had no prior knowledge of the attack but that the police had known the suspects' names within twenty-four hours of the murders but delayed making arrests. It also found one police officer was alleged to have tipped off the suspects about the investigation but the RUC had failed to properly investigate the claims. Most damningly, it found that one of the murder suspects was an RUC informant. The report was sensational. To the families of the victims, it confirmed their long-held conviction that collusion had occurred. Many other victims' families in other cases began to wonder if collusion had also occurred in their loved ones' deaths. However, for many RUC officers it constituted an unfair rewriting of history. Other critics argued that the issue of collusion was so complex and emotive that it was not right for an ombudsman's report to consider it but would require more complex structures, such as a full inquiry or a legal case.

Attention to the collusion allegations was further amplified after a documentary about the murders was screened in cinemas in November 2017. The documentary included many of the findings of the ombudsman's report and also gave the names of the alleged suspects, as well as showing footage of their faces and place of work.

However, soon after its publication, the police ombudsman's report was challenged in court by two retired officers. In December 2017, a High Court judge found the report was 'unsustainable in law'. The judge was highly critical of the report's authors, accusing them of being 'careless, thoughtless and inattentive in the language and structuring of the document' and said the suspects were 'in effect tried and convicted without notice in their absence'. The judge later recused himself from the case, after concerns were raised that he may have been vulnerable to accusations of bias due to previous similar cases he had been involved in. At the time of writing, the ombudsman's report still stands and a new judge is to be drafted in to hear the legal challenge against it. The case has raised a number of serious issues within the handling of legacy cases in Northern Ireland in relation to collusion allegations. It raised serious questions about whether there are adequate legal structures and processes in place for those who believe collusion was a factor in their loved ones' deaths, and for officers who believe they were wrongly accused of collusion.

The decision of the documentary makers to name the alleged suspects raised further controversy, with critics arguing it was a form of journalistic vigilante justice to name those who had never been tried in a court or found guilty. However, the victims' families have stood by the documentary, arguing it was a last resort after they had exhausted the few legal avenues available to them.

The Loughinisland case encapsulates the difficulties and sensitivities that can be involved in cases of alleged collusion. It appears that the current legal structures in place are not adequate for dealing with the hugely emotive and politically significant nature of such cases. Indeed, in order for them to be properly addressed in a way that is legally balanced and emotionally sensitive to families' needs, perhaps it is one area where an official public inquiry into all collusion allegations might be appropriate. This would allow a specific, tailored process to be put in place which could be appropriately funded and resourced and could deal with the issue definitively rather than on a piecemeal basis, death by death and atrocity by atrocity. However, many unionist politicians have opposed this move, due to their support of the RUC and their belief that nationalists are falsely using collusion allegations to discredit the force. If the British government were to order such an inquiry, this could remove the need for the plans to be supported by a unionist–nationalist consensus locally. However, some nationalists fear the British government will not do so because of the state's vested interest in not being found to have colluded in deaths. They argue that the reputational damage this would cause, as well as the fear of expensive legal claims from victims' families, will ultimately deter the state from ordering an inquiry. In the meantime, in the absence of any political leadership or appropriate legal structures, controversy over collusion allegations is likely to remain a highly emotive and deeply divisive aspect of cold-case murders for some time.

* * *

Northern Ireland is at a critical juncture over cold-case inquiries. The Good Friday Agreement was conspicuously silent on what should happen in unsolved cold-case murders from the conflict. That silence has becoming deafening in recent years, and only grows louder with time. At a global level, other international examples of post-conflict truth and reconciliation mechanisms provide templates for dealing with similar circumstances as used in post-apartheid South Africa and post-genocide Rwanda.

Amid the backdrop of debates in Northern Ireland about treatment of ex-soldiers and the botched work of the Historical Enquiries Team, time is running out. In many cases, witnesses or suspects are dying of old age or are no longer able to engage in a meaningful way with inquiries due to age-related illnesses such as dementia.

If Northern Irish society does want to see people brought to trial for historic Troubles deaths, there is realistically only a window of a few more years in which this can be done before almost all those involved are too elderly or have died.

Despite this, there appears to be insufficient momentum or understanding of many of the issues around cold cases, both at a political and a societal level, for a clear and consistent final push to occur. At a political level, politicians in the DUP and Conservative Party have derailed the debate into a narrow and inaccurate narrative that cold cases are a witch-hunt against ex-soldiers. At a societal level, there is little or no agreement on how the past should be dealt with. Many have ethical concerns over putting elderly people on trial or in prison for wrongs committed thirty years ago. Among younger generations, many simply do not know enough about the horrors of the past to realise the grief families feel and instead wonder why they can't simply quietly come to terms with their relatives' deaths without a prosecution.

Having been in court to hear many cold-case inquests and having spoken with both victims' families and alleged culprits, it is an issue I have spent considerable time reflecting on but cannot offer a solution. It is an ethical minefield and there is no clear correct answer as to what should happen now. Sadly, I do not anticipate that this is an issue which is likely to be resolved in the time that there is left.

It seems to me that Northern Ireland is slowly sliding into a system of immunity through incompetence. Declaring an official amnesty for those who killed during the conflict would be too controversial politically and legally. Similarly, however, putting elderly people, particularly soldiers, on trial or in prison is ethically disturbing for many and likely to be equally controversial.

Therefore, we have instead sunk into an unofficial *via media*, or middle road. The legal system is currently slowly working its way through the cases, but without sufficient finance, resources or legal powers it is unlikely that many, if any, cases will result in convictions. Politicians and lawyers in Northern Ireland know this. The system is simply not fit for purpose and lacks the competence or direction to get convictions.

This is tantamount to an amnesty, as killers will not be held to account for their actions. However, it will happen with a whimper rather than a bang, as culprits and witnesses slowly die off one by one. Rather than the headline-grabbing controversy of an official amnesty being announced, we will reach the point in a decade or so where people will look back and realise there is no one left to stand trial or take to the witness stand.

This system of effective immunity through incompetence has

the effect of appeasing both sides of the debate: those who do not wish to see convictions and those who find an official amnesty morally abhorrent. However, it does nothing to help victims' families, who are cruelly strung along to police stations and coroner's courts in pursuit of closure which will almost certainly never come. In the meantime, they fight on, die out, relive the horrors of their loved ones' massacres in a system incapable of dignifying their efforts with return. They make the long journey from home to court and the even longer journey from the public gallery to the witness stand. Waiting, hoping, reliving.

While reporting on several cold-case inquests in Northern Ireland, I began to recognise one man's face as he sat in the public gallery in different cases for different victims. The man was of advanced age, perhaps in his early seventies. He would sit quietly by the various families, calmly, wordlessly and focusing intently on what was said in each case as the different barristers sparred back and forth and different witnesses took to different stands. After recognising him a few times, I wondered why he was there so often – had he been dealt an exceedingly hard hand by fate in losing so many relatives and friends?

One morning, a case was delayed in beginning as the judge hearing a case was held up by a previous trial overrunning. As we waited on the benches outside the courtroom, the man struck up a conversation with me. As we were chatting, I asked if he was in court as a friend or a relative of the deceased. Neither, he told me. His brother had been killed forty years ago in the conflict. There had never been a proper investigation or inquest. No one had ever been held to account for the murder. The man wanted one to be held, out of a duty to his brother, whom he felt he owed a proper day in court where the truth could emerge. He has no particular hope of one happening now, as neither politicians nor the police have shown interest in his brother's specific case.

Nevertheless, he wants to be ready and familiar with court processes and legal cases so that, should the time ever come, he'll be ready to take a strong legal case for his brother. He retired a few years ago and, as he lives in the countryside, he gets up at first light to take multiple buses snaking through rural Northern Ireland to get to the Belfast courts using his pensioner's bus pass. He sits in the public gallery and simply listens and takes it all in.

We don't discuss it, but we both know the chances of his brother's death coming to court within his lifetime, if at all, are next to none. This fact simply hangs in the area outside the courtroom, as I wish him well. When the case begins, we go our separate ways as I troop off to the press benches and he takes his position in the public gallery. He sits in the back row, fantasising that it is him in the witness box, his brother's name on the listing, the court in rapt attention, his brother looking on in the afterlife as he sees justice finally done.

CHAPTER FOUR

INTERGENERATIONAL TRAUMA

In my memory, he jerks like a marionette with imperceptible strings. His head twitches at an unnatural angle to his neck, presumably as he absorbs the impact of the gunshot wound to his head. Then he keels over and slaps the ground with his full torso.

There is no sound in my memory; no gunmen, no instigators, no sense of anything that comes before this time or after.

Then a second memory fuses with this first: my mother kneels beside the man and places the scraps of what are left of his head on her lap, gently scoops the fragments of his brains and skull off the tarmac, softly prises them back to where they once were in an attempt to bring him back to life by reversing the shooting. Her efforts do not work and the man, long dead, stares back with vacant eyes ungrateful for her gesture.

This is my earliest memory – an impossible scene which I now know cannot be right, yet feels as real to me as events which happened yesterday. When I was three years old, the IRA executed a man in front of me by shooting him dead. This much has since been confirmed by my parents and by histories of the Troubles. But the rest is complex.

My parents had moved from Northern Ireland to England to start our family there, in the hope that this could shield their children from the horrors of the Troubles. But the pull of home was still strong and when the IRA declared a ceasefire in 1994, they decided to move us to Belfast. As the history books now show, this optimism was misplaced and although the ceasefire felt at the time like the end of the conflict, it was in fact to be the first of many short sojourns in the war that would take many more years to gain permanence.

Shortly after we moved to Belfast to start our new life in what we thought was the peace process, the ceasefire was broken and, with disturbing irony, we were to be witnesses to the event.

My parents' memory of what happened is that they had been visiting friends in South Belfast, along with myself, then a toddler, and my two brothers, then aged five and ten months. As we returned to the family car to drive home, a crackling sound rang out. My mother was frightened, but my father told her not to worry and that it was just fireworks. As the noise persisted, they looked up and saw gunmen volleying shots into a man, blowing his head apart. My father has no recollection of their faces, but my mother recalls one of the gunmen looking at her and laughing. The men then scurried off.

My mother recalls unwrapping the baby blanket in which my little brother was swaddled and placing it around the dead man to keep him warm as blood stopped pumping around his body and his corpse slowly turned cold. An unmarked van pulled up and two men jumped out, explaining they were from the RUC. They then dragged his body into the boot of the van and drove off, with my brother's baby blanket still wrapped around him. My mother says she tried to give a police statement but the RUC were uninterested. The memories that stay with her most strongly are of seeing the man dragged into the boot and his corpse colliding with the metal in their careless haste to leave. The bloodied torsos of cattle and pigs in butchers will hereafter always make her wince.

The death we witnessed became a crucial point in the conflict, as the IRA was officially on ceasefire. As a result, the shooting was attributed to a separate affiliate group named Direct Action Against Drugs, who claimed they were an IRA offshoot focused on killing drug dealers out of respect for communities harmed by drug addiction. This pretence was not probed by the authorities, who, perhaps desperate to see the ceasefire opportunity for peace not squandered, seemingly agreed to accept this unconvincing explanation. No one was ever held to account for the murder. My parents were never asked to testify. We got back in the car and drove home. The RUC only contacted my parents on one occasion – to ask my mother to come back to the station for the baby blanket in which she had wrapped the dying man. She duly did; rust-brown smears of blood had seeped into the fabric – the only outside verification beyond our memories that it had actually happened.

* * *

As I was so young when it happened, it is unlikely that my memories of that evening have any basis in fact at all. I assume that the memory I have is at best a memory of a memory, bastardised fusions of what limited memory I may have had mixed with my parents' own subsequent retellings of events on the rare occasions that we have discussed it. It may be further mixed with my memories of other contemporaneous reports from news bulletins throughout my childhood of graphic Troubles deaths, which have since intermingled with my own experiences, forming a Frankensteinian false memory. Or it may merely be due to the frequent flair for drama and exaggeration characteristic of some children's minds.

My mother tells me that no, she did not reach into this man's head and try to put it back together. Of course she didn't; what an odd and disturbing thing that would have been to do. Yet this memory is as real and disturbing to me as anything else I have experienced in my life.

Like most people who were victims of or witnesses to Troubles violence, my family has never been offered any support, counselling or advice from any state or government agency about what we saw or how to live with it.

We have learnt to live around it. Years go by without us mentioning it. The street on which it happened is at the centre of what is now the student quarter. In my teenage years, my friends and I would often drunkenly stumble along the same street on our way to and from nightclubs and friends' flats. In my job now as a journalist reporting on Northern Ireland, I routinely talk to and interview men who were in the IRA. Some of them may have been involved in what happened that evening, or know who was. Sometimes during an interview or a press conference at Stormont, this thought slides into my head along with the memories. I close my eyes for a second or two, push these thoughts out and get back to work.

Then, at other times, it is unavoidable. The sound of fireworks at Guy Fawkes Night. A facial expression. A motorbike engine backfiring. A stain on a blanket. Pigs strung up in a butcher's shop window.

Throughout the Troubles, the impact of the conflict was often viscerally visual and overt. As bombs and bullets ripped through communities and lives, they left in their wake clear signs of the harm they had wrought: melted metal frameworks of buildings gutted by fireballs, raw flesh where limbs had been ripped from torsos by shrapnel, blood smears on pavements.

In other ways, however, the harm incurred by the violence was less clearly identifiable. Some damage was silent and elusive, leaving behind nothing that could be photographed by forensic officers or scooped up into evidence bags.

Despite this, the mental health impact of the conflict is no less real and no less deserving of attention than physical wounds. For each life that was lost or person who was maimed, considerable trauma rippled around the individual and the event, from loved ones bereaved, to bystanders in the wrong place at the wrong time, to police and hospital staff whose daily job it was to sift through unimaginable horrors.

It is impossible to quantify exactly how and to what extent the mental health of Northern Irish people has been affected by the Troubles. Yet the few imperfect metrics which are available raise serious red flags.

In 2015, research by academics at Ulster University found that 30 per cent of people living in Northern Ireland have a mental health issue. Of these, researchers found that half were directly related to experiencing a traumatic incident connected with the Troubles.

In addition, Northern Ireland in the present day continues to have considerably higher suicide rates than the rest of the UK. Data from the Office for National Statistics released in 2016 showed that in 2014, there were 16.5 suicides per 100,000 people in Northern Ireland. This was much higher than the rate for Scotland (14.5), England (10.3) or Wales (9.2).

More curiously, mental health professionals have begun reporting that children who were either young toddlers during the Troubles or in some cases had not even been born at the time of the conflict are now presenting with Troubles-related trauma. In an evidence hearing to the Dáil Parliament in Dublin about legacy matters from the Troubles in 2017, Sandra Peake, CEO of the Wave Trauma Centre, which supports people affected by the Troubles, told a committee of Irish politicians that the charity have had referrals made to them of children as young as six years old displaying signs of Troubles-related trauma.

Some experience self-harm, suicidal ideation, PTSD or anxiety about events they were scarcely old enough to remember or which occurred before they were born. Precisely why is unclear.

The most developed research on intergenerational trauma comes from the horrors of the Holocaust, where the phenomenon has been noted in what has been called second-generation Holocaust trauma. In this context, researchers have noted that considerable trauma is noted not only in survivors of the Holocaust but also among survivors' children and grandchildren.

Theories suggest that a similar phenomenon is now occurring among people traumatised by the Troubles in Northern Ireland. Of course, while the Troubles were deeply traumatic, the horrors experienced in the conflict were not on the same scale as the Holocaust, where entire families and communities were destroyed on a much larger scale. Nevertheless, intergenerational Holocaust trauma is the closest sociological phenomenon to the current patterns observed in Northern Irish society among families affected by the conflict and so deserve serious consideration.

There are two theories as to how this trauma can be passed on to the second generation. The first is that the trauma is biological; the second is that it is behavioural, or learnt. The biological theory stems from research conducted by scientists at Mount Sinai Hospital in New York, which compared the genetic makeup of thirty-two Jewish people who had been interned in a Nazi concentration camp or had seen or undergone torture or had been forced into hiding during the Second World War. They also analysed the genetic makeup of the first cohort's children and found they were much more likely to have stress-related issues such as trauma than a separate control group of Jewish people living outside Europe whose parents had not experienced the Holocaust. The scientists concluded that the extreme distress and trauma was passed on to the second generation through 'epigenetic inheritance'.[*]

---

* Rachel Yehuda et al., 'Holocaust Exposure Induced Intergenerational Effects on FKBP5 Methylation', *Biological Psychiatry*, Vol. 80, Issue 5 (1 September 2016), pp. 372–80

The second theory is that the trauma is transferred behaviourally, i.e. through children seeing their parents behave in a traumatised way. A 2012 study by academics at by Haifa University conducted in-depth interviews with 196 Israelis who are second-generation descendants of Holocaust survivors. The study found that parents who had survived the Holocaust were often traumatised, subsequently being emotionally cold or distant as well as overprotective of their children. In some cases, this resulted in the children not forming secure attachments with their parents or developing excessive anxiety.

A third theory may be worth considering within the Northern Irish context. While the Holocaust affected millions of people's lives, obliterating whole families and communities across Europe regardless of class or income, the Troubles conflict was largely confined to particular streets and areas. Broadly, the most intense violence tended to happen in working-class and impoverished areas, such as West Belfast and East Belfast or the Bogside of Derry-Londonderry, while middle-class areas such as South Belfast, for instance, were less affected. There is considerable overlap, therefore, between areas which were already in poverty and those which later came to see bloodshed and trauma. Other studies have suggested a link between growing up in an impoverished household and later having a mental health problem. For instance, the Children and Young People's Mental Health Coalition highlighted in a 2015 report that 'being born into poverty puts children at greater risk of mental health problems and, for many, this will lead to negative consequences through their lives, affecting educational attainment and social relationships, and can be cumulative'.

Therefore, it is worth considering whether this affects the data in a Northern Irish context, perhaps exacerbating the issue further.

It appears to be the case that people traumatised by the Troubles whose trauma was never addressed or given attention by mental health professionals can pass this trauma on down to successive generations, similar to Holocaust survivors.

In 2009, the Eames–Bradley Consultative Group on the Past published its report, giving the first major assessment of how Northern Ireland was dealing with its past, a decade on from the end of the conflict. The report gave one of the first indications of intergenerational trauma, recording: 'Inter-generational trauma is similarly not recognised as a root cause of the problems many young people face. Many are affected by the legacy of the past while often having only indirect experience of that past.'

This finding was echoed the following year in a report from the Irish Peace Centre, which found that:

> the intergenerational transmission of the experience of conflict in Northern Ireland corresponds with international trends identified in the research literature. Namely, that the effects of harm (broadly defined) and the experience of injustice carried by a particular generation can, if not addressed and resolved, be passed on to the next generation to produce a range of social and psychological pathologies, such as self-harm, suicide, anti-social behaviour, anomie and inter-personal violence.

In 2012, the Commission for Victims and Survivors published a study noting a 'dearth of research specifically examining transgenerational trauma in the specific context of "The Troubles"'.[*] The research was based on a small sample of people affected by the Troubles, who were found to transfer their trauma to the generation below by being obsessively afraid of the outside world and being hyper-protective of their children. The study's assessments of children and young people 'provided evidence that transgenerational trauma is a very real issue in Northern Ireland today with all but 3.4% of respondents reporting that they had experienced trauma related events, but also ... that their family's experiences of "The Troubles" have had a greater impact on them than their own experience'.

Mental health professional David Bolton writes in *Conflict, Peace and Mental Health*, a seminal text on Troubles-related trauma, that poor mental health in a first generation can also result in worse living conditions for a second generation if their parents are unable to work due to poor mental health. This case also indirectly exacerbates the second generation's mental health, as they not only see the direct psychological effects of trauma but also suffer from the socio-economic disadvantages related to growing up in poverty:

> Harsh, neglectful and otherwise poor parenting styles, especially where worsened by economic and social stressors, impact on the developing child – limiting the development ... capabilities. These then place the child at increased risks of a range of disadvantages in childhood, adolescence and later in adulthood

---

[*] Donncha Hanna et al., 'Young People's Transgenerational Issues in Northern Ireland' (Commission for Victims and Survivors, 2012)

– including poorer mental health, which is made worse by poverty and other basic deprivations. In turn, this secondary wave of adversity and disadvantage is more likely to impact negatively on the next generation, and so on.

A 2014 report by the Wave Trauma Centre in Belfast contains a number of insightful case studies of both parents and children, which prove revealing on the topic of intergenerational Troubles trauma. One woman explains how, as a young child, her life changed when her father was killed in the conflict:

I always remember such a lonely empty feeling in the house. It was just me and Mum because my sister was newly married and was living in her own house. So it was just such a lonely feeling, so empty and Mum I suppose has had bad health ever since … Mum would not have been interacting or sitting with me, she didn't play often with me. Mum was dealing with her own struggles and her own grief. So she would have just have lay and watched TV and maybe fell asleep.

Later, as an adult with children of her own, she describes having an obsessive interest in her children's lives and desire to protect them. She says:

Nobody was allowed to touch my kids. When I took them to nursery school, I roared and cried, and when they started primary school I roared and cried! My son's friend laughs, because I think I brushed his teeth up until the age of eleven or twelve, in case he didn't do them properly and when he went to the toilet he would shout, 'Finished, Mummy come and clean me,' and I would.

Another interviewee, who was just a teenager when his sister died in the Troubles, explains how the loss affected him and his mother:

My mum didn't cope at all, there was too many doctors coming in and out of the house and putting her on these tablets, she didn't know what she was doing herself so basically I was looking after myself to be honest and she tried to take me over to the Royal Victoria hospital after it happened to see a psychiatrist but I bluffed my way through that and pretended there was nothing wrong as any teenage boy would. Mum couldn't cope, she didn't even know what planet she was on because of the tablets she was taking, she was crying every day, she had to get her breakfast made for her, things like that.

Later, as a grown man with children of his own, he describes how the trauma has seeped through the generations and now affects his own children, who had not been alive at the time of his sister's murder and had no first-hand experience of the Troubles:

My daughter stays in Mum's every weekend and Mum has a shrine [to the interviewee's sister] and she knows it's her auntie, they know who she is, they know what happened to her and that's as far as it goes. I've had to explain it to them because there's days when they have seen me crying and they've seen me upset or they've seen me drunk or they've seen me stoned so I've had to sit them down and explain to them and they understand perfectly even though they're only kids themselves ... They understand better why I used to be upset all the time and why I used to be depressed because they were probably thinking why is daddy like this? And now that they're a lot older it's gonna make them understand why.

He admits it affects his parenting approach now:

I'm very, very over-protective ... I don't like my eldest going into Belfast because there has been a number of bomb scares in [the town where they live] and on a Saturday afternoon I'll try and do anything to give her something else to do so that she doesn't go into town in case something happens to her and it's the same as my mum: I don't like her going into town and I try and stay out of the town on a Saturday afternoon as much as possible, I freak out too much because it proved to me that anything can happen in one short moment. I know that I sound paranoid but it's just how I feel.

In another case study, one young man describes how, on the day of his father's death, authorities discussed but then dismissed concerns about traumatising him with the details on the grounds that he was so young he would scarcely understand or remember. He recalls:

I was off school ... I can remember the event well, the police spoke openly in front of me and named people who had been involved in the murder. One of them said, 'Sure let him stay in the room, hasn't he been through enough, a child will pick nothing up'. I have a vivid memory of every detail and of every name ... the names and details stuck with me. It sort of burned into the hard drive of my memory and stayed there.

* * *

Jayne Olorunda is all too aware of the lasting harm that can be inflicted on families when trauma is left untreated. She was just two years old when her father Max was killed by an IRA bomb in 1980. He was an accountant from Nigeria who had moved to Northern Ireland and fallen in love with a local nurse, Gabrielle. The couple married and had three daughters together, Jayne and her two sisters Alison and Maxine.

Max was murdered while on a train travelling through Dunmurry, a suburb of Belfast, when an IRA bomb in the carriage detonated prematurely. As Jayne was so young, she does not remember the terrible moment that her mother was informed and their family was shattered. What is burnt deep in her memory, however, is how the trauma affected her family throughout her childhood and to this day.

In her powerful and moving memoir *Legacy*, Jayne tells a deeply worrying story which perhaps epitomises the ways in which families traumatised by the Troubles can be shut off from support and left to suffer alone. It is a narrative that is seldom discussed in Northern Irish society, as few victims' families have publicly spoken out about the mental health impact of trauma from the

Troubles. In her book, Jayne explains how her mother was left severely traumatised by her father's murder, but struggled to have this suffering acknowledged or addressed by state services over the course of decades. As a result, Jayne and her sisters experienced an at times chaotic and highly stressful childhood in which her mother's acute trauma went unaddressed.

She writes of the moment her father died:

> In theory, I was there but in practice I was too young to remember and I thank God for that. However, I did not escape from the events of that night in January 1980. The accounts of that night have been retold so many times that they are like the stuff of fable in mine and my sisters' histories. Every year from Christmas to January 17, Mum walks us through the chronicle of events leading to and the aftermath of my dad's death. She needed to tell someone I suppose and in the absence of any form of therapy who better to tell than the only people she was left with? ... That night has become a tangible part of Mum, the events relived so many times that they are as solid and real as I am. It is a night she will never forget; she will take it with her to her grave. For my sisters and me, it is likely that we will too.

Her ensuing childhood was marked by poverty and instability, during which she often had to provide emotional support for her mother, who struggled to cope with life in the wake of the bomb. At times her mother would hallucinate and see things and people that weren't there. Her mother experienced serious depression. She struggled to work or gain financial stability and the family moved some seventeen times in a decade. Jayne says that throughout this she approached multiple victims' agencies and her family's situation was known to medical professionals but she was still never offered any meaningful support. Instead, she and her young sisters were simply expected to look after their mother and her severe trauma.

She explains:

Once a woman who had taken such pride in her appearance, she now thought nothing about stepping out with her night dress under her coat. Her shaky hands meant that the buttons were never matched right, always some were missed or in the wrong place, the result was that her nightdress was visible to all. I did not worry about this too much, as Mum rarely went out. She would panic when I left her in the house alone.

She became angry and confused. Everything angered her, she would sit scowling at the TV, swearing at whoever's poor face happened to grace the screen. Her tablets were once again increased, but this time even they didn't help. Every time I would wander up the stairs I would find her talking. What was more alarming was the fact that she often invited me to join her and her acquaintance. Or worse, she would be talking to me and I hadn't even opened my mouth, yet she would lie responding to my every non-existent comment. Often she would talk as if she lived in the 1970s and talk about her three little girls. Once, she ran downstairs and asked why there were police in the living room – who had died?

Then the suicide attempts began, I had started another job and wasn't at home with her as often as I should have been.

Every job I started, I had to give up. Mum's condition, whatever it was, demanded that she have someone with her constantly.

Jayne says she tried on multiple occasions as a teenager to try to access help through a number of different charities set up for victims' families, but found them disinterested. She explains:

I was all alone, I was all alone with Mum and my misery. To say I felt frightened, isolated and vulnerable would be an understatement. I didn't know where to turn. Even if I had found somewhere to go or someone who would listen, where would I even start? Words would fail me. I didn't feel capable of even articulating our situation, words couldn't describe how desperate we had become.

Eventually, after becoming acutely distressed, Jayne's mother was taken to a secure mental health unit in 2010, where she was finally assessed in a comprehensive way. Life is still not easy for Jayne and her mum, but things have got better. She writes: 'Yes, we still have our bad days but they are becoming lesser. Mum will never be fully recovered and she has the wherewithal to accept that, but now that she is receiving the appropriate treatment I feel I have her back, albeit intermittently.'

However, this belated support does not erase how her mother's trauma affected her childhood. Reflecting on her experiences now, Jayne tells me:

I think that it is assumed that victims are supported as that is what any decent society does, it looks after its wounded.

Northern Ireland in reality gives it victims very little. There was no support for Mum or indeed my sisters and I as children. Had there been, then I believe the outcome of our lives would have been very different.

She tells me that her alienation from support services may have also been heightened by racism in Northern Irish society. As a mixed-race person, she found it particularly hard to access support, and her family were perceived as being not 'really' Northern Irish or not 'truly' victims due to their ethnicity.

At the time of our interview in 2017, Jayne had recently left Northern Ireland and moved to England for a new life. She tells me this was fuelled in part by a desire to escape the relentless racism in her home country. However, she says the final indignity that caused her to leave came in 2016, when she learnt that Sinn Féin had selected the daughter of one of the bombers who killed her father to be a politician representing their constituency at Stormont. Jayne tells me that she holds nothing against the young woman personally but the distress of seeing her, and facing the person she considers the young woman to represent, became too much. The little closure she had been able to gain was once again undermined and the traumatic wounds of the past were reopened. Speaking to me from her new home in England, she tells me she has no plans to ever set foot in Northern Ireland again.

Jayne's experiences are a damning example of how state services can fail to support the children of victims and the bereaved. They also highlight how, twenty years on from the Good Friday Agreement, many victims and their children have been left to simply cope alone with major trauma and denied the dignity and support they deserve.

INTERGENERATIONAL TRAUMA AND THE GOOD FRIDAY AGREEMENT

The Good Friday Agreement did not include provisions for the possibility of intergenerational trauma. This is perhaps understandable, as the phenomenon has only more recently been understood by researchers.

Nevertheless, the issue cannot be neatly detached from the peace process or written off without responsibility. The trauma experienced by both first and second generations of Troubles victims has been exacerbated in many ways by the failings of the Good Friday Agreement in other areas.

For instance, the peace process failed to set up mechanisms for Northern Ireland to deal with unsolved Troubles deaths. Many deaths were not investigated properly at the time, meaning that little or nothing is known about the circumstances in which loved ones died. In many cases, relatives have been subject to mental anguish not knowing where, how or why their family member died. In the cases of the IRA's 'disappeared' victims, family members still do not know where the bodies are buried and have been unable to give their loved ones a Christian burial. In the 2010s, some inquests and investigations have been reopened following campaigning by victims' families after it has been accepted that the RUC failed to investigate properly at the time. However, these 'lucky ones' have often been subject to further trauma as the processes have been botched and subject to excessive delays due to lack of funding or resources. The peace process has roundly failed to establish appropriate mechanisms for relatives to seek justice, resulting in further anguish and trauma as they continue to fight through the courts.

In many cases, as the older generations age, it is the younger generations tasked with pushing for justice. In 2017, the Victims Commissioner Judith Thompson, who is the official representative of victims and survivors of the conflict in Northern Ireland, told the *Irish News*:

It is shocking when you sit down in a room with people and you see the impact that has on their lives every day right up to the present. People feel they have an obligation to the person who died, no matter how difficult it is, and you see individuals within families who have taken on that role at great personal cost. One elderly man I met had shouldered responsibility for trying to get an investigation into his brother's death, for his brother's sake and his mother's sake and his family's sake. And he found himself bewildered by what they had to encounter, he had this battered folder and he said, 'I know which one of my sons is going to pick that up when I die and I know he'll ask one of his sons to do it if we don't get there', and you could just see that folder being passed from generation to generation.

We still do not know the extent and ways in which the Troubles conflict traumatised people in Northern Ireland. Due to the elusive, unquantifiable, stigmatised nature of mental health, it is something we may never fully grasp. Nonetheless, the limited research that is available suggests serious mental health issues exist in post-conflict Northern Ireland. This has largely gone untreated in first-generation victims, many of whom are now elderly.

As the children and grandchildren of these victims come of age, it is increasingly clear that the issue is not one that can be ignored in the hope that the trauma will 'die out' with the traumatised. Rather, as the mental health of victims and their families goes untreated, it continues to live on in a generation freshly traumatised not by the conflict itself but by our failure to deal with the past.

CHAPTER FIVE

EQUALITY AND
HUMAN RIGHTS

At the core of the Good Friday Agreement are the principles of equality and human rights. These values formed the cornerstone of the Agreement, in an acknowledgement of how the conflict had been sparked by inequality between the two communities, with the nationalist community initially being subjected to inequalities in voting rights, employment and access to housing. Furthermore, the conflict itself had been marred by human rights breaches, ranging from allegations that suspects had been subjected to torture in interrogation suites, to claims that the British state had been operating a 'shoot-to-kill' policy against suspected terrorists.

In order to prevent such issues continuing in a post-conflict era and undermining the peace process, multiple protections were built into the Good Friday Agreement, including:

- The establishment of an Equality Commission to promote and protect equality;

- The establishment of a Human Rights Commission to promote and protect human rights, which would have a membership reflecting the 'community balance' in Northern Ireland;
- A pledge of office for Stormont politicians to take, including a commitment to 'serve all the people of Northern Ireland equally, and to act in accordance with the general obligations on government to promote equality and prevent discrimination';
- An agreement that all people in Northern Ireland should be entitled to equal opportunity 'regardless of class, creed, disability, gender or ethnicity';
- An agreement that the British government would create a statutory obligation for public authorities in Northern Ireland to 'carry out all their functions with due regard to the need to promote equality of opportunity in relation to religion and political opinion; gender; race; disability; age; marital status; dependants; and sexual orientation';
- The existence of a mechanism called a Petition of Concern (described in Chapter One), which required potentially discriminatory legislation to secure a majority of support among both communities.

However, despite this focus on human rights and equality, twenty years on from the Good Friday Agreement such provisions are beginning to show their age, as they have been outpaced by society's changing conceptions of what constitute equality and human rights issues. The Agreement's provisions were specifically designed with sectarianism in mind and therefore consider oppression and discrimination primarily through the lens of Northern

Ireland's unique ethno-national divisions. This focus is evidenced in how, for instance, the Human Rights Commission guarantees equal representation of both the Catholic/nationalist community and the Protestant/unionist community, while remaining silent on gender equality and representation of ethnic minorities, the LGBT community and people with disabilities. Where these other discriminated groups are mentioned in the Good Friday Agreement, they tend to be referred to as general vague principles but no specific action is agreed.

While this focus on sectarian discrimination was understandable in the immediate aftermath of the conflict, it has come under strain with the passage of time. While Northern Ireland has strong bulwarks against sectarianism, it is a far from healthy political system when it comes to other forms of discrimination. In particular, the rights of women and the LGBT community continue to be marginalised in Northern Ireland, often due to decisions taken at Stormont.

Most notably, the Good Friday Agreement focused on ending sectarian violence, while ignoring ways in which domestic and sexual violence increased during the Troubles due to the increase in availability of firearms and the breakdown in normal policing, which limited women's access to justice. Although such violence was not strictly sectarian in nature, it was also related to the conflict. The Good Friday Agreement did not address this tension. As we will see later in this chapter, the lack of a gendered approach to violence has resulted in a reductive and male-centred definition of violence and victimhood both in the Good Friday Agreement and in the peace process more generally.

In some cases, the equality provisions embedded in the Agreement actually facilitate the oppression of other marginalised groups. For instance, as we will explore in this chapter, the Petition of Concern is currently being used to block legislation to advance LGBT rights, while the principle of devolution is being used to block legislation to reform Northern Ireland's abortion ban.

This chapter therefore considers the ways in which the narrow definition of equality and human rights in the Good Friday Agreement has been outpaced by changing social attitudes, and explores whether limiting concepts of equality to a purely Catholic/Protestant dynamic has stilted equality for other vulnerable groups.

DOMESTIC VIOLENCE DURING THE TROUBLES

As we have seen, throughout the Troubles, Northern Ireland regularly became engulfed by violence. From daily bombings to sectarian tit-for-tat executions and armed soldiers swarming through neighbourhoods, the daily reality of violence often felt relentless.

But alongside these overt displays of aggression, a parallel system of violence was playing out behind closed doors. It was not recorded in news bulletins, nor the subject of emergency Cabinet meetings. Nor is it remembered in murals painted across the city or in memorial services flanked by bowed heads of state.

Although it is seldom discussed in political discourse or recorded in histories of the Troubles, gender-based abuse took on a particular edge when the sectarian conflict in the region began. In fact, there is compelling evidence to suggest that as the Troubles increased, both the regularity and the lethality of domestic violence worsened. Not only did domestic violence increase, but the number of women who died as a result of it also soared, and women's recourses to justice plummeted as the nature of law and order was fundamentally altered by the conflict.

Occasionally throughout the Troubles, a sectarian attack would include a form of sexual violence. For instance, in 1972, when a loyalist gang broke into the home of a Catholic woman and raped her in front of her severely disabled son before shooting him dead, the attack provoked outrage from both sides of society. However, more often than not, sexual and domestic violence were not used as a war tactic, but occurred within communities and families as men attacked their own wives, girlfriends, sons, daughters and mothers.

In reality, when we talk about 'violence' in the Troubles, we as a society tend to view this through a deeply gendered lens. Such discussions almost always involve male definitions of violence by unacknowledged default – bombs, bullets, torture and executions – all of which occur in the public or male sphere. In so doing, they silently and often without realising it erase the experiences of women and girls, who are subjected to additional violence in the domestic or female sphere.

DOMESTIC VIOLENCE INCREASE DURING THE TROUBLES

Data shows that during the conflict, women in Northern Ireland were more than twice as likely to be killed as a result of domestic violence than women elsewhere in the UK during the same period. For instance, the number of women killed by intimate partners during 1991–94 amounted to twenty-six women per million couples per year in Northern Ireland. This is considerably higher than other comparable areas such as England, where ten women per million couples were killed in the same period.[*]

Furthermore, the Ardoyne Women's Research Project also found that the number of adult women who were identified as currently being victimised by or having previously been the victim of domestic violence was particularly high in the Ardoyne area of North Belfast, which was home to some of the most brutal murders in the conflict, earning it the ominous moniker 'Murder Mile'.[†] This indicates that in areas where the conflict was particularly bad, gendered violence was also higher.

There are a number of reasons domestic violence was exacerbated by the Troubles. They are chiefly: an increase in availability of both legally and illegally held guns, which increased domestic abuse control and even femicide; and extreme disengagement with the security services such as the army and the police, which meant women were unable to access support services to leave abusive situations or receive effective, neutral mediation or protection.

Research by academic Monica McWilliams, who went on to found the Northern Ireland Women's Coalition which helped negotiate the Good Friday Agreement, records how the conflict rapidly increased the availability of firearms in domestic settings both for men in paramilitary groups such as the IRA, the UVF and the UDA, and for state actors such as the army, the RUC

---

[*] Monica McWilliams and Lynda Spence, *Taking Domestic Violence Seriously: Issues for the Civil and Criminal Justice System* (Stationery Office Books, 1996)

[†] Monica McWilliams and Joan McKiernan, *Bringing It Out in the Open: Domestic Violence in Northern Ireland* (HM Stationery Office, 1993), p. 5

and politicians. Due to the illicit and secretive nature of such operations, it is impossible to estimate the number of guns handled by paramilitary groups. However, data on legally held firearms is clearer and suggests that up to 134,000 firearms were legally held in Northern Ireland during the conflict, which amounts to one in every seventeen people in Northern Ireland holding such a weapon legally.*

The researchers noted:

[A] significant feature of the Northern Ireland domestic homicides was that the majority of victims had been married to members of the security forces, showing that it was legal, and not just illegal, weapons that had to be accounted for. As a direct result of the political conflict, members of the security forces (police, prison service and army) were able to apply for personal protection weapons, as were a number of politicians, business people and others working with the security sector. This led to a much larger number of households holding firearms compared to any other part of the UK or the Republic of Ireland. The result being that women in these households (homes containing men 'protecting' the state) were at significantly higher personal risk of harm.†

Their research records one ordeal relayed by the wife of a man who had been issued a 'personal protection' gun by the state for him

---

* Monica McWilliams and Fionnuala D. Ní Aoláin, '"There Is a War Going on, You Know": Addressing the Complexity of Violence Against Women in Conflicted and Post-Conflict Societies' (*Transitional Justice Review*, Vol. 1, Issue 2, Art. 2, 2013), p. 13
† Ibid., p. 32

to keep in their home: 'He would put a gun to my head and play Russian roulette with it.'

Similarly, women's refuge workers have recalled treating women during the Troubles with circular bruising on their necks and temples caused by pressure points of gun barrels.

HOW THE TROUBLES CUT OFF ACCESS TO POLICE OR CRIMINAL JUSTICE FOR DOMESTIC VIOLENCE VICTIMS

The conflict greatly changed how both communities interacted with the state and policing. Among many Catholic communities, the police were seen as being anti-Catholic and were not welcome in many Catholic areas as locals feared police brutality. For women experiencing domestic violence, this meant many in Catholic areas felt they could not report their abusive partners to the police for fear that attending officers could harm their own communities, or they would be alienated by neighbours for being 'disloyal' by inviting officers into the area. One woman said at the time: 'We look after ourselves. When we look for help, the police are never included. They are always seen as the harasser." Furthermore, Catholic women have stated that on some occasions when they did report domestic violence to the police, officers refused to attend, as for them Catholic areas were 'no-go zones' where they feared they would not make it out alive, due to extreme anti-police sentiment in some Catholic neighbourhoods. Indeed, even more concerningly, on some occasions when Catholic women reported their abusive partners to police, the police not only refused to go

---

* McWilliams and McKiernan, op. cit., p. 56

but instead sent the army, whom they considered more able to deal with the threat of travelling in Catholic areas. This was inappropriate on two levels: firstly, armed soldiers are not trained in the sensitivities involved in treating domestic violence victims, who are often extremely vulnerable and traumatised, nor are they versed in child protection law. Secondly, this move exposed the women to ostracism and backlash from their communities as they were perceived as 'inviting' the British Army into their neighbourhoods and exposing locals to potential arrests or brutality.

Conversely, while the Troubles saw many Catholics become severely alienated from the police force, for many Protestants the reverse happened: they became intimately and intensely connected to state services in a way that had not occurred prior to the conflict. The surge in violence meant that more personnel were recruited and came almost exclusively from the Protestant community, as they were considered loyal to the state. This meant that many Protestant women found that they became personally connected to security agents in the form of brothers, fathers, husbands and other male community figures who become officers. These connections may have resulted in stigma about contacting the police or other security agents, as the women could not receive impartial advice, help or intervention but must rely on people who were already personally known to them and their attackers or abusers as well.

Indeed, for both communities, domestic violence became sidelined in Northern Ireland during the conflict as police told women they were too busy attending to the more serious violence of sectarianism. This is shown in how RUC officers coined the term 'ordinary decent murders', which they used to describe offences not directly related to the conflict, distinguishing them from those they deemed terrorism-related and motivated by sectarian hatred. Twenty-five per cent of 'ordinary decent murders' were domestic violence homicides. That this term was used by police officers to apply to domestic violence murders reveals how, to a certain extent, violence against women was normalised and seen as inevitable.

Similarly, one woman from the deeply conflicted Republican area of West Belfast contacted the RUC to report a domestic violence incident, only to be informed by the officer: 'There are worse crimes in your area." This suggests that this was not only an opinion expressed within RUC ranks but communicated to domestic violence victims in order to minimise the severity of the crimes against them.

Sadly, this tendency to minimise domestic and sexual violence occurs not only in conflict situations but in non-conflict or 'normal societies', in which an implicit hierarchy of violence is maintained that places violence against women near the bottom. However, during times of conflict, this can take on a particular edge as violence against women and girls is minimised even more when compared to terrorism.

Furthermore, the nature of the conflict made it easier for abusers to control victims as it resulted in many people retreating from public life and spending more time at home with their families due to safety fears about being out in public where bombings and shootings could often occur, especially in town or city centres.

---

* Ibid., p. 92

These factors may have been particularly pronounced for women, who even in 'normal' societies experience far greater restrictions on their behaviour and movement in the guise of protecting their safety. During the Troubles, therefore, it was often the case that women were particularly restricted to their family homes and could have their movement and behaviour controlled by abusers, subsequently leaving them isolated at home.

DOMESTIC VIOLENCE AFTER THE GOOD FRIDAY AGREEMENT

Research in international comparative conflicts has noted a phenomenon whereby women experience 'backlash violence' coinciding with the end of conflicts such as civil wars. It appears that women experience a sudden spike in violent attacks by men in the months and years following peace agreements. This may be due to men who were formerly engaged in armed violence outside of the domestic sphere suddenly returning to the home and turning this violence against their own family, or due to traumatisation of men who participated in armed conflict struggling with mental health issues including alcohol dependency or drug abuse, which have been known to exacerbate domestic violence.

It is not clear to what extent 'backlash violence' occurred in Northern Ireland following the signing of the Good Friday Agreement. However, compelling evidence from international comparative conflict zones suggests that such an analysis of the Northern Irish context could prove illuminating in considering how violence was experienced by women. Crucially, Belfast Rape Crisis noted as recently as 2006 that the number of women being raped at gunpoint was considerably higher than elsewhere in the

UK or in the Republic of Ireland, which they believe is due to the greater number of Troubles-related firearms in circulation between men in Northern Ireland. This continued trend suggests that some guns have remained in circulation long after the ending of the conflict and continue to be used as part of gender-based abuse. This is an issue that needs to be urgently addressed, given the serious repercussions for the current safety of women and girls in Northern Ireland.

DEFINING 'VICTIMS' OF THE TROUBLES

The Troubles-related spike in domestic violence has never been acknowledged by the UK or Northern Irish state. Opportunities to acknowledge the rise have been further hampered by the fact that the UK state never declared the conflict a war. The British government's avoidance of such a declaration may have been due to fears that to do so would further destabilise the region by admitting that they had lost control of events. Furthermore, such a declaration may have left the region open to military intervention by other countries such as the Republic of Ireland, which occasionally considered intervening but was prevented from entering the UK jurisdiction in the absence of an official declaration of war.

This problem has been further compounded by the definition of 'victims' of the Troubles, which is enshrined in law. As we have seen, throughout the Troubles, women and girls were subjected to domestic and sexual violence at a considerably higher rate than elsewhere in the UK, largely due to: an increase in both legally and illegally held weapons; being cut off from police help; and the conflict aiding opportunities to control their behaviour. Despite this, women and girls who experienced these forms of abuse are not considered victims of the conflict and have been silenced and sidelined in the discussion about violence during the Troubles.

The official definition of a 'victim or survivor' of the Troubles is defined by the Victims and Survivors (Northern Ireland) Order 2006. It regards a victim as:

(a) someone who is or has been physically or psychologically injured as a result of or in consequence of a conflict-related incident;

(b) someone who provides a substantial amount of care on a regular basis for an individual mentioned in paragraph (a);

(c) someone who has been bereaved as a result of or in consequence of a conflict-related incident.

The order adds:

An individual may be psychologically injured as a result of or in consequence of –

(a) witnessing a conflict-related incident or the consequences of such an incident; or

(b) providing medical or other emergency assistance to an individual in connection with a conflict-related incident.

According to the order, a 'conflict-related incident' means 'a violent incident occurring in or after 1956 in connection with the affairs of Northern Ireland'.

People who meet the official definition of a 'victim or survivor' are entitled to some limited resources such as potential compensation and the use of specialist services from the Victims Commissioner.

When I contacted the Victims Commissioner's office in 2017 to ask them if women and girls who experienced domestic violence during the Troubles are included in the definition, they could not give a clear response or point to any specific resources offering help for them. Instead, they said they address each person on a case-by-case basis and if a woman provided enough evidence to prove she had been victimised directly as a result of the conflict they would be happy to consider her one.

It is impossible to tell how many women can or indeed have done this. There is no evidence to suggest that women who experienced gender-based abuse are seeking and receiving redress for their victimisation on a mass scale. I fear it is more likely that they have been written out of both history and contemporary reparations processes by systems that don't deliberately seek to exclude them but simply ignore the particular ways in which violence against women is committed.

It is not enough to have a catch-all definition of victims and survivors of the Troubles. Rather, as has been shown throughout this chapter, women and girls clearly experienced domestic and sexual violence in particular ways. Rather than having to navigate a piecemeal definition of victimhood not designed with their experiences in mind, they merit a particular subsection relating to gender-based issues, for the matter to be treated with the seriousness it deserves and for women to be given a clear and comprehensive means of engaging with victims' services.

Furthermore, it is worth considering how gender-based violence fits into ongoing legacy 'cold cases' from the Troubles. As has been discussed earlier in this book, thousands of 'cold-case' or legacy murders are being considered by courts, which occurred during the conflict but were not subject to full and fair investigation at the time.

Should 'cold-case' legacy investigations be expanded from murders to include gender-based violence which occurred during the Troubles but which soldiers or the police failed to respond to? Should the Northern Irish police issue an apology or at least an acknowledgement that their decision to distribute firearms on a mass scale to the homes of their officers worsened domestic violence? Should the UK government issue an apology or least an acknowledgement that by not declaring the conflict an official war, they have shut survivors of domestic violence off from access to justice?

Sadly, it is unlikely that women and girls who experienced domestic and sexual violence as a result of the Troubles will ever see the wrongs done to them acknowledged or atoned for. As we have seen with cold-case murders, attempts to investigate decades-old cases have now been plagued by issues including political interference and funding barriers, as well as evidence going missing and witnesses and alleged culprits being long deceased or now too elderly to stand trial.

While a limited number of cold-case murders have come to court, this has largely been due to the work of campaigners, lawyers and politicians pushing to keep them on the agenda. Unfortunately, there is no such public support for victims of domestic violence from the Troubles, who have been excluded from political discourse and histories of the conflict. Simply put, there is not enough interest in crimes committed against women and girls for this problem to be properly addressed.

Indeed, some victims may not wish to see legal action taken over their abuse. As can often occur in cases of domestic violence, many women remain trapped in relationships for decades. They may fear speaking out in case they are not believed, or fear the stigma which can come from being considered a 'battered woman'. It may therefore be worth considering other ways in which the trauma of women and girls from gender-based violence in the conflict can be addressed beyond legal frameworks. For instance, specific government funding could be released to support domestic violence charities in Northern Ireland with counselling, legal advice or safe spaces in which affected women can discuss their experiences in a supported environment if they wish to do so.

There may also be merit in further academic research on the topic in the hope that, even if it is now too late for many women in Northern Ireland to be protected or access justice, their experiences can still be of use in helping other societies to learn from the trauma of our past and help women and girls in other conflicts in the future.

The issue is an extremely complex one, with no clear or catch-all solutions. However, important first steps may come from the issue merely being acknowledged, as women's experiences in this regard have been silenced for so long. Through acknowledgement, perhaps some movement may finally be made towards the sensitive and serious discussion that gender-based violence deserves.

The Good Friday Agreement failed to recognise gender-based

violence and in so doing failed to outline opportunities for women and girls to address the ways in which domestic and sexual violence increased as a direct result of the Troubles. Although this violence was not sectarian in nature and most often occurred within families, it was still connected to the conflict due to the increase in access to weapons among both paramilitaries and RUC officers which some men used to murder or terrorise their own partners. Therefore, it is still important to consider as Troubles-related violence. The Good Friday Agreement's failure to do so represented a failure to recognise women's and girls' suffering and create opportunities for them to access healing and justice.

LGBT RIGHTS

It's a late evening in autumn and I'm sitting in a cabaret club in Belfast, watching punters shuffle in. They shake off rain droplets and stamp their feet free of leaves and other debris of the season, before removing their warm layers and casting a nervous eye around the room. It's an unusual crowd tonight. There's an eclectic mix in the audience, most of whom have been to an evening of burlesque before. In one corner, barristers and drag queens compare notes on wigs, while in another two young women explain to their nervous parents what is about to happen. As the room fills, the crowd settle into their booths and wait for the performance to begin.

Tonight we're here for a special show. The usual fixtures of nipple tassels and naked women in jumbo champagne glasses are on hold for now. Instead, we're here to see something that many people in Northern Ireland consider to be an equally shocking display of sexuality. We're here to see a gay couple get married.

While marriage for LGBT couples in Great Britain and the Republic of Ireland is legal, the same right has never been extended to Northern Ireland. Tonight's ceremony will have no legal value and is instead a protest event organised every year as part of the city's Culture Night. Each year, couples who are engaged but denied marriage under Northern Irish law hold mock marriage ceremonies to highlight the inequality.

This evening we're here to celebrate Belfast couple Eoin and Shane, officiated by a drag queen. They've been together for five years and engaged for two. They want to marry in Northern Ireland but the law will not allow them to.

The pair have written their own vows and although they are peppered with quips and they heckle the audience playfully, the emotion of faking their own marriage does not escape them. As their vows come to a close and the drag queen prepares to announce them husband and husband, tears trickle down the face of one of the grooms.

After their 'ceremony', we chat and Eoin explains:

> We had a really good time tonight, but ultimately we've had to stand up there and try to prove to people that we have worth, that we're the same as you. That's the frustrating part. What it all boils down to is the fact that we're second-class citizens in our own country.

Shane concurs. Today should have been one of the happiest days of his life but instead his overriding emotion is pure anger. He tells me: 'We're going to fight tooth and nail with them. I am done putting on the kid gloves, I'm done pretending this is OK. That's the position I'm at now. What are we meant to do, wait another twenty years?'

The couple are determined to wait until their marriage can be recognised as truly legal, Shane explains:

> We get asked a lot when are we setting a date. My response is always the same: whenever it's legal. I do get frustrated at times. I would've loved our grandparents to be there but they are quite elderly now, and I don't know if they will be around, which is quite upsetting.
>
> This is my country, my home, so why do I have to be separated? I live here, I pay my taxes, I'm governed by Westminster, so why do I not have the rights of someone in England, Scotland, Wales? Am I different? My love isn't second-class and neither should the legal recognition of it be.

SAME-SEX MARRIAGE LEGISLATION IN NORTHERN IRELAND

In 2004, legislation was passed giving same-sex couples the right to enter civil partnerships in the UK. The legislation came into effect the following year and granted similar although not identical legal rights to marriage. It applied to all four regions of the UK, including Northern Ireland, which was under direct rule of Westminster at the time due to a collapse in power-sharing at Stormont.

Indeed, the first civil partnership in the UK took place in Northern Ireland as local couple Shannon Sickles and Grainne Close tied the knot in a ceremony at Belfast City Hall. Photographs of the couple standing in front of the building wearing monochrome suits, pink corsages and beaming smiles have become an iconic image for the LGBT rights movement.

In July 2013, legislation was passed in England and Wales which went one step further and legalised same-sex marriage on a par with heterosexual marriages. The move was largely symbolic as civil partnerships had granted much of the same rights of marriage already, but was welcomed by many LGBT people as an important message that their relationships were just as valid as anyone else's.

The first wedding ceremonies took place the following March. Scotland soon followed suit, passing similar legislation in spring 2014 which took effect from December of the same year.

Prophecies of hellfire and locust plagues made by anti-marriage advocates failed to materialise and the matter came to be largely considered a settled and non-controversial issue in the UK. Many other countries have since passed similar laws, including the Republic of Ireland, which became the first country to legalise marriage equality by popular vote following a referendum on the issue in 2015.

However, in Northern Ireland, couples are still waiting. The same-sex marriage legislation did not extend to the region and instead civil partnerships remain the highest institution same-sex couples can enter into.

What's more, same-sex marriages are not recognised in Northern Ireland at all, even if a couple has entered into a legal marriage elsewhere. If a couple marry in a jurisdiction where marriage is legal (for instance, England, Scotland, Wales or the Republic of

Ireland), once they enter Northern Ireland's legal jurisdiction their marriage ceases to be valid and instead is converted to a civil partnership in the eyes of local law. This is the case even if the couple have never been in a civil partnership.

That same-sex marriage has not been legalised in Northern Ireland is not due to a lack of local support for the issue. Indeed, the overwhelming majority of people in Northern Ireland support same-sex marriage being extended to the region. A 2016 survey by polling group Lucid Talk recorded 70 per cent support for it, with just 22 per cent of respondents against. The latter was a drop from 27 per cent the previous year, suggesting that resistance to the idea is slowly receding.

However, the unique nature of the parliamentary structure used in Northern Ireland as part of the peace process means equal marriage has not been introduced, despite public demand. Since 2012, proposals to legalise same-sex marriage have been put to Stormont on five occasions in total and failed to pass each time. On the first four occasions, the bill failed to achieve majority support. On the fifth time, a majority of MLAs backed the proposal. However, it still failed to become law, as the DUP employed a mechanism of the Good Friday Agreement called a Petition of Concern to veto it.

The Petition of Concern is a mechanism inserted into the Good Friday Agreement to enable political parties to effectively veto or block pieces of legislation they deem to be discriminatory. The mechanism is unique to Northern Ireland and was designed with a view to protecting the rights of minority or marginalised communities. However, recent years have seen the inverse happen, as the DUP have begun using it to oppress marginalised groups and deny them their rights.

Although there is now majority support for same-sex marriage both among the general public and on Stormont's benches, while the Petition of Concern is engaged this majority will not be enough. A Petition of Concern can only be overridden if 60 per cent of MLAs support it, including 40 per cent of both union- ist and nationalist MLAs. While support for same-sex marriage among MLAs is in the majority, it is not strong enough to meet these thresholds. This is particularly the case as nationalists are more likely than unionists to support LGBT rights.

The issue has therefore reached deadlock due to the unique nature of the democratic structure of the Stormont Parliament. Barring some major and unexpected blow to the DUP support, the party will have enough seats to block same-sex marriage legislation and, barring some major and unexpected ideological softening, they will continue to do so. It could take decades before the balance shifts towards same-sex marriage at Stormont. In the meantime, LGBT couples are left in limbo.

LEGAL CHALLENGES TO THE DUP'S VETO ON SAME-SEX MARRIAGE

In recent years, LGBT activists have begun turning to the courts instead, in the hope that lawyers can achieve what politicians cannot. In August 2017, the Belfast High Court handed down a long-awaited judgment on the matter. The case was composed of essentially two distinct cases, heard as one due to their similari- ties. The first case was arguing that same-sex couples should have the right to equal civil marriage in Northern Ireland. The second case was arguing that same-sex couples who get married in places where it is legal should have this marriage count while they are in Northern Ireland, contrary to the present arrangements.

The judgment has been a long time coming. The case was first heard in 2015, but it has been subject to multiple delays and deferral of the verdict. Couples across Northern Ireland prolonged their engagements and delayed their ceremonies, waiting for the verdict they hoped would bring what they considered a 'real' wedding. On 17 August, the verdict was finally handed down. Couples waited outside Belfast High Court to hear their fate, while friends, family and supporters around the region held their breath.

The judge rejected both cases, ruling that marriage was not a matter for courts to decide and that only Stormont had the right to legalise marriage. The day was an extremely hurtful one for many couples. After waiting years in the hope of being able to finally marry, their hopes had been dashed again. Wedding invitations would remain unsent, florist orders were cancelled and wedding dresses were reluctantly returned to the backs of wardrobes.

HOW LGBT RIGHTS BECAME AN ORANGE *V* GREEN ISSUE

Same-sex marriage, or indeed LGBT rights in general, might not appear on the face of it to be a particularly obvious 'Orange' or 'Green' issue in the Northern Irish context. The topic played no tangible role in the conflict, nor did it feature in the peace process.

Globally, the issue of LGBT rights is often framed as one of Christians or other religious groups against secular society, with the former bitterly opposed and the latter ardently in favour. It therefore may not appear to be a particularly divisive 'Catholic' or 'Protestant' issue, as both faith groups in many other countries would be opposed to same-sex unions.

However, in Northern Ireland, like so many issues, same-sex marriage has been sucked in by the region's seemingly ceaseless gravitational pull towards sectarian politics. In recent years the issue has come to be at the centre of a proxy war between the DUP and Sinn Féin.

It is worth once again remembering that although Northern Ireland often uses the terms 'Catholic' or 'Protestant' to refer to the two 'sides', neither group is defined by religious character; rather, they are more complex ethno-nationalist groups which use those terms as a shorthand that fails to capture their complexity. The two communities' differing views on same-sex marriage stem not from theological or biblical differences but from the wider issues of equality and majority rule. The two communities' different experiences during the Troubles shape how they now view LGBT rights.

THE DUP AND LGBT RIGHTS

The DUP are a vehemently and vocally anti-LGBT organisation. Throughout the party's history, its politicians have shown an almost obsessive interest in same-sex intercourse, unparalleled by any other party in the British Isles.

In 1977, the DUP's founding father Ian Paisley led the 'Save Ulster from Sodomy' campaign which saw him collect some 70,000 signatures for a petition against the decriminalisation of homosexuality in Northern Ireland. Senior DUP figures have been against LGBT rights in the strongest and most colourful terms.

In a 2007 interview, DUP MP Ian Paisley Jr said: 'I am pretty repulsed by gay and lesbianism. I think it is wrong. I think that those people harm themselves and – without caring about it – harm society.'

In 2008, Iris Robinson, one of the party's MPs and wife of then DUP leader Peter Robinson, used a Stormont debate on sexual offences to state her view that homosexuality was worse than child abuse, remarking: 'There can be no viler act, apart from homosexuality and sodomy, than sexually abusing children.'

In 2005, DUP councillor Maurice Mills suggested that Hurricane Katrina was sent by God to punish gay people. Of the natural disaster which killed some 1,300 people, he said:

> The recent Hurricane Katrina descended on New Orleans and took many people suddenly into eternity. However, the media failed to report that the hurricane occurred just two days prior to the annual homosexual event called the Southern Decadence Festival which the previous year had attracted an estimated 125,000 people. Surely this is a warning to nations where such wickedness is increasingly promoted and practised.

He then added for good measure: 'This abominable and filthy practice of sodomy has resulted in the great continent of Africa being riddled with Aids, all at great cost to the nations and innocent children.'

The DUP's anti-LGBT approach has not been limited purely to controversial comments, but has a firm hold on party policy, which has seen the DUP consistently attempt to block LGBT rights advancement in the region.

Edwin Poots, who once told a BBC talk show that he found gay sex 'unnatural', served as Health Minister in Stormont between 2011 and 2014. He spent much of his time in office fighting against proposals to allow gay and bisexual men to be permitted to donate blood, taking numerous costly legal cases in a bid to retain a ban on such blood donations. Similarly, he took a number of legal challenges attempting to stop same-sex couples adopting children.

In addition, when Northern Ireland became embroiled in what was referred to in local media by the unfortunate moniker 'gay cake row' in 2014, the DUP again used the opportunity to attempt to limit LGBT rights. The row occurred when a Belfast bakery run by an evangelical Christian couple refused to bake a cake requested by an LGBT rights activist bearing the slogan 'Support Gay Marriage'. The activist subsequently took a legal case against the bakery, arguing that he had been the victim of discrimination and refused service due to his sexual orientation. The case was backed by the Equality Commission for Northern Ireland. The bakery owners argued that they reserved the right to refuse to ice slogans they opposed onto their cakes. To force someone to ice messages they opposed amounted to a violation of free speech, in their eyes.

The DUP came to the support of the bakers, arguing that they were the victims of political correctness gone mad and 'persecution' of Christians. DUP MPs collected a petition against the legal case going ahead. One of the party's MLAs, Paul Givan, announced the party would introduce a 'conscience clause' bill at Stormont which would create an exemption in law so that people with strongly held religious beliefs could be exempt from following equality legislation.

In 2015, DUP leader Arlene Foster wrote to the Scottish government asking them curtail Northern Irish couples' access to same-sex marriage there. The Scottish government declined, saying 'it would not be appropriate' for them to do so.

This staunchly anti-LGBT stance is largely due to the party's strong evangelical Christian bent, which traces its roots back to the Protestant plantation of the seventeenth century and the ensuing belief that they have been given Northern Ireland to rule as a Christian country.

Furthermore, the party's social conservatism has roots in the 'siege mentality' inherent in the unionist/loyalist position that all change is to be viewed with suspicion and the traditional social order to be preserved at all costs. Just as the civil rights movement in Derry-Londonderry in the late 1960s was resisted by some unionists who feared it may have been an IRA ruse under the guise of equality, many in the DUP continue to fear that equality legislation brought in to protect LGBT minorities may in fact be used as a trojan horse for greater rights for the minority Catholic/nationalist community.

Therefore, their anti-same-sex-marriage stance is about much more than mere homophobia itself (although many voters believe that does exist in the party in abundance); it is a core value which goes to the heart of their identity as unionists and loyalists.

SINN FÉIN AND LGBT RIGHTS

In stark contrast, Sinn Féin have adopted a staunchly pro-LGBT and pro-same-sex-marriage position in recent years. Perhaps more than any other party, Sinn Féin has bound itself tightly in the rainbow flag in the intervening period since the peace process.

As the 'Yes' result was announced in the Republic of Ireland's marriage referendum, among the celebrators was Gerry Adams, pictured cheering alongside a drag queen amid a sea of rainbow flags, balloons and confetti. The image was a striking one which for many political commentators encapsulated the extraordinary change Northern Irish politics had undergone, as the rumoured former IRA man took selfies with a drag queen in shared joy at LGBT equality.

How much of a priority this issue had become for the party was strikingly evidenced when Adams used his graveside oration at former party leader Martin McGuinness's funeral in 2017 to call for same-sex marriage to be extended to Northern Ireland. Indeed, at Pride marches around Northern Ireland since then, Sinn Féin political banners have come to be a familiar fixture, often accompanied by senior Sinn Féin MPs and MLAs draped in the rainbow flags and pro-LGBT slogans.

Nor has Sinn Féin's stance on LGBT rights been confined to mere rhetoric. Within days of taking the position of Health Minister from the DUP in 2016, Sinn Féin MLA Michelle O'Neill (who would later go on to be the party's leader) announced that she would end the region's ban on blood donations from gay and bisexual men. On five separate occasions, the party has backed motions at Stormont attempting to legalise same-sex marriage.

When power-sharing collapsed in 2017, the party announced that the DUP committing to the introduction of same-sex marriage for Northern Ireland was one of a small number of non-negotiable red-line issues. Unless equal marriage was legalised, the party simply would not return to government.

This ardently pro-LGBT equality stance can appear at first glance to be a perplexing one, as the Irish Republican movement has previously had little overlap with LGBT rights. However, it is a strategic move that serves a number of the party's needs and is consistent with the party's wider ideology.

Primarily, the issue feeds into how the party frames itself as Northern Ireland's pro-equality and pro-human rights party. Much of the Republican ethos is based on the perspective that the Catholic/nationalist community in Northern Ireland was the victim of systematic discrimination under British and subsequently majority unionist rule. Many Republicans see clear parallels with discrimination that LGBT communities face under a heterosexual society which sidelines them. A Sinn Féin policy document on LGBT rights explicitly embraces this link, stating:

Lesbian, gay and bisexual people suffer from discrimination and harassment in every aspect of their daily lives. Whether in the social, political, economic or cultural spheres, they are denied equality of rights and opportunities. There is no logical or rational defence for such exclusion. Only ignorance and indifference enable such a denial of basic fundamental rights to continue.

Republicans are only too well aware of what it means to be treated as second-class citizens. Our politics are the result of decades of resistance to marginalisation and discrimination. Self-determination is our core demand, not only as a nation, but also as diverse communities within that nation.

When confronted with experiences which are similar to

our own (such as those of ethnic minorities, Travellers, women etc) it should be automatic for us, as republicans, to understand and actively express that understanding through solidarity. The denial of justice from one section of this nation is a denial of the rights of us all.

So it is imperative that Sinn Féin plays an active role in securing equality not only for the nationalist community, but also all those other sections of our society that have been denied the right to play a full and equal part in determining the course of this island.

Sinn Féin has been quick to realise the merits of being associated with this cause, which is increasingly being viewed as a litmus test of progressive values. As more and more countries make progress on LGBT rights and continue to legalise same-sex marriage, the DUP's homophobia has begun to look more and more jarring both at home and internationally. By contrast, Sinn Féin are seen by many as representing the populist, progressive view and look poised to be remembered as being on the right side of history as LGBT equality has become the status quo. By pushing the issue so strongly, Sinn Féin are able to embarrass the DUP with their views, which many people consider to be bigoted and authoritarian.

This sentiment was most acutely seen during the response to the June 2017 DUP–Conservative deal in which Arlene Foster's ten MPs agreed to prop up Theresa May's minority government through a confidence-and-supply arrangement. In the immediate aftermath, many in Britain suddenly became aware of the DUP's homophobic policies and beliefs. British newspapers were suddenly full of the DUP's views on homosexuality. Leader of the Scottish Conservative Party Ruth Davidson contacted Theresa May to seek assurances that LGBT rights would not be changed in Britain as a result of the deal. Capitalising on the situation, Gerry Adams released a statement in which he dryly commented: 'The focus by the mainstream British media on the DUP's policies and history is belated but a welcome education for people in Britain.' In so doing, he capitalised on how the DUP are perceived by many in Britain to be obstinate and bigoted in one regard, and widen it out towards the DUP's treatment of minorities in general. The implied eye roll was palpable – thanks for finally waking up to these dinosaurs that we've been dealing with for years.

For Sinn Féin, becoming LGBT advocates has also had a further benefit in helping detoxify the party's brand, particularly among young people who may have no direct experiences with the Troubles or cognisance of Sinn Féin's IRA links. By focusing on 'feel-good' issues like marriage rights, the party has promoted a rights-based agenda without being overtly Republican, through an issue which younger voters overwhelmingly support. This has also helped diversify the party's policies beyond Northern Ireland's constitutional question and deflect against allegations that they are a single-issue party, obsessed with Irish reunification but without much else to offer.

Finally, the party were heavily involved in the Republic of Ireland's 2015 referendum on same-sex marriage, campaigning for a 'yes' vote. The experience was an overwhelmingly positive one for them and it helped embed Sinn Féin further in politics south of the border.

However, it's important to stress that the issue is not as clear-cut as running down a simplistic unionist versus nationalist, Catholic versus Protestant divide. Although the DUP are Northern Ireland's largest Protestant party and most vocally anti-LGBT group, their views do not represent the unionist community as a whole.

Of course, there are many individuals within the nationalist and Republican community who oppose same-sex marriage on moral or religious grounds. Similarly, there are unionists and loyalists who are pro-LGBT rights or are LGBT themselves. Indeed, there are many DUP supporters who disagree strongly with their stance on same-sex marriage but due to the nature of Northern Ireland's unique politics, they vote for them regardless because their stance on the constitutional question is what appeals to them most. The 2015 Northern Ireland Election Survey found that 31 per cent of DUP voters said they either agreed or strongly agreed with same-sex marriage being legalised. (By comparison, 75 per cent of Sinn Féin voters said the same.) Therefore many people who support same-sex marriage are still casting their ballots for the DUP despite knowing they hold diametrically opposed views.

It's an issue which is all too acute for Stephen Donnan, an LGBT activist who has worked for Love Equality, the main campaign group advocating for marriage equality in the region, and the Rainbow Project, Northern Ireland's main LGBT charity. Coming from a unionist background, Stephen knows that some members of his own family vote DUP despite being aware that he is gay and that their vote translates to him not being able to marry.

He explained to me:

I have members of my family who vote DUP, who want me to be able to get married but they see issues like the union, legacy issues around parades, the past and the Troubles as being higher on their list of priorities than how the DUP defines marriage.

The majority of people I know who are unionists or loyalists have absolutely no problem with marriage equality or LGBT rights. They have gay daughters, gay sons, gay uncles – everybody knows a gay person.

Stephen feels some DUP voters who support LGBT rights turn a blind eye to the party's anti-LGBT policies because they agree with their hardline stances about keeping Northern Ireland in the UK. He says: 'The DUP still get a massive vote due to issues about the union and identity. What people put on a flag pole can be a stronger pull for people here than social issues.'

Knowing that members of his own family back the party can be challenging, he says, but he encourages them to discuss it rather than denouncing them. 'I'm happy to talk to people about it, even family members. When I was younger I was a lot more antagonistic but now I listen more. What I ask them to do is understand that their political opinions and religious beliefs cannot and should not influence law.'

For many unionist voters, the DUP blocking same-sex marriage is regrettable but acceptable collateral damage in order to have DUP politicians strongly advocating for Northern Ireland's position within the UK.

DIFFERENT MARRIAGES, SAME DIVISIONS

Furthermore, it is important to note the historical opposition to 'mixed marriages' between Catholics and Protestants during the Troubles and how this continues to frame the debate about same-sex marriage rights today. During the conflict, marriages across the religious divide became highly taboo, as many viewed them with suspicion. Policing marriages or relationships was perceived as a vital part of keeping communities safe and not bringing the 'wrong sort' of people into an extended family. To this day, just 10 per cent of marriages and long-term relationships are 'mixed' between a Protestant and a Catholic.

The overwhelming majority of people in Northern Ireland support mixed marriages and just 10 per cent of people told a 2016 study that they would object to a family member marrying someone from the other religion.[*] Crucially, this trait was particularly pronounced among DUP members, among whom 75 per cent said they would 'mind a little' or 'mind a lot' if their relative had such a marriage.

It is possible that some of the anti-same-sex-marriage rhetoric and righteousness felt by the DUP is in part linked to their history as an anti-mixed-marriage group. For them, the decision to oppose same-sex marriage is merely another step in their long-held belief that they can critique other people's marriages and private love lives.

Richard O'Leary, a campaigner for same-sex marriage equality in Northern Ireland who himself was in a mixed Protestant–Catholic

---

[*] Northern Ireland Life and Times Survey 2016

relationship during the conflict, wrote a thought-provoking article for the political website Slugger O'Toole in 2017 in which he compared his experiences of the two forms of marriage discrimination. He wrote:

> Come 2017, and the leaders of the Catholic and Protestant churches have grown out of their opposition to mixed marriage. They realise that they got it wrong. Have they learned from their past mistake? Unfortunately, they have not. Instead, they have turned their opposition to the extension of civil marriage to same-sex couples.

Current debates around same-sex marriage tie into wider, generations-old debates over which marriages and relationships are socially acceptable, which have their roots in attempts to police relationships across the sectarian divide.

LGBT RIGHTS AND THE GOOD FRIDAY AGREEMENT

LGBT rights did not feature in peace process talks, nor are they mentioned in the Good Friday Agreement apart from vague commitments to equal opportunity 'regardless of ... sexual orientation'. This is understandable, as in 1998, LGBT rights were far from the political agenda throughout Europe and could hardly have been anticipated at this time.

However, the Good Friday Agreement was left vulnerable to exploitation in its Petition of Concern mechanism, a parliamentary feature unique to Northern Ireland which was introduced in a bid to safeguard minority rights. This device was included due to fears that majority rule could return during power-sharing and replicate the dark days of unionist dominance and marginalisation of nationalist communities.

Rather than a mechanism to protect minority rights, the Petition of Concern has instead been used by the DUP to block them. The mechanism has been used repeatedly by the party on votes about issues including same-sex marriage.

The Good Friday Agreement could not have anticipated that LGBT rights would become an important social justice issue, and cannot be blamed for failing to foresee this issue, which was not on the political agenda at the time. However, it is deeply ironic that one of its mechanisms designed to protect the rights of vulnerable and marginalised groups has instead been used for the exact opposite. Rather than a means of protection, the Petition of Concern is now often a tool of oppression.

The potential harm which could be incurred by the mechanism was not anticipated in 1998. This was largely due to the peace process in Northern Ireland considering concepts of harm and oppression purely on a nationalist versus unionist axis. It failed to consider a time in Northern Ireland when politics could seek to understand or address other forms of oppression. It subsequently has been unable to facilitate recent political developments.

It is a positive step for Northern Ireland that social justice issues considered by the Parliament and wider society have grown beyond the narrow Orange versus Green spectrum. This political maturity is a sign of a normalised society and a result of the peace politics which the Good Friday Agreement secured in 1998. However, it now appears that while the GFA's strict focus on sectarian oppression was necessary to reach a point where other forms of harm could be considered, it is also incapable of facilitating the new politics that it helped to deliver. While the GFA helped Northern Irish politics reach a point where LGBT rights could be considered, its institutions are inherently incapable of delivering this change.

The issue of same-sex marriage shows no sign of imminent resolution. Sinn Féin has vowed to keep introducing bills on the matter, while the DUP have vowed to continue to block it through the Petition of Concern. Recent attempts to reach a resolution through the courts instead have also been met with the legal judgment that it is not for the judiciary to get involved and only Stormont can introduce change.

The only realistic chance of change would come through a fundamental shift in Stormont's makeup. For instance, if the DUP suffered a considerable drop in seat numbers, meaning they lose the figures required to mount a Petition of Concern challenge. In the March 2017 Assembly election, the DUP lost the numbers required to engage the mechanism. However, it is likely that there would be enough hardline politicians within the Ulster Unionist Party (who are the second largest unionist party in Northern Ireland) who are anti-same-sex marriage who would break ranks with their party to support such a petition. It is also likely that this drop in seat numbers for the DUP is momentary, as the election was a particularly difficult one for the party, being called in the immediate aftermath of a major scandal in which the DUP were accused of allowing millions of pounds of public money to be misused. Their vote drop may have been due to voters seeking to punish the party for the scandal, which was fresh in their minds as they entered polling booths; however, the party faithful appear to have since returned, as the June 2017 Westminster election saw the DUP enjoy record figures. It is likely that in the event of the next Stormont election, the DUP will return with enough seats to regain power over the Petition of Concern.

Therefore, it is highly probably that the issue will be subject to further legal appeals and cases, as well as bills submitted to Parliament for many more years to come.

ABORTION RIGHTS

It was when the bleeding started that she began to feel relieved. It was the first relief she'd felt since she had first discovered she was pregnant some weeks before.

Earlier that same evening, Claire* had calmly walked into the bathroom of her student flat and locked the door carefully behind her. She then ran a bath in order to have a convincing alibi should her flatmates wonder why she had been in there for so long. As the water gurgled down through the taps and she watched the bath slowly fill, she thought about what she was about to do and found her breath involuntarily quickening into sharp, shallow bursts tightly within her chest.

She then sat down on the tiled floor and took out the pill packet

---

*   Not her real name

she had squirreled into the pocket of the fluffy dressing gown she was wrapped up in.

The pill had arrived unceremoniously that morning encased in anonymous packaging within a nondescript envelope. However, for her, there was no doubting what it was. She had researched the tablets meticulously online before finding the website of a women's charity that supplied such pills. She had completed an online consultation with a doctor and watched the charity's video how-to guide on what to expect. She had memorised the instructions and possible side effects before carefully deleting her browser history.

She then waited for the package to arrive, checking the post each morning with a feigned nonchalance in front of her flatmates. They didn't pick up the sinews in her jaw that flickered as she clenched them, betraying her angst while her eyes remained cheerful and calm. She had only recently moved into the flat with three other girls also at the university. They seemed like decent girls but she didn't know them well enough to know for sure how they'd react or what they might do.

Then, on the fourth day, the package arrived. She stuffed it into her bag along with her usual bills and junk mail as calmly as possible before heading out to the university campus, so as not to arouse suspicion. Throughout her seminars and lectures that day she felt acutely aware of the package, nestled between a university grant form and a pizza delivery flyer.

By the time she had arrived back at the flat that evening, stomached as much small talk as possible with her flatmates and then slunk off to the bathroom, she felt relieved to get it over with. She didn't feel nervous about taking the pills themselves. Plenty of people she knew had taken them before. Friends of friends, boyfriends' exes, the outspoken girls in the university feminist society. Stories would trip out after a few drinks, and rumours spread round the campus.

Despite official denials, everyone knew someone who had had one.

Sitting on the bathroom floor as the tub continued to fill, she took a deep breath, pierced the packet's film and held the pill in her palm. With one gulp of water it was gone and she reclined her back against the bathroom wall, breathing a sigh of relief.

The past few weeks had been some of the most stressful of her life since finding out about the pregnancy. She resolved that she was certain she would terminate the pregnancy; the only question was when and how. Flying to England to have an abortion in a clinic there had been her first thought, but it was simply not an option. Working part-time in a local shop around her studies, her pay packet was hardly enough to get her through each month with Belfast rent, books and bus tickets, without last-minute flights, a hotel stay and private medical bills on top.

Asking friends or family for a loan was also too risky. Instead, she resolved that online pills would be her best option.

So, as she waited for the pills to take effect, she found herself relieved when the bleeding started. When she had run out of toilet paper and the trickles had not ceased, she began to get worried. Ringing a friend for advice was too risky, in case they revealed her secret. Contacting her GP for advice or going to A&E could result in life imprisonment. Instead, she lowered herself into the bath to wait it out. Her blood slowly mingled with the water as it spread throughout the tub, turning the liquid a curious pink.

* * *

It's a phrase that jars grammatically – to commit an abortion. To most people in the UK, this mismatched pairing of medical and criminal terminology has an odd linguistic cadence that snags in the ear. Elsewhere in the UK, one could no more commit an abortion than be found guilty of having a heart bypass or stand trial over appendix removal.

Yet, in Northern Ireland, abortion remains something that women commit. Unlike the rest of the UK, abortion in Northern Ireland remains a criminal offence on a par with murder and carries a sentence of life imprisonment.

In 1967, the Abortion Act effectively legalised abortion in England and Wales, subject to term limits and doctors' approval. In Northern Ireland, however, the legislation was not extended as the bill was passed during a rare period in which Northern Ireland had its own government. The hyper-religious government at Stormont was intensely Christian and socially conservative. It resolutely opposed introducing any legislation which the politicians considered tantamount to murdering unborn children.

Instead, Northern Ireland continues to be governed by the Victorian-era legislation that criminalised abortion throughout the UK and the wider British Empire 150 years ago. Written before women had the right to vote or the light bulb had been invented, the 1861 Offences Against The Person Act makes abortion a criminal offence which carries a life sentence. The act states:

Every woman, being with child, who, with intent to procure

her own miscarriage, shall unlawfully administer to herself any poison or other noxious thing, or shall unlawfully use any instrument or other means whatsoever with the like intent, and whosoever, with intent to procure the miscarriage of any woman, ... shall unlawfully administer to her or cause to be taken by her any poison or other noxious thing, or shall unlawfully use any instrument or other means whatsoever with the like intent, shall be guilty of felony, and ... shall be liable to be kept in penal servitude for life.

Northern Ireland is almost unique in the world as a country which actively enforces its abortion ban. Although abortion is illegal in many countries (including the Republic of Ireland), few states actively enforce the law by arresting women and putting them on trial. However, in Northern Ireland this is happening – and at an increasing rate.

POLICE CRACKDOWN

For many decades, the ability to fly across the Irish Sea to a clinic has proven something of a pressure value for Northern Ireland. It has meant that most women and girls have been able to have terminations (if they have sufficient resources, contacts and the right immigration status) by going elsewhere. However, this status quo has recently been disrupted, bringing Northern Ireland's abortion crisis to an unexpected and urgent head.

An increasing number of women are now performing abortions on themselves in Northern Ireland. It is difficult to obtain information on the precise number of women involved, due to the illegal nature of such self-induced abortions. However, the Northern Irish police are arresting an increasing number of women for doing so.

In 2016, a woman was arrested on suspicion of breaking the abortion ban. It has since emerged that she is accused of helping her daughter, then aged fifteen, to access abortion pills. It has been claimed that the daughter was in an abusive relationship. After helping her daughter to access the pills, the mother disclosed to her GP what had happened. The doctor subsequently contacted authorities and the woman was arrested. Despite the fact that the girl was below the age of consent and therefore her pregnancy could constitute statutory rape, no charges were brought on these grounds. At the time of writing, the woman is still awaiting trial.

The case shocked many people in Northern Ireland, as it was assumed that the pressure valve provided by the option to travel to England, Scotland or Wales would mean that women and girls would not feel the need to perform abortions on themselves.

However, rather than an anomaly, the case was a sign of things to come.

In April 2016, a disturbing case was heard at Belfast High Court. A 21-year-old woman was accused of committing an abortion. The court was told that the woman was nineteen years old when she had experienced an unplanned pregnancy. She had little money and desperately tried to raise enough funds to travel to England in order to have a termination in a clinic there. However, she failed to do so in time. She then ordered abortion pills online and took them at her home. Her flatmates discovered bloody clothing and foetal remains in a communal bin. They phoned the police, who attended and subsequently arrested the woman.

In court, the woman pleaded guilty to the charges. Her lawyer explained that she now had a young child and was trying to put her life back together after the traumatic incident. She was given a three-month sentence, suspended for two years.

The following January, another case appeared before the courts. A young woman and her partner were accused of committing abortion offences after ordering pills online in 2015. The woman was described as 'vulnerable and immature' and was said to have experienced serious mental health problems including self-harm. The couple accepted a formal warning. The judge issued an order banning media from identifying the woman, citing a risk that she could die by suicide if her identity were known to the public.

In March 2017, the police carried out raids at two properties while searching for pills. The raids were conducted on International Women's Day, when pro-choice activists were away from their homes at a feminist rally. No charges were brought.

It is not entirely clear why an increasing number of women appear to be performing abortions on themselves in Northern Ireland. It may be the case that women and girls are increasingly struggling to afford the cost of travelling to Britain. The effects of the 2008 financial crash reverberated around the world and Northern Ireland was no exception. Amid a culture of mounting student debt, precarious zero-hour contracts and squeezed pay packets, the costs of such a journey can be prohibitive, as last-minute flights (often booked at short notice by necessity), can cost several hundred pounds, combined with needing to stay in a hotel for a few days either side of the procedure. Prior to a policy change in 2017, women and girls were also required to pay several hundred pounds for the procedure itself; the NHS could not cover it, as the procedure is not legal in Northern Ireland.

Another reason may be the overall increasing role that the internet has in people's lives. Consumers feel more comfortable ordering products online than they would have a mere decade ago. Now that women and girls have the option of ordering pills, they may be more likely to seriously consider this as an option.

Ordering pills online has a number of benefits for some people when compared with travelling to England for an abortion. For many of the most vulnerable women and girls, travelling simply isn't an option. In addition to potentially prohibitive costs, which only the wealthiest women can afford, it also requires taking an unexplainable length of time away from home. While in England for the days required, alibis must be given to friends and family, as well as leave granted at short notice by an employer. For women in abusive relationships, it can be the case that their partner does not permit them to leave and already controls access to money or passports. For undocumented women, such as asylum seekers, refugees or those who have otherwise precarious immigration status, travelling can be impossible.

However, performing an abortion at home remains illegal under the abortion ban. Every woman and girl who does so is at risk of prosecution, making it a high-risk choice. This can be particularly concerning in the event of medical complications. While most women who have abortions do not experience complications, those who do are unable to get medical aid in Northern Ireland for fear of discovery, thereby exposing them to further risk.

ABORTION AND THE TROUBLES

There has been little discourse on the ways in which the Troubles fuelled Northern Ireland's abortion laws. However, the links between the conflict and the ban merit serious consideration.

It is often said that Northern Ireland is a very religious society and it is thereby assumed that the abortion ban stems from this. However, this belies the specific ways in which the unique circumstances of the Troubles heighten the extreme abortion laws of the present day. After all, many countries are religious, and indeed many continue to outlaw abortion, but few actively pursue and prosecute women who break these laws in the way that occurs in Northern Ireland, which is one of the few states in the world to actually enforce its abortion ban by conducting raids on women's homes, arresting them and putting them on trial.

During the Troubles, Northern Ireland experienced a heavy-handed and authoritarian approach to policing and security, as evidenced in internment without trial, widespread stop-and-searches and the army forcibly searching homes without warrant. This history may go some way in explaining why Northern Irish people accept the heavy-handed manner in which women are criminalised under the abortion ban, due to a wider social acceptance of authoritarian and aggressive policing.

The nature of the Northern Ireland conflict has meant not only that the society is hyper-religious, but that there is also a social acceptance of religious groups aggressively asserting their beliefs over others.

In particular, the Troubles pivoted on a political discourse containing dramatic, total-sum moralising pronouncements about life and death, often denouncing other politicians and political parties as murderers. For instance, the SDLP (which supports the abortion ban) sought to distance itself from Sinn Féin and the IRA, through their stance that it is unjustified to take a life. Similarly, the DUP's (which also supports the abortion ban) modus operandi is centred on its vocal anti-IRA rhetoric; denouncing them as murderers and terrorists. For decades, the nature of the conflict has meant that political discourse has been centred on if and when it is permissible to end a life, to the extent that the issue is central to many of the parties' identities in Northern Ireland, in a way that doesn't occur in non-conflict societies such as England, Scotland or Wales. This may have given parties more entrenched views on abortion, which they consider ending a life.

In addition, the breakdown of civil society during the Troubles increased the role and stature of the churches, particularly the Catholic church among nationalist communities. The nature of anti-Catholic discrimination, particularly in areas such as Derry-Londonderry, alienated Catholics from the state as they were denied housing, education, employment rights and fair electoral representation. Many Catholics subsequently turned to the local church to fulfil this role through housing advice, food donations or other aid.

Furthermore, the nature of the peace process elevated church leaders to a higher position in society. Most famously, the DUP's leader during the peace process was the Reverend Ian Paisley, who led his own church. In addition, it was often the case that during negotiations both 'sides' would send a priest or minister as an intermediary. This way, they knew that they had someone clearly from their community representing them, but the representative would be palatable to the other 'side' as a man of the cloth and therefore to be respected. For instance, during decommissioning, it was agreed that a priest and a minister would watch the paramilitaries destroy their weapons and then report back to their own communities to confirm it had happened. This gave church leaders a more prominent social and political role.

In addition, much of Northern Ireland's conflict has been defined by debates about 'demographics', i.e. how the Protestant and Catholic birth rates compare. The Northern Ireland state was established by creating a region with a Protestant majority in order to ensure majority support for remaining in the UK. However, since the foundation of the state, the Protestant majority is waning as Catholics tend to have larger families. In the 1926 census, Protestants accounted for 67 per cent of the population, with the remaining 33 per cent Catholic. However, by 2015, this figure was 48 per cent Protestant, with 45 per cent Catholic and 6 per cent identifying as Other. As a result, many politicians, particularly in the Protestant/unionist community, have voiced an anxiety about birth rates. DUP leader Ian Paisley used inflammatory language to this effect at a loyalist rally in 1969 when he said of Northern Ireland's Catholic community: 'They breed like rabbits and multiply like vermin.' Similarly, when the Northern Ireland Woman's Coalition was present at the Good Friday Agreement negotiations, some loyalist politicians told them that if they really wanted to contribute to politics they should go home and 'breed for Ulster'. In this way, birth and reproduction has taken on a particular politicised edge in Northern Ireland, which may explain why some politicians feel so strongly opposed to women having control over their own reproduction, as they attach political significance to 'their women' having as many pregnancies and births as possible as part of the wider demographic fight.

Finally, it is worth noting that the overwhelming majority of people in Northern Ireland oppose the current abortion ban, yet they vote for anti-abortion politicians due to the unique nature of Northern Ireland's post-conflict politics, which means many people will vote exclusively on the basis of where politicians stand on the constitutional question. A 2016 Amnesty International study found 58 per cent support for total decriminalisation of abortion in Northern Ireland. Just 22 per cent supported it remaining a criminal offence. A slightly higher proportion supported decriminalising in cases of rape or incest (72 per cent for, 15 per cent against) and in cases where the foetus will be unable to survive due to a fatal foetal abnormality (67 per cent for, 17 per cent against).

However, these views are not reflected among Northern Irish politicians. The notion that abortion is murder is held by the majority of mainstream politicians, who have consistently voted to keep Northern Ireland's abortion ban despite legal warnings that it constitutes a human rights abuse and despite popular public support for decriminalisation. The DUP and SDLP support prosecution in all circumstances bar where a woman would die if she did not have an abortion. Sinn Féin support changing the law in limited circumstances. This has previously been solely to permit abortion in cases of conception following rape or incest, as well as when a fatal foetal abnormality means the foetus cannot survive outside the womb. However, as the Republic of Ireland began preparing in 2017 for a referendum on its own abortion ban to be held in 2018, Sinn Féin altered its stance in line with signs that the Republic would soon opt for a more liberal legal framework; as an Irish Republican party, they could not justify having different policies for the two different jurisdictions. Sinn Féin therefore changed its policy slightly to include cases where a pregnant person's mental or physical health is at risk. This stance therefore puts the party's policy broadly in line with the legislation currently in place in Great Britain, as the 1967 Abortion Act did not technically legalise abortion on demand but instead made it permissible where doctors agreed that there could be a greater risk to the woman's physical or mental health if it continued than if a termination was performed. For the UUP, the matter is an issue of personal conscience rather than party policy. The fifth party, Alliance, also believe the issue is a matter for their politicians' personal conscience. However, all of their current MLAs support some kind of change to the laws, ranging from abortion access to women who have conceived as a result of rape, to the full extension of the 1967 Abortion Act.

That Northern Ireland's political parties are so out of step with the public on abortion is striking. The fact that the electorate are willing to vote for them regardless is also arresting and has its roots in the unique nature of the Troubles conflict. As the conflict narrowed political focus in Northern Ireland to a single issue (namely, the constitutional question), it subsumed all others to mere side issues. Simply put, voters may not agree with the politicians when it comes to abortion, but they will continue to vote for them as long as they share their stance on Northern Ireland's constitutional status.

ABORTION ACCESS IN MODERN-DAY NORTHERN IRELAND

Of course, the fact that abortion is illegal in Northern Ireland does not mean that it does not happen. There is no evidence to suggest that women have fewer abortions in the region than in other parts of the UK where they are legal. Northern Irish women do have abortions. They just have them at much later dates once they have raised the funds to travel to England, or – increasingly – they perform abortions on themselves at home.

It's difficult to understand the true extent of abortion in Northern Ireland. Due to the inherent nature of the laws, women often fear discussing the issue for fear of legal repercussions or social isolation.

As a journalist covering the abortion ban for many years, I am often sent personal accounts from women who have had abortions. Some send lengthy emails explaining what happened. Others send short snatches to me in private messages on social media. Some want me to write about their stories. Others just want to tell someone for the first time, after years of keeping the secret swallowed inside them.

They write: *I swallowed some bleach, my sister threw herself down a flight of stairs, I stole money to get to England, I ordered pills online, I didn't eat for a week to afford the taxi fare from the airport to the clinic.* Some have escaped abusive relationships; some remain in them; some have conceived after rape; some are too poor to look after a child; some are underage; some simply do not want to have a child.

In the Victorian era, a device called a zoetrope was created as an early precursor to video. The device involved lining up short clipped images of a situation and spinning them in quick succession to give the human eye the impression of movement, as the images merge and flicker to depict a scene. Reporting on Northern

Ireland's abortion laws and being privy to women's testimonies often feels like a zoetrope of sorts. I don't claim to have a clear understanding of exactly how the laws affect women. But these testimonies, the graphic nature of them, their striking similarities to each other, give some image of the impact of the ban – if an incomplete one. The picture it conveys is dark and disturbing.

Data from the Department of Health suggests that 800–900 women who have abortions in clinics in England and Wales give their home address as being in Northern Ireland. This amounts to an average of two to three women per day. It is thought the true figure will be much higher, as many women will give fake addresses out of fear of being found out.

While having an abortion in Northern Ireland itself is tantamount to murder under local legislation, to travel to England, Scotland or Wales for the same procedure is perfectly legal. The policy is a striking example of nimbyism, whereby local people do not object to women having abortions so long as they don't do it locally. Even within the anti-abortion movement in Northern Ireland there has been no appetite to introduce any legislation making it a criminal offence for women to travel to England in order to have a termination. This appears to be logically inconsistent, as the same groups argue that abortion is just as much murder as the taking of an adult life. However, it appears that many even in the anti-abortion movement in Northern Ireland recognise the ability to travel as something of a 'pressure valve' for the abortion ban. If women were not allowed to travel for terminations, it is likely that Northern Ireland would be the site of similar scenes to those which propelled the 1967 Abortion Act in Britain, following

a series of high-profile cases in which women died from performing botched backstreet abortions on themselves.

So you can have an abortion so long as you go across the Irish
Sea to get it. So long as you make up a convoluted alibi about
going to a spa weekend in England or visiting a long-lost cousin.
So long as you go to a strange clinic in a strange part of the world,
with unfamiliar accents and no one to hold your hand. So long as
you bleed quietly on a budget airline flight on your way home. So
long as you smile when you get back and wax lyrical about your
great spa weekend or trip to the theatre. In exchange, Northern
Ireland won't ask why your face is pale and your jeans are stained
and your story doesn't add up. So long as we can continue the
pretence that abortion doesn't happen here. Perhaps in heathen
England. But not here. Not us. Not in God's own Ulster.

ATTEMPTS AT LEGISLATIVE REFORM

In the years following the introduction of the 1967 Abortion
Act in Britain, attempts have been made to reform the law and
bring Northern Ireland in line with the rest of the UK. As the
violence of the Troubles escalated, the Stormont Parliament was
suspended in 1972 and Northern Ireland was instead ruled directly
from London. Direct rule was seen by some as an opportunity for
progressive reform, but English governments have primarily shied
away from making any such moves for fear of provoking backlash
among the Northern Irish political parties.

In 2008, legislation was put to Westminster which could have
legalised abortion in Northern Ireland. However, it was purportedly
blocked by then Labour MP and Leader of the Commons Harriet

Harman in exchange for the DUP (who are vehemently anti-choice) supporting then Prime Minister Tony Blair's controversial policy of 42-day detention without trial for terror suspects. For many pro-choice activists in Northern Ireland, this has been an insult for which they have never fully forgiven the Labour Party. While Harriet Harman is considered by many women in England as a feminist icon due to her work to advance gender equality during her time in office in other regards, for many in Northern Ireland she will always be the woman who sold her Northern Irish sisters down the river.

Since the debacle, as power-sharing at Stormont has seen devolution established in Northern Ireland, MPs at Westminster largely assert that it would be both inappropriate and potentially a violation of the devolution powers outlined in the Good Friday Agreement for them to change the abortion laws, and that only Stormont can do so. This means that the Good Friday Agreement is being used as a justification for the denial of reproductive rights.

In November 2015, the Belfast High Court ruled that Northern Ireland's abortion laws constitute a breach of European human rights law, in criminalising women who terminate following rape, incest or fatal foetal abnormality. The court issued a statement of incompatibility to Stormont, informing the Parliament that its policies are incompatible with human rights legislation. Such statements are rarely issued in the UK.

In 2016, in a bid to address the court ruling, a vote was subsequently held at Stormont on whether to legalise abortion in the specified cases of rape, incest and fatal foetal abnormality. However, politicians voted to reject this and keep the abortion ban as it is.

The 2015 ruling was also appealed by the Attorney General

on behalf of the Northern Irish government. In June 2017, the Court of Appeals gave its verdict on the appeal. This time it did not uphold the previous judgment, instead finding that it was not appropriate for the courts to decide the matter and referred it back to Stormont to decide on.

This decision was again appealed in the Supreme Court, with judgment pending at the time of writing.

Following news of the DUP–Conservative deal in June 2017, which saw the former support Theresa May's minority government in exchange for £1.5 billion funding for Northern Ireland, an unprecedented spotlight was shone on the abortion ban. In the hours after news of the minority government emerged, Google searches for the DUP surged. Media outlets across the UK, who normally never mention Northern Ireland, were full of features about the region's abortion laws, which, previously ignored, were now denounced as barbaric.

In the ensuing weeks, Labour MP Stella Creasy used the issue to embarrass the Conservative Party about their new bedfellows. An amendment to the Queen's Speech was tabled calling for the NHS in England to give free abortions to women who travel from Northern Ireland, as they had previously been charged hundreds of pounds for a procedure granted free of charge to their fellow UK citizens. The stunt worked and the Conservatives announced they would pass the policy separately if the amendment to the Queen's Speech was withdrawn.

This was arguably one of the greatest moments of progress for Northern Irish reproductive rights in a generation. However, while it amounted to progress, it did little to alter the overall structural issues at play or help the most vulnerable women in the region, who would still be unable to travel. The British government continued to maintain that it could not intervene to change the legislation within Northern Ireland itself due to their need to respect the principle of devolution.

In February 2018, the debate was further ignited when a report from the United Nations called on the British Parliament to legalise abortion in Northern Ireland, arguing that the current ban is a human rights abuse and that devolution is no excuse for Westminster not intervening.

Again, the British government declined to act, insisting that the principles of devolution outlined in the Good Friday Agreement mean it is for Northern Ireland alone to decide.

For all of the Agreement's focus on promoting equality and human rights, it is striking that Stormont has ignored the pleas of the UN and local courts that the abortion laws amount to a human rights breach. Furthermore, the British government's argument that it cannot intervene due to the principle of devolution is an instance of the Agreement being used as a means of denying rights for vulnerable groups, similar to the use of the Petition of Concern as a means of blocking LGBT rights.

VULNERABLE GROUPS AND
THE GOOD FRIDAY AGREEMENT

As we have seen, the Good Friday Agreement has at its core principles of equality and human rights. This was designed to prevent a repetition of the sectarian discrimination that occurred in the early days of unionist majority rule and the alleged human rights abuses reported to have occurred during the conflict.

However, these provisions and protections were considered within the narrow frame of the recent conflict, therefore viewing discrimination solely on a sectarian axis and not contemplating wider issues of social inequality. This emphasis is evidenced by the way in which politicians are required to designate as 'unionist' or 'nationalist' to ensure votes receive the backing of both communities; there is no equivalent whereby votes need to be approved by both men and women, for instance. It is also evidenced in the way that Troubles-related violence is largely limited to a narrow definition of sectarian attacks, which excludes and erases the ways in which domestic violence increased in many homes as men had greater access to both legal and illegal weapons.

To a certain extent, this may have been due to the fact that the Agreement was written in 1998 and therefore of a time when LGBT rights were not mainstream in the way that the issue is presently and when there was even more stigma about domestic and sexual violence. However, twenty years on, concepts of oppression and discrimination have evolved to such a point where many people in Northern Ireland consider LGBT rights or gender equality to be of equal importance to anti-sectarianism, particularly among younger voters. In this way, the Good Friday Agreement has been outpaced by social attitudes and is struggling to facilitate protection for minority and marginalised groups in today's society. Indeed, as we have seen, elements of the Good Friday Agreement have been used not only to turn a blind eye to human rights issues, but as a justification to actively block progressive reform.

This does not mean that the Agreement has completely failed to protect marginalised groups, as small reforms or updates to it could be made in the present day to bring it up to date. For instance, the Petition of Concern could be reformed so that politicians can only use it to block legislation if they can prove it meets set criteria. Other reform could include guidance on what should happen when Stormont politicians vote for legislation which the United Nations has specifically stated constitutes a human rights breach; who or what can hold Stormont to account in such an instance; and under what circumstances Westminster can intervene. Similarly, a gender-based approach to legacy issues which includes domestic and sexual violence is still possible – if the political will is there. Stormont-directed policy could be updated to address this issue now by commissioning research on the topic; by directing the Victims' Commissioner to adopt a gendered approach to their work; and by setting up public outreach initiatives giving women and girls opportunities to discuss their experiences in safe spaces and access counselling and other support. However, as we have seen throughout this chapter, considerable division remains within Northern Ireland's main parties on how to address equality outside of sectarian oppression. The parties remain divided on LGBT rights, largely opposed to abortion reform and entirely silent on addressing gender-based legacy issues. It seems unlikely that the political will or leadership is there to address these equality areas where the Good Friday Agreement has failed to provide direction. While the Agreement failed in these areas, the biggest failure has come from the lack of political direction in the twenty years since to make difficult decisions about equality and human rights beyond the old familiar territory of the Orange *v* Green axis.

CHAPTER SIX

BREXIT

Just beyond the Northern Irish city of Newry, the mini metropolis suddenly drops off into the countryside like honey pouring out from a jar, at first in a trickle and then great glugs, of fields, forests and rivers. A small grey slither of a road slices between the hillocks and fields, taking cars and lorries about their business. Every few minutes, objects of mild interest crop up by the otherwise featureless roadside, from the odd pub to a small pharmacy or a placard advertising a day-care centre. The road wiggles through the countryside without much fanfare, lined by untidy trees, occasional rocks and patches of unshorn grass.

The landscape, although easy on the eye, is otherwise unremarkable. However, within it, the terrain harbours the crux of the island's troubled past and present – Northern Ireland's border with the Republic of Ireland. Or, more accurately, one of a total of 275 border-crossing points which are strewn across the border, which measures a total of 310 miles (499 km) as it weaves between the two jurisdictions.

Despite the fact that the conflict in Northern Ireland was fundamentally about partition, surprisingly little focus is paid within contemporary Northern Irish politics as to the actual site where partition occurs, the point at which the island is cleaved in two. To a certain extent this has been deliberate, as a campaign of bomb attacks by the IRA against border checkpoints during the early period of the Troubles has seen both jurisdictions keen to avoid highlighting where one country ends and the other begins. To that end, there are few markings or signifiers of the border at all, which is instead largely tucked between hills and under the foliage of overgrown trees or in watery graves at the bottom of lakes.

However, the border is about to take on new significance in light of the UK's vote on 23 June 2016 to leave the European Union. As Northern Ireland is the only part of the UK to share a land border with an EU country, namely the Republic of Ireland, this is soon to be the UK's frontier with the rest of Europe. The region, which took so long to subdue during the conflict, is to be once again imbued with controversy and political discord.

In this new light, the Irish border's ambiguous and elusive nature is no longer an asset but rather a hindrance as the world's attention is on how this meandering stretch of land can be policed to manage the flow of trade, immigration and security. Furthermore, the Good Friday Agreement has been subject to greater scrutiny than ever before, as Leavers and Remainers alike grapple with the text and seek to understand whether it is compatible with Brexit or whether the Agreement limits the form that the UK's withdrawal from the EU can take.

As a child, during family trips from our home in the North

to visit relatives in the South during the '90s, my parents would distract my bored brothers and I on the long car journey by creating what we called 'the border game'. We were tasked with keeping a keen eye on our surroundings as the car zipped along to see who could spot the point at which we passed from one country to the other; a uniquely Northern Irish game fusing I Spy with the constitutional question. The keys we developed as primary school children on these trips were chiefly: looking at the signs outside shops to see if prices were given in pounds sterling (Northern Ireland's currency) or punts, later replaced by the euro (the Republic of Ireland's), or at adverts to see if the phone numbers for local businesses were listed with Northern Ireland dialling codes or Republic of Ireland ones. The klaxon alerting us to the key point of fusion would be when our car radio would slowly begin to flicker and stutter on its BBC setting as it lost connection and instead began to pick up signal from the Republic of Ireland's national broadcaster RTÉ. A blurred white noise emitted for the brief overlap period, during which snatches of Belfast accents and Dublin ones would stutter in and out across the fuzzy backdrop, creating an illogical and patchy duet. The din in many ways encapsulates the blurred and flickering existence of the border itself.

I visit again shortly after the UK's vote to leave the EU, to try to find some of these border crossings, to see if I can pin down the physical point at which Northern Ireland ends and the Republic of Ireland begins. I try to draw on the keys we developed then as primary school children, while I attempt to navigate the border now, some twenty years on. Armed with detailed maps and plans of the area, I soon arrive at the crucial mile, guided by the map's heavily inked red line encasing 'NORTHERN IRELAND', as distinct from 'IRELAND'. Pinpointing anything closer than this, however, proves a much harder task.

Visiting in the present day, the modernised version of the 1990s radio white noise appears to be mobile phone signal, which splutters and struggles as I get close to the border. 'Welcome to Ireland', my phone network provider texts me to inform me I am now overseas and being switched from my usual UK network to their sister company in the Republic. As I drive further down some more winding roads, a flash on my screen welcomes me back to my UK phone company. This goes on for some time before my mobile, seemingly exasperated by the constitutional question, simply tells me 'No signal' instead.

After some time mulling over different identical fields, under the nonplussed eyes of some sheep, I drive to the next cluster of shops and homes and find a Garda station in Omeath. The Gardaí are the Republic of Ireland's police, meaning I am certainly on the southern side of the border. After I explain my mission, two bemused but game police officers, apparently unshackled by crime-fighting duties and with little else to do on a Sunday afternoon, agree to explain how they mark the border within their area. This is key for them, as they are not permitted to step one boot or slip one patrol care tyre into the Northern Irish jurisdiction, and vice versa.

They cite two border crossing points in the immediate vicinity and their directions are as follows. The first is marked by a presence of a large yellow pub on one side of a thin road; flanking the road on the other side is a petrol station. In front of the pub is a flock of geese and in front of the petrol station is a flock of sheep.

Everything in front of the pub is Northern Ireland, everything behind and including the pub is the Republic of Ireland.

The second is a little further on. It lies beyond the pub, requires two right turns up narrow country road offshoots and, out of the corner of your eye, a little stone wall will appear. Where the wall ends, the border begins.

I set off for the latter and, armed with this new knowledge, soon find it. The scene itself would be easily missed by any traveller except one on a specific mission to find the border. On my right, I see a small wall about four feet tall, a makeshift barrier composed of mismatched stones piled atop each other. On my left, a small metal barrier cuts off the undergrowth from mingling, not unlike the metal arm of a barrier in a car park. Immediately before me, the white line painted down the centre of the road suddenly stops and becomes plain tarmac. Where the paint stops, the border lies. The road with white paint is the Republic of Ireland; where the paint ends is Northern Ireland.

That this border has been the inadvertent focus of so much bloodshed and loss of life is arresting and might appear almost comic, were it not so dark. It appears strikingly rudimentary. Particularly now, in light of the Brexit vote, it is jarring that this collection of rocks, painted tarmac and a metal bar form what will soon be the UK's frontier with the EU. Few borders in the world have as much need to be forgotten as this one before me and, thanks to the UK's EU withdrawal, it is about to become one of the most famous and most examined in the world.

As I leave, I take the second route out of the Republic of Ireland and back to Northern Ireland. As I pass the pub on my left, the geese and the sheep are both out in their respective paddocks, now the inhabitants of the Brexit frontier. One weathered and lumpy ewe stands ahead of her herd and, careless of the political situation, criss-crosses the UK's frontier with the EU to get a fresher patch of grass a few yards ahead in the Republic of Ireland. Around her, unburdened by qualms over constitutional law or global political events, her fellow flock graze calmly on.

NORTHERN IRELAND'S PLACE WITHIN THE BREXIT DEBATE

The Irish border was seldom discussed during the Brexit referendum campaign by either side. Nor, for that matter, was Northern Ireland's unique stake in the debate identified or acknowledged during campaigning in any significant way. It did not feature as a distinct talking point in televised debates, policy documents or campaign material leading up to the referendum. Simply put, there was very little awareness of Northern Ireland as a place or an issue by either Leavers or Remainers. This is particularly evidenced in the name 'Brexit', which refers to Britain's exit from the EU, a revealing Freudian slip as it is not just Britain (England, Scotland and Wales) which is leaving the EU but the UK (England, Scotland and Wales plus Northern Ireland).

This was largely due to the fact that Northern Ireland is very seldom considered in UK-wide debates, as people in Britain rarely give the region much thought even when it comes to UK-wide issues, nor have they done so since the region's inception.

However, this age-old dynamic took on a particular edge during the referendum, due to the nature of the issue at hand. Although Brexit was a UK-wide vote, it was primarily about Little Englanders and their struggle to grapple with Britain's decreasing importance in the world due to the decline of the British Empire. Many in England had been fed on a diet of British superiority for generations by successive governments. Much of this was based on a sense of English pride, which seldom acknowledged that much of the reason England has held wealth and political power internationally has been due to colonialism and the exploitation of foreign countries, particularly the exploitation and oppression of people of colour. As the British Empire has shrunk, British power has shrunk with it and an identity crisis has ensued at home.

However, rather than accept this new dynamic or question the nature and ethics of the colonialism which had been the source of Britain's lost 'greatness', many in England turned this anger outwards. As many other European nations increasingly treated England as an equal partner, rather than the wise and superior grandfather of the world, anger grew against structures like the European Union. Public opinion turned against immigrants to the UK, as there was a growing sense among many that English identity was shrinking and had to be protected.

With no apparent sense of the great irony at play, many in England developed a fantasy that England itself was being subject to a colonisation of sorts. After generations of invading countries and subjugating nations by forcing them to adopt Anglo-culture, they began to fear the same was now being done to them through globalisation, as an increasingly international economy saw migration to the UK increase. Now, the logic went, the UK was being enslaved by a foreign and unfeeling super-state in the form of the EU.

Within this narrative, Brexiters have very little to say to or about Northern Ireland. While British identity is complex, fragile and hotly contested in Northern Ireland, concepts of British nationalism operate in a vastly different way in Northern Ireland than in the UK. While in England British nationalism is often defined in relation to a sense of native dwellers versus foreign-born immigrants, within Northern Ireland the focus has instead been on British identity as defined in opposition to the perceived hostile nationalist or Catholic community within. Northern Ireland's place within the British Empire had never been as an agent or beneficiary. Nor was Northern Ireland home to many EU nationals, as fewer immigrants come to the region than come to England. For instance, in 2014, net migration from the EU to Northern Ireland stood at 2,237, which out of the region's 1.8 million population was scarcely perceptible. Therefore, the Leave campaign had very little to offer Northern Ireland within its England-centric narrative.

While the UK as a whole voted to leave the EU, Northern Ireland voted to remain. Of 1.2 million eligible voters, 790,000 votes were cast, with 55.8 per cent backing Remain, while 44.2 per cent backed Leave. Perhaps not unsurprisingly, there was a sectarian divide within the vote. The 2016 Northern Ireland Assembly election study, headed by Queen's University Belfast academic Professor John Garry, found that 85 per cent of nationalist/Catholic voters backed Remain, compared to 40 per cent of unionist/Protestant voters.

The Brexit debate within Northern Ireland took on a different form to the Little England narrative taking place in the 'mainland'. It did not focus on issues such as claims the EU was having too much input in UK legislation, or fears of immigration. Instead, in characteristic Northern Irish fashion, it became another proxy war through which people debated the region's constitutional position. The Brexit issue became a debate on whether Northern Irish voters backed greater or fewer links with the Republic of Ireland. The two largest nationalist parties in Northern Ireland, the SDLP and Sinn Féin, both backed remaining in the EU, and ran campaigns to that effect focusing on the need to maintain links with the rest of the island, warning that people's sense of Irish identity could be harmed by Brexit.

By comparison, Northern Ireland's unionist politicians were largely pro-Brexit. The DUP were ardent Leave campaigners, spending hundreds of thousands of pounds on campaign material. They argued that breaking off from the EU would leave Northern Ireland more closely embedded in the UK, under the logic that it would be the little collection of islands against the world. As unionists identify as British, many feel strong pride in the union and hold an ardent belief in its political and economic strength (which nationalists in Northern Ireland do not share). The more moderate unionist party, the UUP, was more circumspect, with party leader Mike Nesbitt warning voters that Brexit could see Northern Ireland's links with Britain loosened due to the border being unsettled. The hardline loyalist group the Traditional Unionist Voice (TUV) strongly backed Brexit. In the middle ground, Northern Ireland's anti-sectarianism Alliance Party backed Remain, as the party's liberal, pro-diversity and outward-looking ethos lent itself to a pro-immigration stance.

Therefore, the UK-wide Brexit debate did not realise the

significance of Northern Ireland in the event of EU withdrawal, and debates within Northern Ireland tended to divide on traditional sectarian lines without giving serious consideration to the objective merits or drawbacks of Brexit. However, Northern Ireland had a unique stake in the Brexit debate, due to both its geographical positioning within the UK and its post-conflict society. Its distinctive vulnerabilities from EU withdrawal include:

- Being the only part of the UK to share a border with another EU country and subsequently being home to the new Brexit frontier, at the coalface of whatever immigration or customs changes are implemented;
- Receiving special 'peace money' grants from the EU for post-conflict projects;
- Having a greater reliance on agricultural subsidies than the rest of the UK due to being more rural;
- The special role the European Court of Human Rights plays as a neutral arbiter in debates about the conflicted society;
- The Good Friday Agreement being co-signed by another EU country (the Republic of Ireland);
- The unique security issues relating to the EU border being in Northern Ireland, due to the ongoing presence of paramilitary groups in the region which could potentially see the border as a legitimate target for terrorist attacks;
- The unique constitutional status of Northern Ireland due to the Troubles conflict (e.g. the Good Friday Agreement enshrining in law the right of Northern Irish people to hold either a British or Irish identity).

The Good Friday Agreement does not specifically state that the UK must remain in the EU in order for the Agreement to be respected; however, many argue that while Brexit may not be against the letter of the document, it is against its spirit and could breach the GFA through secondary means, as it makes the North–South and East–West links harder to maintain.

THE BORDER

Throughout the Brexit referendum campaign, the rallying cry of the Leave lobby was the demand that the UK 'take back control of our borders'. However, throughout the campaign, talk of 'borders' was solely hypothetical and used as a grand metaphor for concepts of security and safety.

Leave campaigners did not seem to realise until long after the referendum result that the UK has a very real border with the EU, beyond the realm of the metaphorical.

As we will see, the history of the Irish border is a complex and colourful one.

THE HISTORY OF THE IRISH BORDER

The border in Ireland first came into effect in 1922, when the Republic of Ireland (then the Irish Free State) gained independence while Northern Ireland remained in the UK. Provision for the border lay in the Government of Ireland Act 1920, which outlined partition on the island to create both a northern and a southern state. The reason for this partition was that while the majority of people on the island wished to leave British control and see Ireland self-governed, a minority opposed this and they were largely concentrated in the northern region of the island. This geographical variation was due to northern unionists largely being the descendants of British planters from the seventeenth century, who continued to feel an affiliation to the British identity of their forefathers. As those in the rest of the island continued to agitate for independence and those in the north continued to petition London to remain, consensus grew among the ruling classes that a two-state solution would be required for the island.

Northern unionists petitioned for the creation of an Ulster state as part of this two-state solution, as Ulster was one of the historic kingdoms or provinces on the island, comprising nine counties out of the island's total of thirty-two. However, taken as a whole, the province had a nationalist majority, which meant unionists feared that the province as a whole could still agitate for independence from the UK and their British identity would be only marginally more secure than in an all-island state. They therefore decided that the Ulster province would need to be shrunk, to just six counties out of nine, in order to select those with enough unionist/Protestant residents to create an overall unionist region. Therefore, Cavan, Monaghan and Donegal were dropped from the new 'Ulster' state, despite being in the province of Ulster. However, the term 'Ulster' continued to be used by many unionists to describe the new state in an attempt to give it a sense of legitimacy by invoking a familiar and historic, albeit now outdated, term for the region.

The new northern state therefore comprised the six counties of Antrim, Down, Fermanagh, Tyrone, Derry-Londonderry and Armagh. Of these six counties, Antrim and Down had sizeable unionist/Protestant majorities, while Derry-Londonderry and Armagh had slight unionist/Protestant majorities and Fermanagh and Tyrone had nationalist/Catholic majorities. Combined, the six counties had a unionist/Protestant majority overall and formed a substantial geographical chunk of the island.

The border used around this new northern state to partition it from the rest of the island was the parliamentary constituency outline for these six counties, as used in elections. The constituency boundaries had long been the subject of suspicion over claims that they were a form of sectarian gerrymandering. At the time, unionists/Protestants mostly owned land in the lower-lying, more fertile areas due to the nature of the Plantation historically, whereby the planters were given what was considered to be the more valuable land while nationalists/Catholics were pushed up to the more mountainous areas. Many nationalists continued to harbour a sense of injustice about this division of land, as well as suspicion that the electoral boundaries were drawn to maximise the unionist vote while suppressing that of nationalists. In short, these electoral boundaries were not perceived as a neutral mechanism of measuring out the new state.

The 1920 Act that created this northern state was drawn during a period when it was thought that a Belfast Parliament for northern unionists and a separate Dublin Parliament for the rest of the island could see the whole island remain within the UK, as it was hoped the move would satiate agitations in the south for full independence.

As a result, little considered discussion was given as to precisely where the border was physically placed, nor was much consideration given to potential constitutional or territorial disputes, as any such issues which arose were expected to be internal UK matters. The border was never intended to be an international one.

However, these plans were soon overtaken by events. Imminently, it became clear that a devolved Dublin Parliament would not be enough to quell agitation for full independence in the region and that full separation from the UK would be inevitable. The 1921 Anglo-Irish Treaty saw the 'rest of Ireland' leave British control while Northern Ireland remained. In 1922, Northern Ireland officially exercised its right not to be included in the Free State and so the border became an international frontier. When this happened, the 1920 act's definition of Northern Ireland and the border it contained was used, despite the fact that it had been drawn up with a view to being an internal UK boundary rather than an international border with the new, foreign Irish state.

The Irish border that was created was therefore one that had been designed for a different purpose altogether, and demonstrated little understanding of how customs or immigration would now work, as well as being mired in controversy not only due to the inherently controversial nature of partition but also on a local level over grievances stemming from alleged sectarian division of land and alleged gerrymandering.

This fragile border was acknowledged at the time to be piecemeal and imperfect. It was always meant to be temporary and a commission to review its boundary was set up with a view to working out the minutiae of exactly where it would fall. Article 12 of the Anglo-Irish Treaty established an Irish Boundary Commission to reconsider the boundary in accordance 'with the wishes of the inhabitants, so far as may be compatible with economic and geographic conditions'.

Turbulent events in both jurisdictions meant it was some years before the commission would meet, as the UK administration changed hands several times and the Irish Free State (as the Republic of Ireland was then called) was engulfed in civil war.

The commission adopted a quasi-judicial approach, whereby they invited affected locals to submit evidence to them petitioning why their land or their village should lie in one country or the other. The documentation submitted to the commission makes for fascinating reading. One man named John McHugh petitioned the committee over his horror in finding that his whole house was in Donegal (Republic of Ireland) and his 'rear garden in Fermanagh (Northern Ireland)'. A Protestant church petitioned that their church building was on one side of the border while their church hall was on the other, causing an administrative headache as babies would be born or couples married in one country but the paperwork physically signed a few yards up the road in the other.

However, despite the commission's work in gathering evidence, it soon fell apart when one of the three commissioners dropped out and the Irish and British governments eventually shelved the proposals the remaining two commissioners had made.

Confusion and controversy over the border was to rumble on for decades. In 1923, the Common Travel Area was established, in part due to the difficulty of managing this new frontier. It allowed freedom of movement for people across and between the island of Ireland, Great Britain, Isle of Man and Channel Islands and was formalised in the Ireland Act of 1949, which stated that the Republic of Ireland was not a 'foreign country' for legal purposes. This avoided requiring a wall or physical structure at the border, or passport checks as people moved across the island of Ireland.

However, while people were free to move, some customs checks were imposed on some goods such as certain foods and agricultural animals. One such example was a fierce dispute which reigned for years over who had the right to fish for salmon in the Lough and River Foyle. The water's shores lay on both the county of Derry-Londonderry (Northern Ireland) and that of Donegal (Republic of Ireland), but the water between and the fish that swam in it were unbound by the border, which only delineated land. Salmon are a migratory species of fish, which hatch upstream in fresh water before travelling seaward. The fish showed a brazen disregard for the delicate constitutional and boundary matters unfolding around them and they slipped through the jurisdictions.

In 1923, the Northern Irish authorities ordered the Republic of Ireland fishermen to desist from fishing in the waters and, when their compliance was not forthcoming, sent bailiffs to the area to confiscate their nets. The row escalated and was eventually the subject of a number of legal challenges. In Northern Ireland, the courts ruled in favour of the Northern Irish fishers and in the Republic of Ireland, the courts ruled in favour of the Republic of Ireland fishers. The case ground to a stalemate as the decades wore on. During the Second World War, tensions escalated further as the UK began using Lough Foyle as a military site, positioning submarines, seaplanes and destroyers there. Eventually, in 1952, a cross-border commission was established by mutual agreement to decide on the matter through joint authority over the waters. As Northern Ireland erupted into the violence of the Troubles not long after, the issue of fishing rights swiftly became a minor issue in relations between the two countries.

During the earlier period of the conflict, the border was often the site of violence. In the 1950s, the IRA conducted a 'border campaign' whereby they undertook violent attacks in the region. This violence escalated in the late 1960s and early 1970s as the Troubles began. Terror groups, in particular the IRA, allegedly exploited the fact that Northern Ireland's police could not leave their own jurisdiction by crossing the border into the Republic, committing attacks near the border before slipping away to the South, where they could not be pursued by the RUC. Some Republicans were said to believe that while the Gardaí police in the Republic ostensibly pursed them, they were less dogged due to having more sympathy with their actions than their counterparts in the RUC. The Gardaí have strenuously denied this and say they have always diligently sought to pursue and apprehend the IRA. The IRA also conducted gun-smuggling operations in the border regions, whereby they would covertly transport illegal firearms into Northern Ireland to use in terrorist attacks.

Perhaps the most notorious terror attack in the border regions was what came to be known as the Kingsmill massacre. In 1976, a group of a dozen men were travelling home from work together in a minibus. According to a witness account, while they were travelling near the quiet village of Kingsmill, a twenty-minute drive from the border, they noticed through the dark January night that a man dressed in combat uniform and standing at the side of the road was flagging them down to stop. Thinking it could be the British Army stopping them to carry out a search of the vehicle, they complied. As they left the vehicle, armed men emerged from the surrounding darkness. The twelve workmen were ordered to line up beside the bus. They were asked their religion and the one Catholic man was ordered to leave and not look back. The eleven remaining men were shot repeatedly at close range, with ten dying at the scene. The eleventh man was shot eighteen times including in his head but remarkably survived. Security documents from the time reportedly state that authorities believed the attackers then slipped across the border into County Monaghan, avoiding detection. The attack is one of the most notorious of the entire conflict due to the nakedly sectarian way in which the men were divided by religion and the Protestant men subsequently slaughtered. The perpetrators were never caught, although a subsequent probe by the Historical Enquiries Team concluded that the IRA were the culprits. For many people, the horrors of that night encapsulated how the border itself could be used as a deadly weapon.

In the 1970s, as violence escalated, the British Army was increasingly deployed to patrol the border regions. Many roads were sealed off by soldiers erecting barricades, while others were rendered impassable as army personnel used plastic explosives to deliberately blow up roads by blasting craters in the ground which cars could not pass. Large watchtowers were erected at some strategic points along the border, giving soldiers a clear view of activity in the surrounding roads and fields, which enabled them to limit the routes passing across the border and to conduct checks on people and vehicles as they crossed. This became a major security operation for the army and a key method of identifying and stopping the IRA on their way to or from an attack, as well as preventing future attacks by uncovering gun-running operations and stopping weapons in their tracks.

The presence of the British Army was not without controversy locally, as not all who lived nearby welcomed their new neighbours. One 1971 BBC report on soldiers blowing craters into roads around the border noted: 'Local residents on both sides of the border are likely to find "cratering" a major inconvenience. One local farmer looked at a gaping hole between himself and his farm further down the road. Asked how he was going to get to it he was at a loss for words. He shrugged.'

Beyond the inconvenience, some locals also felt intimidated and frightened by the soldiers' presence. Some complained that the newly obliterated roads and looming watchtowers were stains on the area's natural beauty. Others said life became tense as they felt they were constantly being watched by the soldiers in the towers above. Rumours grew that the army had also developed technology to hear conversations happening the homes below, fuelling paranoia further still.

However, soldiers insisted they were merely doing their best to protect the public and thwart the IRA on their way to commit untold horrors. One soldier told *The Guardian* in 2001:

> It's hard on the people who keep the law, yes, but the towers are a necessary part of the operation here. It's either that or more foot patrols tramping over land. It's no picnic for soldiers here.

Many of them are working seven days a week and most are away from their families for months. Yes, the watchtowers are ugly. But they provide vital cover and information that cannot be disclosed because it would jeopardise future security. What do these people want? They're complaining about the view while we're saving lives.

Following the signing of the Good Friday Agreement and the end of the conflict, the army's presence along the border slowly shrank. In 2006, the last watchtower was dismantled. Since then, the border has reverted to being invisible and seamless.

THE FUTURE OF THE BORDER AFTER BREXIT

At the time of writing, it is hotly contested what the border on the island of Ireland will look like after Brexit. Of particular concern is whether the border will be altered, whether it will be required to harden and whether such changes would be a violation of the Good Friday Agreement.

The concerns pivot on whether the UK will leave the single market and the customs union as the country withdraws from the EU. Presently, there is no requirement for checks on goods or vehicles travelling between Northern Ireland and the Republic, as the two regions' shared membership of these two mechanisms means they are both subject to the same standards and regulations. Many pro-Brexit politicians, campaigners and voters in England believe passionately that the UK must leave the single market and customs union in order to be allowed to strike their own international trade deals and to be free of EU trade regulations and oversight, which many believe to be unnecessary red tape holding back businesses. However, if the UK does choose to exit the single market and the customs union, considerable disparity will exist between Northern Ireland and the Republic of Ireland as goods and vehicles travelling across the border will likely need to be checked and monitored. Different standards of quality could apply to goods which were previously subject to EU-wide standards, resulting in goods needing to be checked at the Irish border to establish whether regulatory standards are met for them to be accepted into the EU. Similarly, tariffs may be put in place between people moving goods from one side of the Irish border to the other, if the tariff-free single market ends.

Such a border could be a bureaucratic nightmare for both the UK and the Republic of Ireland, requiring huge amounts of staff and documentation on the border, operating several hundred checkpoints on narrow rural roads and painstakingly stopping each car or pedestrian that passes to enquire about the purpose of their journey and whether they are carrying any goods with them. The financial and procedural cost would be significant if required at all 275 border crossing points between Northern Ireland and the Republic. It is possible that trade in Northern Ireland (which is already far behind the rest of the UK, due in part to damage in reputation and confidence during the conflict) would slump as businesses in the rest of the UK and in the Republic ceased to see the benefit in trading with their northern neighbours under such convoluted and costly provisions.

Yet border structures would not only be a burden for businesses and for bureaucracy. Of perhaps far greater concern would be the psychological impact of sealing up the border and effectively shutting Northern Ireland off from the rest of the island. Many in the Republican or nationalist community would recoil at the psychological impact of a hard border on the island, as it reopens debates about the relationship between the two jurisdictions which have lain primarily dormant or at least benign since the peace process. Many would see it as 'their' country being partitioned even further and resentment would likely grow towards the UK government. It has been argued that a 'high-tech' border would be a possible solution to the dilemma, whereby cameras could be erected at the border crossing points which could subtly scan and record the number plate of each passing vehicle, or that drivers could register online before making journeys, in order to avoid tailbacks and heavy traffic jams at checkpoints. However, even a high-tech solution is likely to cause considerable distress to border communities in Northern Ireland by giving them a sense that they are being constantly watched, which would be concerning for any community but is particularly problematic for one which may already have trust issues with surveillance and UK authorities due to their trauma from the British Army's and the IRA's activities not so long ago.

Furthermore, the presence of any structure at the border could be vulnerable to attack from Republican paramilitaries, whether that is full-scale customs checkpoints or surveillance cameras. This could have the unintended but concerning effect of exposing both customs staff and border communities to potential serious harm or even threat to life. The head of the Northern Ireland police, Chief Constable George Hamilton, told *The Guardian* in February 2018 that such a presence at the border would potentially be seen as 'fair game' for attacks by Republicans. He said:

> The last thing we would want is any infrastructure around the border because there is something symbolic about it and it becomes a target for violent dissident republicans. Our assessment is that they [customs staff] would be a target because it would be representative of the state and in their minds fair game for attack.

He added:

> Anything that makes the police presence predictable in places where terrorists are active of course raises the threat and increases the harm to my officers. We deal with risk every day and we are good at it but unfortunately the terrorists only have to be lucky once and get a result with catastrophic consequences. I think it would be a poor use of police resources if we are going to have to protect physical infrastructures at the border.

The debate over the future of the Irish border is not merely political or economic but represents a serious security calculation, as the UK government could potentially be putting staff at serious risk by positioning them in the region.

Furthermore, it is possible that UK officials stationed there could represent security risks, even if it is not their intention.

Following the Brexit vote, a former colonel for the British Army who had been positioned at the border during the conflict told me he was deeply troubled by the possibility that British authorities there may one day feel they need to use excessive or deadly force to maintain the border. He told me: 'What happens one day if you tell someone to stop and they keep going [across the border]? How do you police that in a split-second decision? How far do you go to stop them? Do you shoot them?' In order for customs officials to conduct their jobs with authority, they would need to have powers or means to enforce checks. However, arming officials could represent a serious threat to life if wielded wrongly under pressure. During the conflict, a number of people were shot dead by soldiers stationed at the border due to officers appearing to misread events or accidentally discharging their weapons. Armed customs officials could find themselves in a similarly difficult position. However, if they are not armed and are unable to stop persons or vehicles to conduct checks, their powers may be entirely toothless and their jobs impossible.

SPECIAL STATUS FOR NORTHERN IRELAND

One option posed as a means to dealing with the 'Northern Ireland question' in Brexit has been to give the region 'special status'. For instance, if a hard Brexit were established for England, Scotland and Wales, Northern Ireland could have separate rules that would essentially amount to a soft Brexit instead. For example, if the rest of the UK left the single market or the customs union,

Northern Ireland could remain. This would have the advantage of avoiding the need for a hard border on the island, or any impediments to trade with or immigration to the Republic. However, it would mean that the effective Irish border would move to being around the island as a whole. It could result in trade barriers between Northern Ireland and the rest of the UK, such as tariffs or the need to conduct checks on goods travelling from Northern Ireland to Britain and vice versa.

The 'special status' idea has been met with positive responses from the Republic of Ireland and the European Union. Within the UK, backers have included Labour's shadow Secretary of State for Northern Ireland Owen Smith. Closer to home, both the SDLP and Sinn Féin have advocated for it. However, the suggestion has been met with horror by many unionists, including the DUP.

Of course, as the Northern Irish unionist identity is predicated on the belief that the region is just as British as any other part of the UK, unionists cannot accept being treated differently than the rest of the UK, even if it would appear to be in their best interests to do so for Brexit. Unionists fear special status would make them less British and more Irish, by giving Northern Ireland laws and regulations that would align more closely with the Republic of Ireland than with Britain.

In September 2017, following a visit from the European Parliament's chief Brexit coordinator, Guy Verhofstadt, to Stormont, DUP MEP Diane Dodds held a press conference in Stormont's Great Hall, where she told press categorically: 'We will not countenance a solution that makes us different from other parts of the United Kingdom.'

Owing to the nature of Northern Irish politics, the DUP will always put their British identity above any other issue. In light of Brexit and their rejections of a special deal for Northern Ireland, the DUP indicated that they will prioritise their links to the rest of the UK above all else, even if it means taking an economic or trade hit at least in the short term.

Indeed, in December 2017, a leaked draft document between the Republic of Ireland and the UK government appeared to reveal the proposed Brexit agreement on the border. It suggested that Northern Ireland would be subject to a form of special status which would allow it to have some form of regulatory alignment with the Republic, thereby eliminating the need for border controls or checkpoints on the island. However, this was immediately rejected by the DUP, who saw it as an attempt to undermine their Britishness by making them similar to the Republic of Ireland and moving the border to be effectively around the island as a whole. Within hours of the draft leaking, party leader Arlene Foster gave a press conference at Stormont in which she expressed her horror: 'We have been very clear: Northern Ireland must leave the EU on the same terms as the rest of the UK. We will not accept any form of regulatory divergence which separates Northern Ireland economically or politically from the rest of the UK.'

Sources say that Theresa May, who was in Brussels at the time, meeting negotiators there, had a phone call with Ms Foster shortly after this speech. Within hours, the deal between Ms May and her EU counterparts was off, with the Prime Minister acknowledging that she could not accept the deal without the DUP's approval.

The debacle was a surprising show of strength for the DUP.

They are a relatively small party within the UK context, as they do not run candidates outside of Northern Ireland, and even within the region receive only around 28 per cent of the vote. It is also worth noting that at the time of Ms Foster's comments she was not acting as Northern Ireland's First Minister at Stormont, as she had lost that position almost a year prior due to the power-sharing collapse that brought the institution down in January 2017. Furthermore, as Northern Ireland had voted to remain overall, the authority from which she was making her decree appeared debatable.

However, due to the DUP–Conservative pact made in June 2017, when Theresa May lost her majority at Westminster, the DUP had been elevated to an unnaturally high position in both Northern Irish and UK politics, which meant that for once Ms Foster's comments carried clout with No. 10. In any other time, her comments would have elicited little more than a vague murmur of sympathy and a pat on the head from Downing Street, but due to the electoral arithmetic at Westminster she now appeared to have an effective veto on the Brexit deal.

Indeed, only days earlier, one of the DUP MPs had appeared to threaten as much when he told the BBC that if the Conservatives appeared to be settling on a Brexit deal that would be disagreeable to them, the DUP's MPs would pull out of the pact and effectively destroy Theresa May's government.

The impact of the Conservatives appearing to pander to the DUP in this way over the Brexit deal was considerable. It not only shaped the Brexit deal significantly, but also resulted in considerable frustration in Northern Ireland as many began to view the Conservatives with greater suspicion and alienation, as the party appeared to be putting their need to keep the DUP onside above the expressed wishes of the overwhelming majority of Northern Irish people.

It is worth noting a central and obvious point of contention in the DUP's protestations that they could not accept any Brexit deal that would give Northern Ireland a different political and economic framework from the rest of the UK. Of course, the DUP have always been perfectly happy to have different laws from the rest of the UK when it comes to issues like abortion and same-sex marriage. Indeed, the DUP have often defended keeping such laws on the grounds that Northern Ireland is different culturally and politically from the rest of the UK and has argued that Westminster cannot, therefore, intervene to overturn those laws and bring them in line with the rest of the UK.

It is therefore possible that while the DUP ultimately succeeded in ensuring that Northern Ireland would receive the same Brexit deal as the rest of the UK, its stance will undermine the party in the long term, weakening their arguments that Westminster cannot intervene in Northern Ireland's same-sex marriage or abortion laws. While it is unlikely that Theresa May's government would risk intervening on any of these issues for fear of upsetting the DUP's ten MPs, on whom her majority depends, the same cannot be said with as much certainty for her successor, whoever he or she may be. Indeed, if a subsequent Labour government were to consider legalising abortion or same-sex marriage for the region via a vote at Westminster, strongly worded proclamations from senior DUP figures arguing in favour of the UK having the same laws and regulations could come back to haunt them.

REIGNITING THE CONSTITUTIONAL QUESTION

As a consequence of Brexit, the constitutional question of Northern Ireland's status, which had been deliberately minimised and excluded from political discourse with great pain and effort in the peace process, is now considered a live issue. On news bulletins and on newsstands around the world, the question of what Northern Ireland's relationship with the Republic is, or should be, is the subject of serious and frank debate in an unprecedented manner. In Parliaments from Brussels to Belfast to London to Dublin and the world over, serious discussion is taking place about Northern Ireland's relationship to the rest of the island.

One of the primary aspects of the Good Friday Agreement was that all signatories agreed Northern Ireland's position in the UK or in a united Ireland would only be decided based on the will of its residents, in a process known as the 'principle of consent'. A united Ireland can only come about if a majority in Northern Ireland vote in favour of it. At the time of the Agreement's signing, the nationalist and Republican view was a minority one and so unionists were happy to agree to the principle of consent as they were confident that such a majority would take a long time to come, if it came at all. Meanwhile, nationalists and Republicans were content with its inclusion as they were confident in the strength of their arguments and hopeful that a majority could be achieved. The Good Friday Agreement was conspicuously vague as to how this support would be measured, stating only:

If the wish expressed by a majority in such a poll is that

Northern Ireland should cease to be part of the United Kingdom and form part of a united Ireland, the Secretary of State shall lay before Parliament such proposals to give effect to that wish as may be agreed between Her Majesty's Government and the Government of Ireland.

No specific or official ways of measuring an appetite for a united Ireland were outlined in the Agreement, due to a desire not to spook unionists or loyalists. For instance, there are no official government polls conducted on such support, as the data would likely have the effect of proving a flashpoint for discord between the two communities. Therefore, the data mainly used to measure support for Irish reunification tends to be conducted by academic researchers or private companies. The polls often fluctuate but have never shown a sizeable enough support for reunification for nationalists and Republicans to convincingly argue that the threshold outlined in the Good Friday Agreement has been sufficiently met. However, the polling data produced following Brexit suggests that may have now changed.

Brexit has not only reignited the united Ireland debate, it has also reframed it. Brexit has detoxified the question of Irish reunification for many people, particularly among younger voters. It is an opportunity for Irish reunification to be framed not through the lens of IRA violence but instead as a positive means of retaining EU membership and associated benefits like immigration, diversity and an outward view of the world. The toxic memories of the past are shed and the united Ireland debate is reframed for a post-Troubles era.

Indeed, the very morning after the Brexit vote result was announced, Republican agitation for a border poll began as Sinn Féin's Martin McGuinness used the opportunity to call for a vote on reunification. While the UK government declined to take him up on his offer, arguing that they felt the conditions to trigger such a poll were not met by Brexit occurring, data suggests the move was not entirely unfounded as demographics on both sides of the border have shifted in favour of reunification.

Importantly, speculation that Brexit will increase the likelihood of a united Ireland has not come only from traditionally Republican lips. Former Prime Minister Tony Blair, who oversaw much of the peace process and establishment of the Good Friday Agreement during his time in No. 10, said in May 2017:

> Brexit means that a lot more people are arguing for a united Ireland. I hope that Northern Ireland remains part of the United Kingdom but Brexit was always bound to have this effect.
>
> This is the first time that the UK and the Republic of Ireland have not been in step with each other, either outside the EU together pre-1973 or in it together since then.
>
> This is also the first time that the status of the North and the Republic will be different.

A study commissioned by BBC Northern Ireland following the Brexit vote and published in August 2016 surveyed people living in Northern Ireland about whether the referendum result had influenced their position on the constitutional question. It found that 17 per cent of people interviewed said this was the case. What's more, 33 per cent of respondents wanted a border poll about Irish reunification to be called, while 52 per cent opposed this and 15 per cent said they did not know.

A study by one polling company in light of the referendum saw support for Irish reunification among people in Northern Ireland jump 5 percentage points between 2013 and 2016, from 17 per cent to 22 per cent. The figures by no means suggest that a united Ireland is immediately on the horizon. However, there is a clear demographic shift towards Irish reunification gaining greater support. Due to the controversial nature of the issue, this alone could go a considerable way in unsettling community dynamics.

Indeed, the biggest demographic shift towards a united Ireland came among voters for the Alliance Party, Northern Ireland's centre-ground, anti-sectarianism party, which has traditionally attracted votes from middle-class 'soft unionists'. An Ipsos MORI study conducted after the Brexit result saw support for a united Ireland among Alliance voters stand at 21 per cent, up from 12 per cent in 2015 and 8 per cent in 2014. While hardline unionists were still unlikely to change their fiercely held stance on the matter, it appeared many in the middle ground were open to persuasion. This is most likely due to the fact that just as Alliance's liberal ethos lends itself to the party's anti-sectarian stance, it also fuels its pro-immigration and pro-EU stance. Therefore, a considerable number of Alliance voters with loosely held opinions on staying in the UK appeared to find their loyalty swayed by the Brexit vote.

A further poll by Northern Irish polling company Lucid-Talk found in December 2017 that in the event of a hard Brexit, 47.9 per cent of people in Northern Ireland said they would vote for a united Ireland as a means of staying in the EU. Just 45.4 per cent said they would vote to stay in the UK and out of the EU, with the remainder undecided.

Some of the most interesting shifts in attitudes have occurred in the Republic. Typically, opinion polls there show support for a united Ireland standing at around two thirds. However, when it is explained to respondents that such a move would likely cost the Republic financially (due to Northern Ireland's weaker economy), support significantly drops. For instance, a 2015 poll jointly commissioned by the BBC and RTÉ found 66 per cent of respondents in the Republic said they desire a united Ireland. Yet, when they were asked whether they would support reunification even if it resulted in them having to pay higher taxes (to absorb the cost of taking on Northern Ireland), support plummeted to just 31 per cent. However, opinion polls suggest the landscape is shifting post-Brexit and an increasing number of people in the Republic seek reunification, even if it means them having to take a financial hit.

A series of Ireland Thinks polls for the *Irish Daily Mail* surveyed residents of the Republic about their attitudes towards reunification. Researchers asked: 'If it cost the Irish government €9 billion per annum [the estimated cost of reunification for the initial transition period, in the event of a united Ireland] for Northern Ireland to unite with the Republic of Ireland, how would you vote in relation to a referendum on a United Ireland?' In March 2017, when 'do not know' responses were excluded, 50 per cent were in favour while 50 per cent were against. The same question was asked in December 2017 and found, with 'do not know' responses excluded,

60 per cent in favour and 40 per cent against a united Ireland. Researcher Dr Kevin Cunningham from Ireland Thinks commented: 'The fiery Brexit negotiations appear to have galvanised support for a united Ireland in the Republic of Ireland.'

It is impossible to tell from the data precisely why this apparent shift in support is occurring. One reason may be that there has been a general surge in Republican sympathy in the Republic, as Britain's apparently blasé treatment of Northern Ireland during Brexit talks has increased their sense of protectiveness towards their northern neighbours. Another reason is possible too: the Republic is set to take an economic hit as a result of Brexit, particularly if a hard border is imposed between them and Northern Ireland, as they may have to pay import and export tariffs with the UK as well as being financially liable for costly custom checks. In light of this, it is possible that people's qualms about the cost of a united Ireland will diminish as the cost may be similar to or less than the price of a hard border on the island of Ireland. Similarly, many of the arguments against a united Ireland often posited include that such a move would plunge people into a period of uncertainty and require a huge bout of negotiations and restructuring of relationships within Ireland. Arguably, this is already happening due to Brexit and so this prospect looks less frightening for some.

At a senior political level, some further support has been expressed in the Republic for a united Ireland. The Tánaiste (Deputy Prime Minister), Simon Coveney, who is also responsible for both Northern Ireland and Brexit for the Republic's government, told his parliament's Good Friday Agreement committee in December

2017, 'I would like to see a united Ireland in my lifetime – if possible, in my political lifetime,' and described himself as a 'constitutional nationalist'. His view is not uncommon for politicians in his position, many of whom have avoided discussing reunification over the past decades for fear of upsetting people in Northern Ireland but when asked directly about the matter will state that they would like a united Ireland to come about by consent and peaceful means. His comments frightened many unionists, who began to suggest that politicians in the Republic were using Brexit as an excuse to snatch back Northern Ireland from the UK. Leader of the UUP Robin Swann said Mr Coveney's remarks undermined 'the very basis of the Belfast Agreement – the consent principle'. Similarly, leader of the hardline unionist TUV party Jim Allister said the Tánaiste's comments were 'another manifestation of the aggressive attitude of his government towards unionists and go well beyond the scope of the Belfast Agreement'. If the Republic of Ireland were to insist on a united Ireland in the absence of popular support in Northern Ireland, that would indeed be a major breach of the Good Friday Agreement, as it would disregard the principle of consent. However, there is no credible reason to believe the Republic would do so. Mr Coveney had been clear about describing himself as a 'constitutional nationalist', i.e. one who wished to achieve reunification through peaceful means and mutual consent. However, some unionist politicians appear to be conflating politicians in the Republic expressing personal support for reunification with the possibility that they would insist on it happening against Northern unionists' will. This may be due to them feeling particularly vulnerable due to the ongoing Brexit debate, resulting in an attempt to slap down any discussion about a united Ireland immediately.

Their sense of unease was further embedded when, in August 2017, an Irish parliamentary report that had been commissioned to look at the impact of Brexit on the island returned with the verdict that a poll on reunification was now inevitable.

Furthermore, in April 2017, the EU announced its official stance that in the event of a united Ireland, Northern Ireland would be allowed to rejoin the EU automatically as a full member. The decision followed lobbying from the Republic of Ireland government for the EU to adopt its position that Irish reunification could come about in a similar manner to German reunification after the fall of the Berlin Wall. Such an announcement may appear innocuous to many on the international stage as it merely outlined technical processes but in Northern Ireland many found it unsettling to see serious international discussion about the practicalities of Irish unification – a taboo subject which is largely discussed only in very abstract ways.

IMPACT OF BREXIT ON ANGLO-IRISH RELATIONS

Another considerable consequence of Brexit has been a sharp decline in relations between the UK and the Republic of Ireland. As the two countries are co-guarantors of the Good Friday Agreement, the agreement is predicated on both nations engaging in respectful and mature relations. Following the EU referendum, however, there has been a marked souring of relations between the two countries. In particular, this has occurred during Brexit negotiations, as there has been a growing narrative in the right-wing British media that the Republic is attempting in some way to botch Brexit for the UK and may be responsible for them getting a bad deal.

This was evidenced in August 2017 by the *Telegraph*, which ran an op-ed headlined 'Britain is fighting to save Ireland from an EU-imposed hard border'. The narrative being outlined was an extraordinary retelling of the events at hand, in which the UK was trying to help Ireland through Brexit but the pesky EU was making things difficult. The narrative was poorly received in Ireland and took on a particularly biting edge in the context of the UK's colonial relationship with the Republic, in painting Britain as the great protector out to save the world while denying responsibility for its own actions.

In November 2017, as Brexit negotiations were further underway, *The Sun*, a right-wing, pro-Brexit tabloid newspaper often accused of bordering on hate speech in its anti-immigrant ethos, published an editorial titled 'Ireland's naive young prime minister should shut his gob on Brexit and grow up', in reference to Taoiseach Leo Varadkar. In this narrative, plucky Britain, grandfather of the world, was trying to stride out into a post-EU world but was being scuppered by Ireland's puerile insistence on taking seriously issues like the Irish border and the Northern Ireland peace process.

Anti-Irish rhetoric was also evidenced in some political circles. As Brexit negotiations advanced, President of the European

Council Donald Tusk announced that the Republic of Ireland would have an effective veto on any Brexit deal, as the other twenty-six EU member states would all back the nation. In response, DUP MP Ian Paisley Jr told the House of Commons Northern Ireland Affairs Committee that the UK should punish the Republic of Ireland by deliberately giving them a bad trade deal in another area if they would not concede to the UK's Brexit demands.

Labour MP and pro-Leave campaigner Kate Hoey also made a remarkable proclamation in one interview when she suggested that if a hard border were erected after Brexit, the Republic of Ireland should be forced to pay for it. The suggestion was derided for its similarities to US President Donald Trump's suggestion that America would build a wall along the border with Mexico and force the Mexican state to pay for it. Hoey's comments did not have popular backing in the UK or even among Leave campaigners, but represented a considerable souring of relations with the Republic of Ireland and an increasingly bullish approach to what had once been one of the UK's closest allies.

It was clear that across the UK political establishment, many politicians were uneasy with the idea that the Republic of Ireland could ever be considered an equal partner to them. What had once been a colonial outpost was now an equal, and one with the backing of twenty-six other EU states. It was a recalibration that for many British politicians was far from welcome.

Furthermore, as the Irish border issue continued to threaten to derail Brexit talks, the topic of Irish politics began to feature more regularly in UK media. Irish politics very rarely appears on the UK radar, bar the occasional mention of the outcome of a general election on a slow British news day, or perhaps discussion of the abortion laws. By contrast, UK news and politicians are strewn across Irish newspapers and broadcast bulletins every day. This is due in large part to the colonial relationship between the nations continuing to be played out in Britain's general indifference in Ireland's internal affairs.

As Ireland continued to rear its head in Brexit negotiations, politicians and journalists were required to have more than an extremely vague and superficial awareness of their nearest neighbour. Unfortunately, this starkly exposed many people's knowledge deficit. Newscasters and MPs appeared to have great difficulty pronouncing the words 'Taoiseach' (pronounced 'Tee-shock'), which is the Prime Minister's title in Ireland, 'Tánaiste' ('Tawn-ish-tah'), meaning Deputy Prime Minister, or 'Dáil' ('Dawl'), denoting Ireland's House of Commons equivalent. That so many journalists and politicians butchered the pronunciation of such terms made it clear that they had never come across them before, encapsulating Britain's ignorance of Ireland and evoking particular sensitivities around historic oppression of the Irish language by the British. Ignorance was not limited to language, however, but also to basic facts. Brexit minister David Davis said in one Channel 4 TV interview in November 2017 that it was his view that the Republic of Ireland's position on Brexit was being shaped by the fact that they had 'a presidential election coming up'. This ignored the facts that 1) the election wasn't due to take place for a further year and 2) the President in Ireland is purely a ceremonial position rather than a political one.

A similar gaffe occurred when Conservative MP and core Brexit cheerleader Jacob Rees-Mogg boldly stated in a live BBC TV interview that the Republic of Ireland's Brexit position was being dictated by an upcoming election and a no-confidence motion in a government minister. This was very much out-of-date information as the no-confidence motion had been abandoned after the government minister in question had resigned the previous week. The BBC interviewer, Andrew Marr, appeared not to realise what a political howler Rees-Mogg had made, and failed to challenge him on the point.

The same week, arch-Leaver and Conservative MP Bernard Jenkin told Sky News that his position on Brexit and Northern Ireland had been informed by assurances from Bertie Ahern and 'Enda Kelly', whom he described as 'two former Taoiseachs or Prime Ministers of Northern Ireland'. This appeared to be an attempt to refer to Enda Kenny, and Jenkin seemed to be confusing the Republic of Ireland (where the men had in fact been Taoiseachs) with Northern Ireland (which does not have a Taoiseach). Such factual clangers would elicit a tut and an eye-roll from most Northern Irish or Irish people under different circumstances, but to come from the lips of a senior pro-Leave figure so far into Brexit negotiations was a deeply concerning error which suggested he didn't know if Northern Ireland had its own Prime Minister.

A core plank of the Good Friday Agreement is a close and amicable working relationship between the UK and Republic of Ireland, who were co-guarantors of the Agreement and jointly lodged it as a treaty with the United Nations. The dynamic is referred to as 'East–West' cooperation, describing the geographical positioning of the two islands. The Agreement text includes a pledge that 'We are committed to partnership, equality and mutual respect as the basis of the relationship within Northern Ireland, between North and South and between these islands.' Of course, the concepts of partnership, equality and mutual respect are vague and elusive. It is hard to identify a specific way in which these qualities have been lacking and therefore the Agreement has been breached. The text gave no way of quantifying disrespect or a specific number of gaffes or insults which would amount to 'partnership' being lost. It is therefore hard to say the accord has definitively been violated. However, a fair assessment of souring relations between the UK and the Republic following Brexit would likely conclude that the spirit of this sentiment had been breached.

IMPACT OF BREXIT ON NORTHERN IRELAND–GREAT BRITAIN RELATIONS

Perhaps one of the most significant revelations from the Brexit result was how little people in the UK knew about not only the Republic of Ireland but also Northern Ireland. As has been discussed, Northern Ireland scarcely received a mention over the course of the referendum itself, as few on either side of the debate seemed to be aware of the particular issues Northern Ireland would face in the context of EU withdrawal. Many appeared to not realise Northern Ireland was in the UK, while others lacked sufficient understanding of the politics and geography of the region to discuss the possible consequences with any nuance or authority.

Most people in Northern Ireland, even among the unionist and loyalist community, do not kid themselves that people in Britain know much about the region. But despite this, the extent of the casual ignorance of the region exposed by Brexit still managed to shock.

In one video clip by *Channel 4 News*, filmed in November 2017, which soon went viral, a presenter stopped passers-by at random on a street in England and asked them to draw the Irish border on a map of the island of Ireland. The process was akin to a constitutional law version of pin the tail on the donkey. None of those asked had any real idea where Northern Ireland ended and the Republic of Ireland began. The video showed participant after participant awkwardly using the marker to obliterate sections of Donegal, Monaghan or Cavan, repatriating great swathes of land and entire counties with a stroke of their pen.

For Northern Ireland's unionist and loyalist communities, watching clips like this combined with senior English politicians' gaffes and knowledge gaps, the situation was humiliating and hurtful. The core of their identity and culture was based on their Britishness and how different they are from the Republic of Ireland, but now they were seeing how unapologetically clueless the English were about where their country began and ended, how it was run and who its politicians were. The facts were unavoidable. Few in England appeared to know or care where they were. In fairness, it is likely that many English people may also struggle to understand or explain the politics or geography of either Wales or Scotland. However, the intensity of national identity in Northern Ireland due to the conflict makes lack of awareness particularly hurtful for those who live in it, especially those who have a British identity and cherish their place in the UK. Among the most hardline loyalist communities in Northern Ireland, there are a considerable number of people who have died or been willing to die in the Troubles to prove their Britishness. Frequent displays of English ignorance and indifference will have been deeply unsettling for them as it appeared this loyalty was far from reciprocated.

Furthermore, while the Brexit process has been a belated education for many in Britain who have suddenly realised Northern Ireland is in the UK, many British people will not have taken this new information as a positive development. While many British people have previously not had any particular awareness of Northern Ireland's existence in the UK, few have objected to it. However, as Northern Ireland has been pushed to the fore of UK politics through Brexit, it is possible that their new familiarity with their previously obscure neighbour will now turn to dissatisfaction. A growing number of people in Britain may now become unsupportive of Northern Ireland remaining in the UK – for instance, if the region is perceived by Leave supporters as a stumbling block that prevents a hard Brexit due to concerns about the Irish border. Similarly, if Remain supporters feel Northern Ireland is given a 'special deal' to protect against what they consider to be the harshest effects of Brexit, frustration may grow as to why Northern Ireland but not they receive special treatment.

Many pro-Leave politicians appear to be viewing Northern Ireland as little more than a nuisance which has the power to scupper or at least soften the Brexit deal they wish to see. It is possible that among such factions, they will begin to look on Northern Ireland unfavourably as a thorn in their side and something the UK would be best to cut out in the interests of getting on with Brexit.

Indeed, dissatisfaction about Northern Ireland being in the UK is not limited to pro-Leave factions of politics but appears to be growing among pro-Remain camps too. During a September 2017 committee hearing in Westminster by MPs about Northern Ireland and Brexit, Labour MP Stephen Hepburn, who represents an English constituency, asked:

> How important do you think this is for the future of Northern Ireland in the UK? For example, if Northern Ireland get a cherry-picking deal and the rest of the UK, say the likes of the north-east, we don't. Are we going to be that much of a big supporter of Northern Ireland being in the UK?

Similarly, as the first tranches of a Brexit deal were announced in December 2017, Labour MP Steve Reed objected to special measures which would see Northern Irish people with Irish passports being allowed to retain EU citizenship, tweeting: 'How is it fair that NI citizens keep EU membership but my constituents in Croydon North don't? Should apply to the whole of the UK.' The glib answer to his rhetorical question is of course that Croydon North was not invaded and occupied by another country for hundreds of years before being partitioned and engulfed in a civil war in which 3,000 people died before the conflict was ended through a peace treaty co-signed by another EU country. It is very clear that the case for Northern Ireland to receive special treatment in the Brexit deal is different from arguments about special status for other regions in the UK, as the challenges and vulnerabilities facing the region are without parallel elsewhere. Nevertheless, there appears to be a perception among some pro-Remain factions in the UK that Northern Ireland is receiving an unfair advantage in Brexit, and many seem to be harbouring a political grudge towards the nation as a result.

The Good Friday Agreement states that 'it is for the people of the island of Ireland alone, by agreement between the two parts respectively and without external impediment' to bring about a united Ireland or not. That is to say, a united Ireland could not come about if people in the rest of the UK vote for Northern Ireland to leave it against their will. Northern Ireland is in the UK whether the rest of the UK likes it or not. The rest of the UK cannot decide to cut Northern Ireland out. This has largely been considered a purely abstract or academic issue, as few in the UK object to Northern Ireland's presence or are even particularly aware of it. However, it is possible that this situation could change, particularly among hardline Brexiters if they cannot get the hard EU withdrawal they want due to concerns about the Irish border. A YouGov poll conducted for LBC in March 2018 asked people living in England, Scotland and Wales which was a greater priority for them: the UK leaving the EU or Northern Ireland staying in the UK. More people opted for the UK leaving the EU, by a small but worrying margin. Also concerning was the number of Britons who expressed no preference on the issue.

Q: Which of these is a greater priority for you?
- That the United Kingdom leaves the European Union (36 per cent)
- That the union between Northern Ireland and the rest of the United Kingdom is maintained (29 per cent)

- Neither of these is important to me (22 per cent)
- Don't know (14 per cent)

As the UK's tolerance of Northern Ireland in the union has always been tacitly assumed and never seriously debated, there is no mainstream data regularly assessing how many people in Britain support Northern Ireland being in the UK. Therefore, it is impossible to measure potential pre-Brexit and post-Brexit shifts in attitudes on the issue. It is important not to read too much into one poll, as replication by other studies has not occurred to indicate statistical validity. However, the YouGov poll will cause concern for the unionist community in Northern Ireland and raise the possibility that a hitherto unquestioned aspect of the Good Friday Agreement could be tested if such attitudes continue.

Other limited research in this area appears to back up this wider trend. For instance, research conducted on Scotland's presence in the union indicates the potential for such attitudes among Leave voters towards Scotland leaving the UK. A 2017 study conducted by academics at Cardiff University and the University of Edinburgh found that 88 per cent of Leave voters said that Scotland voting for independence would be an acceptable price to pay in order to 'take back control'. The same study did not ask respondents whether they would be happy for Northern Ireland to leave the UK in order for them to achieve the Brexit they desired. However, it did ask them if they would be willing for the peace process to be damaged in order to achieve Brexit – with 81 per cent of Leave voters saying yes. This suggests a wider casual attitude towards both the union and Northern Ireland's prospects.

If a growing number of pro-Brexit people in England begin to resent or question Northern Ireland's membership of the UK, this would put Northern Ireland in a tenuous position, as the Good Friday Agreement would ensure it stays regardless – a position which could cause considerable social unrest in both England and Northern Ireland.

IMPACT OF BREXIT ON RECOURSES TO JUSTICE

A cornerstone of the Good Friday Agreement was guaranteeing human rights protections and a 'rights-based society'. The Good Friday Agreement includes within it an obligation on the UK government to 'complete incorporation into Northern Ireland law of the European Convention on Human Rights' as well as giving citizens the right to take legal cases where they feel the convention has been breached and requiring the Stormont Parliament to ensure its legislation meets its standards. In addition, the Good Friday Agreement gave provisions for Northern Ireland to have its own Human Rights Commission.

This focus on human rights was largely due to the fact that much of the conflict had stemmed from structural discrimination against the Catholic/nationalist community under unionist majority rule. Robust human rights and anti-discrimination laws have been prioritised to ensure a repeat of such breaches does not occur. In addition, a number of serious human rights abuses were alleged to have occurred during the conflict, ranging from collusion between paramilitaries and state forces, to torture during the interrogation of terrorist suspects and deprivation of civil liberties through internment without trial.

However, while human rights legislation may have been originally perceived as a nationalist cause, perhaps one of the most interesting aspects of human rights discourse in the region has come from unionists' unexpected embrace of the same language in line with their own objectives. For instance, following a Parades Commission ruling blocking them from marching down a nationalist area, the Loyalist Orange Order announced it would contest the decision on the grounds that their human right to peaceful assembly (Article 11 of the European Convention on Human Rights) was breached. Due to the nature of the conflict, Northern Ireland has largely looked beyond the Belfast and Westminster Parliaments in guaranteeing these rights, amid obvious neutrality concerns. Instead, much of this human rights provision has occurred at a European level.

Brexit will likely have a considerable impact on human rights provisions currently enshrined through EU membership. Throughout the Brexit campaign, much prominence was given within Leave campaigns to the sentiment that British courts were being defied by foreign laws, articulating a sense that the UK's sovereignty was being undermined by the EU's human rights provisions. For instance, one official Vote Leave leaflet claimed: 'EU law overrules UK law. This stops the British public from being able to vote out the politicians who make our laws. EU judges have already overruled British laws on issues like counter-terrorism powers, immigration, VAT and prisoner voting.' Much attention has been given within right-wing media in England in recent years to the notion that Europe is being unfairly liberal in giving human rights protections to people, at the expense of 'common sense' and the sovereignty of British courts. For instance, in 2014, as momentum for a Brexit referendum was mounting, Conservative Cabinet minister Chris Grayling wrote in a column for the right-wing *Daily Mail* newspaper:

> Over 60 years, the system of human rights laws set out in those early days [of the establishment of the European Court of Human Rights] has been drowned by measure after measure, court decision after court decision that have little to do with the original principles that people like Winston Churchill signed up to.
>
> Prisoners being allowed artificial insemination treatment in order to protect their family rights, votes for prisoners in our jails, no whole-life sentences for the most brutal murderers, no deportation for terrorists – some of the decisions that the European Court of Human Rights has taken in recent years – and we came within one vote from one judge of being required to permit US-style political TV advertising. These are not great principles of human rights. They are decisions taken by a Court, made up of people who are not by any means all legally qualified, that sees the original European Convention as a 'living instrument', to be rewritten as the years go by. All of them should be matters for our Parliament and not for the Courts to decide. But right now they aren't.

Many within the Conservative Party and media outlets like the *Daily Mail* have been campaigning for the UK to withdraw from the European Convention on Human Rights and instead replace these provisions with a 'British bill of rights', which would be narrower in scope and contain fewer provisions.

The ECHR outlines a number of political, social and economic rights that EU institutions must respect when exercising their powers. Many of these are of particular significance in the context of Northern Ireland. For instance, when First Minister Arlene Foster blocked the release of funding for legacy inquests into Troubles deaths, the legal challenge to the decision (discussed in Chapter Four) was brought on the grounds that the absence of funding breaches Article 2 of the Convention – which obliges the government to conduct 'a full, open and transparent investigation' into any case where the state has taken a life.

Similarly, the British government has also been accused of committing torture when interrogating terror suspects, most notably in what is known as the 'Hooded Men' case. The men allege that they were captured by state authorities, had hoods held over their heads and were then flown by helicopter to an unknown location. The men had not been subject to any criminal trial or charged with any offences. They claim that they were then forced into holding stress positions, as well as being subjected to white noise, sleep deprivation, physical beatings and deprivation of food and water. One of the detainees said the experience was so distressing and harmful that he suffered hallucinations and prayed for death. A case was brought against the government in 1978 claiming that this treatment amounted to torture. In 1978, the European Court of Human Rights ruled that the threshold for torture was not met but the men had suffered inhuman and degrading treatment. In 2014, the

Republic of Ireland government decided to ask the ECHR to revise this verdict, following concerns about the quality of the original case.

It is important to note that the European Court of Human Rights (ECtHR) is not a European Union institution. Rather, it was set up by the Council of Europe, which has forty-seven members including a number of non-EU members such as Russia and Ukraine. Therefore, Brexit will not exempt the UK from following its decisions. However, as anti-Europe and anti-human-rights rhetoric escalates, it is possible that momentum on this issue will see the UK eventually push for withdrawal from the ECtHR too. Many within the Leave movement struggle to differentiate between the ECtHR and the European Court of Justice, often wrongly conflating the two despite the fact that they are vastly different institutions. As Professor Louise Mallinder from Ulster University writes in her report on 'Brexit and Dealing with the Past in Northern Ireland':

> Leaving the European Union would not alter the UK's relationship with the European Court of Human Rights. However, it may embolden those seeking to replace the ECHR with a UK Bill of Rights. This could be negative for efforts to deal with the past, as it would remove one source of pressure on the UK government to address the needs of victims. It could weaken or remove a system of safeguards to ensure that mechanisms that are established are adequate to the task.

Once Brexit occurs and Leave voters realise their long-standing bogeyman of European human rights has not been felled, focus is likely to switch to the European Court and European Convention on Human Rights, risking a weakening of Northern Irish people's recourses to justice for human rights abuses.

'PEACE MONEY'

Since 1995, the European Union has given more than €1.3 billion to support peace projects in Northern Ireland and along border communities in the Republic. This funding, known locally as 'peace money', has been spent on projects with an ethos of promoting better relations between the unionist and nationalist communities. Major ventures have included the so-called peace bridge in Derry-Londonderry, which links the two communities, as well as groups that work to promote anti-sectarian principles, often among at-risk youths or vulnerable adults in marginalised or working-class communities. It is, of course, impossible to accurately assess how much these projects have benefited Northern Ireland, as there is no objective measurement by which to capture and compare sectarian sentiment. However, many within communities on both sides of the divide have spoken positively of the changes they feel these projects have been able to cement locally.

The EU also funds a number of projects which are not directly related to anti-sectarianism but indirectly support the goal through the wider aim of normalising society and thereby reducing the effects of the conflict; for instance, large subsidies have been given to Northern Ireland's train service. As Northern Ireland continues to be one of the most impoverished and underdeveloped parts of Europe, this funding has provided employment opportunities locally, as well as improving quality of life through infrastructure.

Furthermore, the money has played a crucial role in the peace process due not only to the cash involved but also to its source. While many Leave campaigners criticised the EU for being a largely faceless organisation where bureaucracy reigned over personality, this quality has been a strength in the context of the Northern Ireland peace process. The EU is largely perceived as being an uncontroversial body (or at least it was prior to Brexit), which is not biased towards any one side in the conflict. Therefore, it has been widely considered neutral and it has been uncontroversial for charities or organisations to receive 'peace money' funding where it may have been an issue if the UK government or the Republic of Ireland were the distributors.

A total of £133 million per year has been earmarked for Northern Ireland in the current funding round, which runs until 2020. Beyond that, the future of the funds, and the community groups for which it is a lifeline, is uncertain. Following the UK's withdrawal from the EU, the country could have little justifiable expectation of the funds continuing. It is possible that the EU could continue to commit funding for a further period purely out of a sense of moral duty to the Northern Irish peace process. However, the likelihood of this is unclear.

In an August 2017 position paper on Brexit and Northern Ireland, the UK government suggested:

The UK proposes that, without prejudice to the wider discussions

> on the financial settlement and Structural and Investment
> Funds, the UK and the EU should agree the continuation of
> funding … for the duration of the existing programme and,
> with the Northern Ireland Executive and Irish Government,
> explore a potential future programme post-2020.

This, like many Brexit position papers from the UK, was vague and gave little practical detail. However, it did appear to hint at the possibility that the Republic of Ireland government could, as a remaining EU member, ask to receive the 'peace money' after Brexit and then forward it on to Northern Ireland. This is one possibility worth considering. However, it could be met by objections from those in unionist or loyalist communities not wishing to receive money from the Republic of Ireland.

Of course, it is possible that the UK government could instead send equivalent 'peace money' funds to Northern Ireland after Brexit occurs. However, this could face a similar problem with nationalist or Republican groups, who would face pressure not to accept money from the British state they reject. In addition, a further issue could arise here if people in England perceive an injustice in Northern Ireland receiving money while the English do not receive similar benefits. Following the DUP deal with the minority Conservative government after the June 2017 election, there was much hostility towards the DUP for securing £1 billion for Northern Ireland in exchange for their support. As Northern Ireland is already perceived by many in England to be on the receiving end of unfair slush funds, 'peace money' secured via London could see this backlash continue.

IDENTITY

Finally, Brexit is likely to test provisions contained within the Good Friday Agreement on identity. Under the Agreement, people born in Northern Ireland are entitled to hold British citizenship, Irish citizenship or both. Following the referendum result, there has been a surge of people in the UK gaining passports from EU countries in a bid to retain some EU rights. In Northern Ireland, this has particular consequences for community relations and the constitutional question. In 2016, the year of the Brexit referendum, the number of Irish passport applications submitted from Northern Ireland rose by 27 per cent from the previous year.

The EU and the UK are in agreement that Northern Irish people with Irish passports will continue to be EU citizens following Brexit. In the UK government's August 2017 position paper, they stated:

> As long as Ireland remains a member of the EU, Irish citizenship also confers EU citizenship, with all the rights that go with this. This is true for the people of Northern Ireland who are Irish citizens – or who hold both British and Irish citizenship – as it is for Irish citizens in Ireland. The UK welcomes the commitment in the European Commission's directives that these EU rights should continue to be respected following the UK's departure from the EU: 'Full account should be taken of the fact that Irish citizens residing in Northern Ireland will continue to enjoy rights as EU citizens.'

This position could cause considerable issues in Northern Ireland, in creating differences between the rights accorded to unionists (who are more likely to have British passports) and nationalists (who are more likely to have Irish passports). While both Ireland and the UK have been in the EU, there have been no differences to the international rights afforded to Northern Irish people. However, this could now change. For instance, members of the unionist community in Northern Ireland may have less of a right to live abroad in some countries, while nationalists retain that right. An imminent division between those in Northern Ireland who have EU citizenship and those who do not may therefore alter the rights of people in the region along sectarian lines, with considerable consequences for the peace process. For instance, on flights from Northern Ireland to EU countries following Brexit, passengers lining up for passport checks as EU citizens or non-EU citizens could effectively mean Protestants in one queue and Catholics in another. This would add a concerning element of 'othering' the two communities in a way that would be deeply unhelpful for community relations.

Central to the Good Friday Agreement was the understanding not only that people had the right to identify as British or Irish, but that those identities would be equal to each other and no one 'side' would have more rights than the other. This was based on a tacit assumption of continued EU membership for both countries and did not consider a circumstance in which holders of one passport would have considerably more rights to movement or travel than the other. Brexit therefore unsettles this provision as the two identities are no longer analogous or equal.

CHAPTER SEVEN

POWER-SHARING

Looking back, it is hard to pinpoint the exact moment at which power-sharing stalled in Northern Ireland and the grand peace process project launched in 1998 seemed to finally run aground. In reality, it was a collection of smaller and disparate moments which accrued over many months and years. Just as a frog in a pan of boiling water does not notice the rising temperature around it until it is too late to jump, it is only in retrospect that we can see that much of the 2010s was spent pushing the peace process too far and not realising the perhaps irreversible damage until it had been done.

Technically speaking, the moment it all fell apart was when Sinn Féin's Martin McGuinness resigned as Deputy First Minister on 9 January 2017 and his party refused to share power with the DUP any longer.

In the nineteen years since the signing of the Good Friday Agreement, power-sharing had not been without its problems, especially in its early years. On a number of occasions, power-sharing was suspended at Stormont and the region returned to being ruled from London, as it had been during the Troubles, in a process known as 'direct rule'. In 2000, this occurred amid concerns the IRA had not fully decommissioned its weapons. Following a pledge from the terror group that it would do so, devolution was once again restored to Stormont. However, in 2001, concerns about decommissioning once again arose and power-sharing was suspended on two occasions for 24-hour periods in order to give the parties time for further negotiations. Power-sharing then limped on until 2002, when police raided Sinn Féin's Stormont offices amid allegations of Republicans illegally collecting information through a spy ring. The Assembly at Stormont was once again suspended and was not reintroduced until 2007.

In the first decade of power-sharing, the two largest parties had been the moderate unionist/Protestant group the Ulster Unionist Party and the moderate nationalist/Catholic group the Social Democratic and Labour Party (SDLP). Under the special mechanisms in the Good Friday Agreement, no single party can rule alone; the region can only be ruled jointly by a First Minister and a Deputy First Minister, of equal rank. Politicians would have to declare themselves as being 'unionist', 'nationalist' or 'other' at Stormont. Then the First Minister and Deputy First Minister titles would go to the largest party of the largest designation and the largest party of the second largest designation respectively. They would also receive a certain number of ministries at Stormont each, in line with their popularity. Some of the smaller parties would also receive ministers too, in order to ensure the more hardline or fringe elements of voters' opinions could also have a voice at Stormont.

While the SDLP and the UUP clearly represented one of each of Northern Ireland's divided communities, they were both anti-violence, pro-peace and capable of putting aside their differences in the interests of the peace process. The leaders of the two parties, David Trimble and John Hume, would go on to be jointly awarded the Nobel Peace Prize for their efforts. As the largest parties, the UUP and SDLP won the titles of First Minister and Deputy First Minister respectively and were given control of more departments at Stormont than any of the other parties. As the more hardline factions on both sides also received a considerable chunk of the vote, they also received ministries. On the unionist side, this was the hardline loyalist/Protestant grouping the Democratic Unionist Party, who were opposed to the Good Friday Agreement and known for their aggressive and flamboyant political rallies, which many considered tantamount to incitements to violence. On the nationalist side, this was the staunch Irish Republican party Sinn Féin, who were widely considered to be the political wing of the IRA, the terror group that had been responsible for much of the violence in the conflict.

By the time power-sharing was restored in 2007, the parties' fortunes had changed. Now, the UUP and the SDLP had slumped in the polls and were replaced by the DUP as the new largest unionist party and Sinn Féin as the new largest nationalist party.

It is perhaps one of the saddest ironies of the peace process that the two parties which did the most to broker it were soon thrown out by voters of the very institutions they had made possible, only to be replaced by those who had opposed or threatened to undermine power-sharing. Or perhaps it is a rational response from a nervous electorate who were still wary of the new power-sharing experiment and felt more comfortable having its detractors at its core. Regardless, Northern Ireland's moderate voices were now on the fringe and the hardline factions were at its heart.

This switch was no mere temporary blip on the part of the electorate. To this day, both Sinn Féin and the DUP remain Northern Ireland's largest parties and have only seen their success at the polls improve in the intervening decade.

As the two parties first began power-sharing in 2007, many feared the two hardline groups would be incapable of cooperating in order to share power. However, to much surprise and relief, DUP leader Ian Paisley and former IRA man turned senior Sinn Féin politician Martin McGuinness managed to establish a great personal rapport. Their unlikely friendship even earned them the nickname 'the chuckle brothers' after they were photographed on many occasions roaring with laughter as they shared a joke.

However, with the passage of time, tensions between the two power-sharing partners began to emerge. In 2008, Ian Paisley, who was by that time eighty-one years old, announced that he would be retiring from frontline politics and relinquishing his role as DUP leader and Northern Ireland First Minister. His replacement, Peter Robinson, who held both positions until 2015, was considerably more antagonistic towards Sinn Féin. As he took office, Robinson pointedly announced that Stormont's 'honeymoon period' was over. Upon his resignation in 2015, Arlene Foster took the reins as DUP leader and Northern Ireland First Minister. She took on a similarly frosty approach and was often quick to criticise Sinn Féin in fierce and personal attacks in the chamber at Stormont and in media appearances.

The DUP–Sinn Féin dichotomy at Stormont was strengthened when, in May 2016, the smaller parties decided they would no longer take ministries and instead set up an official opposition at Stormont. The UUP and the SDLP were the largest drivers behind this move, as they were increasingly frustrated with playing small parts in the Stormont political drama alongside the behemoths of the DUP and Sinn Féin. Instead, they calculated it would be better to give up those small roles and enter an opposition from which they could attack and criticise their rivals more openly and perhaps even be rewarded in the polls for it.

By the time Sinn Féin pulled the plug on power-sharing in January 2017, Northern Ireland had had a decade of continued and stable government. While few in the region would have considered power-sharing perfect, almost everyone agreed it was infinitely preferable to the dark days of Northern Ireland's violent past and so should be protected nonetheless. For many, particularly younger generations, it was no longer a novel peace experiment but an almost mundane fact of everyday life now more associated with drudging bureaucracy than the dramatic scenes and frequent suspensions characteristic of its first years.

Therefore, when Sinn Féin announced they were pulling out of power-sharing with the DUP and walking away from the institutions at Stormont, the initial surprise was met with a sense of incredulity by many in Northern Ireland. By now, power-sharing was taken for granted. Politicians may make dramatic threats from time to time, but it was here to stay.

However, voters were soon to find that this occasion was different. The spark that lit the fuse on the eventual implosion of power-sharing was the allegation that a government-run green energy scheme had been very badly mismanaged. Called the Renewable Heat Incentive scheme, but dubbed locally 'cash for ash', the scheme was designed to give businesses a financial reward for using renewable rather than non-renewable heat sources. However, the scheme appears to have been badly flawed and it later emerged that it was in fact giving out subsidies far higher than the price of the fuel, meaning that people were being paid to burn fuel pointlessly. The scheme was primarily used by farmers and others in the agriculture industry. Reports soon emerged alleging one farmer had been paid £1 million to heat an empty shed for no reason, while others were earning hefty sums pointlessly heating horse boxes. It is estimated that the scheme will have cost the taxpayer close to £1 billion due to the flawed implementation, a considerable sum considering Northern Ireland has only 1.8 million inhabitants.

The debacle caused public outcry. The image of public money going up in flames was a visual hook that touched a nerve among many voters. Further subtext to the scandal was the public perception that Northern Ireland's agriculture and farming community is still predominantly unionist/Protestant due to the history of land confiscation and redistribution in the Plantation centuries before. Concerns that a sectarian edge may have existed in the scheme, as it may have been designed to deliberately aid one side of the community, who were still profiting from generations of land ownership, added to some voters' dissatisfaction.

An inquiry into the affair was soon ordered to get to the bottom of how and why the flawed scheme had been allowed. As the Minister for Enterprise, Trade and Investment between 2008 and 2015, the DUP's Arlene Foster had been responsible for implementing the scheme. Now in post as First Minister, Foster faced calls from Sinn Féin, among other parties in the Northern Ireland Assembly, to step down. Foster refused, insisting that she had done nothing wrong and her name would be cleared by the inquiry, which would take several years to complete its probe and present its findings.

Then, in January 2017, Sinn Féin's Martin McGuinness resigned as Deputy First Minister, citing concerns about the DUP's 'arrogance' in their handling of the 'cash for ash' debacle.

Under the rules of the Parliament as set out in the Good Friday Agreement, Stormont could only continue to rule while the largest nationalist and unionist parties governed together. When Sinn Féin pulled out of the partnership, therefore, the DUP could no longer govern either. Nineteen years on from the Good Friday Agreement, the power-sharing partnership was paralysed.

After everything that Northern Ireland had been through in recent decades, spanning massacres and bombings, terrorist spy rings and human rights abuses, to pull the government down over something as trivial as a green energy scheme seemed almost farcical. In many ways, that such a banal political scandal could bring down a government in Northern Ireland was perhaps a sign of how normalised politics had become in the region thanks to the peace process.

Upon McGuinness's resignation, Northern Ireland Secretary James Brokenshire was faced with two options. He could either introduce direct rule from London or call a snap election in the hope that different parties could be elected who would agree to share power – or at least the month-long election campaign period might give Sinn Féin and the DUP time to resolve their differences. There was little appetite in London to govern Northern Ireland, as 10 Downing Street had become engulfed in Brexit talks and had little time for much else. Similarly, Brokenshire was no doubt mindful of the step backwards it would have been in the peace process to see Stormont fall.

Calling an election also had its downsides, however. Northern Ireland had undergone local elections in May of the previous year, as well as going to the polls in June 2016 for the Brexit referendum. The year before that had been the May 2015 general election for Westminster. It was possible the electorate could have voting fatigue and simply not turn out to vote in a snap election for Stormont. A low voter turnout could be seriously damaging for public confidence in the power-sharing government, undermining its credibility.

After some deliberation, Brokenshire announced that Northern Ireland would once again go the polls. Although it would be the third time in twelve months that voters were asked to traipse to the polling stations, it was hoped that they would make the effort nonetheless as this election was in many ways like no other. This time, the election was not so much a poll of individual parties as a proxy poll on faith in power-sharing itself.

THE 2017 SNAP ELECTION

The election was called for March, and Northern Ireland once again snapped into election mode. Candidates were chosen and volunteers were assembled to knock on doors at homes across the region. Election placards bearing politicians' beaming faces were once again sprouting from trees and lamp-posts throughout Northern Ireland, blossoming like strange fruits. Social media channels, television listings and radio airwaves became clogged with party propaganda once again.

Sinn Féin ran their campaign on the basis that they were stalwarts against a corrupt and incompetent DUP whose arrogance was making them impossible to work with. The DUP, by comparison, ran on the basis that Sinn Féin were cynically creating a melodrama about the 'cash for ash' scandal in order to undermine unionism and stage a Republican takeover. The smaller parties, the SDLP and the UUP, hardly featured in the campaign. Their decision the previous year to enter official opposition at Stormont appeared not to have had the desired effect of framing them as clear alternatives to the DUP and Sinn Féin. Instead, they appeared increasingly irrelevant as the political stage shrank to the narrow ground inhabited by the two main parties.

After six weeks of intense campaigning, the election was held on 2 March. That night, election counters assembled at makeshift centres across the region and sifted through a flurry of ballot papers to ascertain the result. Politicians and political correspondents held their breath to see the future of power-sharing decided.

As different areas declared slowly over the course of the next day, the news came in trickles. By that afternoon, a picture had emerged. The good news was that the election had produced a turnout of 64.8 per cent, a healthy figure in the face of speculation that voters might shy away from another day at the polls.

The turnout would give credibility to the verdict produced and indicated that Northern Irish voters' patience in democracy had not yet been totally exhausted. The bad news, however, (from the perspective of the future of power-sharing, at least) was who the voters had cast their votes for.

Far from electing a different set of politicians, voters had opted to continue to support the DUP and Sinn Féin as the largest parties in Northern Ireland. The DUP took 28.1 per cent of the vote (a small drop from 29.2 per cent the previous year) while Sinn Féin took 27.9 per cent (a considerable increase from 24 per cent the previous year). There was now just over 0.2 per cent vote difference between the DUP and Sinn Féin – the smallest gap between unionists and nationalists that any election in Northern Ireland had ever produced. Rather than end the DUP–Sinn Féin dichotomy, the electorate had entrenched it.

The result was also affected by changes to the number of seats at Stormont, which had been planned before the election was called as a means to reform the legislature. When Stormont was first established under the Good Friday Agreement, the rules allowed for 108 elected Assembly members – six for each of Northern Ireland's eighteen constituencies. For a region as small as Northern Ireland, with a population of 1.8 million, this was an extremely high number of elected representatives, giving one politician at Stormont for every 16,700 residents of Northern Ireland. If the same ratio were applied to the Westminster Parliament, for instance, this would be equivalent to the UK having 3,930 MPs in the House of Commons. In the context of Northern Ireland's peace process, this extreme number of politicians (sometimes dubbed a 'democratic surplus') was deemed necessary as it enabled smaller fringe groups to be elected and so feel they had a stake in the power-sharing Assembly. However, in the 2010s, discontent grew about the large number of politicians at Stormont, particularly regarding the cost to the taxpayer. The expenses scandal at Westminster brought an attitudinal shift towards politicians across the UK and greater awareness of the financial costs of running a Parliament. Similarly, austerity across the UK under the 2010–15 Conservative–Lib Dem coalition government also reignited debate about excess costs. As many other public sector workers were refused pay increases or had their budgets and resources slashed, public opinion shifted towards politicians being required to cut their costs and lay off some staff as well. It was therefore decided that the eighteen constituencies would drop from six politicians each to five. This would reduce the number of politicians at Stormont from 108 to 90 and make considerable savings for the taxpayer.

The reduction in the number of politicians had been agreed long before the power-sharing collapse and received cross-party support at Stormont. However, in the context of the snap election of March 2017 it took on a new meaning and had unexpected consequences. The drop in the number of Assembly members meant the gap between the two largest parties shrank dramatically, and thus the binary extremes of the DUP and Sinn Féin were only entrenched further.

Small shifts in voting patterns were therefore amplified and distorted, making the gap between the two parties narrower than it would normally have appeared. For instance, while the DUP experienced a vote drop of 1.1 per cent on the previous year, they lost ten seats. Now, instead of a sizeable ten-seat gap between the DUP and their arch rivals in Sinn Féin, there was just one seat difference between them.

The seat allocation from the 2017 election was as follows:

DUP	28 seats
Sinn Féin	27 seats
SDLP	12 seats
UUP	10 seats
Alliance	8 seats
Green Party	2 seats
People Before Profit	1 seat
Independent	1 seat
Traditional Unionist Voice	1 seat

In the previous year's 2016 Assembly election the seat allocation had been as follows:

DUP	38 seats
Sinn Féin	28 seats
UUP	16 seats
SDLP	12 seats
Alliance	8 seats
Green Party	2 seats
People Before Profit	2 seats
Independent	1 seat
Traditional Unionist Voice	1 seat

POWER-SHARING NEGOTIATIONS

The snap election of March 2017 therefore did little to solve the stalemate at Stormont. Indeed, if anything, it bolstered the two main parties' positions. Sinn Féin had arguably been rewarded rather than punished at the polls for their hardline approach to the DUP. Meanwhile, the DUP held supremacy at Stormont by merely one seat and were even less likely to make concessions to Sinn Féin, instead amping up their rhetoric in a bid to restate their authority over their nationalist rivals. Delegations of negotiators from both parties met for a series of talks aimed at reaching an agreement, but to no avail.

Then, three weeks after the election, senior Sinn Féin politician and former Deputy First Minister Martin McGuinness died. The 66-year-old had been suffering from a genetic condition and had appeared frail in recent months. In mid-January, shortly after he had pulled his party out of power-sharing, he had also announced his resignation from politics due to his ailing health. Michelle O'Neill, a former government minister for the party, was appointed to replace him as the party's leader in Northern Ireland.

McGuinness's death marked a turning point in the party's history. He had been on the front line of Sinn Féin politics for decades. McGuinness had been open about his past as an IRA commander in Derry-Londonderry during the conflict and how he had come to embrace politics rather than violence as a means of achieving his Republican aims. In many ways, he epitomised the peace process, as he had spent his earlier life engaged in violence before later dedicating himself to peace and reconciliation. Yet for many in Northern Ireland, in particular victims of IRA violence, he was a deeply divisive and controversial figure. Following his death, his life and legacy were debated in obituaries and news bulletins the world over.

In the days that followed, McGuinness's death was a major talking point both locally and internationally. He was perhaps the best-known Irish Republican from the peace process to die to date and so assessments of his life often amounted to de facto reflections on Sinn Féin's history, as commentators and news producers sought to understand what his and his party's legacy would be.

Some in the Republican movement may have held their breath with nervous uncertainty as they awaited the verdict. However, most obituaries recorded McGuinness as a political icon and historic leader. It was acknowledged that he had participated in violence, but the general consensus seemed to be that he would above all be remembered for his work for peace. Among the dignitaries and heads of state who attended his funeral was former US President Bill Clinton, who paid a touching tribute to the man he got to know during their joint work on the Good Friday Agreement, further cementing the former Sinn Féin politician's place as one of the most significant figures in Northern Ireland's peace process.

Such obituaries and tributes buoyed Sinn Féin in the weeks after the election, confirming to many of their members that they were on the right side of history and should not be cowed by or apologetic about the party's violent origins. It is possible that this strengthened the party's sense of purpose and resolve, while also bolstering them against the usual attacks from the DUP that the party were terrorists with blood on their hands.

Indeed, a further breakdown of relations between the DUP and Sinn Féin occurred when DUP leader Arlene Foster wavered over whether or not to even attend McGuinness's funeral. Foster has always been staunchly anti-IRA, having been partly inspired to enter politics after her father was shot by the IRA during her childhood. However, many people in Northern Ireland had hoped that as Foster had worked with McGuinness for almost two years as First Minister and Deputy First Minister at Stormont, she would be able to put that aside in order to pay her respects to him at the funeral. Foster appeared to dither. In the days after his death, the DUP press office would not confirm if Foster would attend the service, prompting many voters on both sides to criticise her for appearing to drag the region back into the politics of the past. On the day itself, Foster was seen entering the funeral chapel and shaking hands with McGuinness's successor Michelle O'Neill. However, the damage was already done. Many in Sinn Féin felt Foster had insulted McGuinness's memory by even dithering on whether to attend. The incident did little to improve party relations in the days and weeks after the funeral when the two parties sat down for more talks on whether or not to return to power-sharing.

Northern Ireland Secretary James Brokenshire gave the parties a deadline in April to agree on a return to power-sharing, warning that if a deal could not be reached, Northern Ireland would face the prospect of direct rule from London for the first time in a decade. The deadline came and went with no progress. It was extended until June to give the parties more time; this again went by without resolution. So too with a July deadline. Hope of a deal being reached soon faded.

Where once Prime Ministers would fly to Belfast during political crises at Stormont, Theresa May stayed put in Downing Street dealing with the dizzying and all-consuming work of Brexit. In the meantime, Mr Brokenshire's calls for compromise fell on deaf ears and the DUP and Sinn Féin careened through yet more deadlines.

Indeed, as negotiations continued, the number of unresolvable issues between the DUP and Sinn Féin appeared only to increase. When power-sharing had initially collapsed in January 2017, Sinn Féin had cited the DUP's 'arrogance' in Arlene Foster's handling of allegations that she had been responsible for the 'cash for ash' scandal. However, other seemingly insurmountable sticking points soon emerged. Sinn Féin's objection over the 'cash for ash' scandal went from the specific to the thematic; it was not Foster's alleged behaviour specifically that was the problem, but rather what it represented more broadly. For Sinn Féin, the issue was no longer the renewable energy scandal but the DUP's general attitude towards power-sharing. Sinn Féin now said the DUP needed to recalibrate its attitudes towards Stormont in order for power-sharing to be restored. They said the DUP had been focused for too long on using their power only to serve the interests of their own party and their own views. They said the 'cash for ash' scandal had merely been emblematic of years of DUP misrule.

Sinn Féin's demands soon spiralled. Their calls for DUP leader Arlene Foster to step aside while the 'cash for ash' inquiry was ongoing were quietly dropped and replaced by a broader range of demands and objections to the DUP which went far beyond the concerns they had initially expressed. The vacuum created by the absence of power-sharing was soon filled with bitter clashes between the two parties. Perhaps Sinn Féin and the DUP had been biting their tongues for a decade in order to get along with their coalition partners, meaning that once the façade of cooperation was finally dropped, ten years' worth of grievances were laid bare. Sinn Féin criticised the DUP for blocking marriage equality for LGBT couples through their use of the controversial Petition of Concern mechanism, which enables parties to block laws they disagree with. Sinn Féin also renewed their criticism of how Foster had blocked funding for inquests into cold-case murders from the Troubles, which she had suggested at the time was due to her desire to stop what she worried could amount to an unfair witch-hunt against former soldiers, many of whom were linked to unsolved killings. In addition, Sinn Féin renewed their calls for an Irish Language Act to be introduced to the region. The other devolved regions in the UK have both passed legislation to promote and protect the local languages, namely Welsh in Wales and Scots Gaelic in Scotland. However, the DUP have resisted the introduction of an Irish language equivalent in Northern Ireland, as the language is primarily spoken by the Catholic/nationalist community. The DUP have said the bill would be a waste of money in supporting a dead language, as well as expressing fears it could give the Irish language and those who speak it a position of supremacy in Northern Irish society. Sinn Féin have fiercely opposed the DUP's attempts to block the legislation, saying their obstinance amounts to discrimination against the nationalist community. Sinn Féin say that in a 2006 negotiation known as the St Andrew's Agreement, it was decided that Northern Ireland should receive Irish language legislation, but the DUP have refused to let such a bill pass at Stormont on the grounds that it was not them who made that commitment in 2006.

Using these three elements (same-sex marriage, legacy inquests, Irish language legislation), Sinn Féin began to argue that they were promoting a 'rights-based agenda' for the LGBT community, Troubles victims and Irish language speakers. They argued the DUP were not fit for office or deserving of power-sharing until it could show commitment to allowing such a 'rights-based' society to form.

IRISH LANGUAGE DEADLOCK

As the months progressed, Sinn Féin whittled down this three-pronged approach so that the Irish language legislation was their only red-line issue. However, the DUP could not agree to return to government on that basis, continuing to argue that it was a dead language which the Catholic/nationalist community were wilfully misusing in order to achieve cultural supremacy in Northern Ireland.

To an outsider, it might appear odd that something as seemingly benign as language legislation could halt the formation of a government. However, in Northern Ireland, where so much of the division is based on cultural difference and history, such things are imbued with a significance without parallel in any other part of the UK.

Throughout 2017, the Irish language became something of a proxy war between the DUP and Sinn Féin, through which they thrashed out the balance of power between the unionist and nationalist traditions.

Few people in Northern Ireland speak Irish. It is difficult to get accurate data on the number of Irish speakers in the region, as many nationalists exaggerate the level of their language skills in research surveys in order to make a political point. However, the proportion of fluent speakers in Northern Ireland is generally estimated to be in the region of 1 per cent or less.

This is largely due to a number of penal laws that were imposed during the colonisation of the island of Ireland, which deliberately sought to suppress and marginalise the native Irish language and replace it with English, as part of Britain's attempts to 'civilise' Ireland. For instance, English was made the official language of most civic institutions in the seventeenth and eighteenth centuries, while Irish was outlawed in courts.

In modern-day Northern Ireland, many in the nationalist/ Catholic community still feel a strong affinity with the Irish language as they believe it represents their native culture and their community's history. Some also feel that speaking is a means of decolonising their own sense of identity and rejecting the historic ways in which the language was oppressed. In a reflection of this, many nationalists have Irish language names, the Irish language is taught as an option in Catholic schools, and street signs in Catholic areas often carry bilingual translations in both Irish and English. By contrast, few people in Protestant/unionist areas speak the language or feel a connection to it.

Sinn Féin demanded that the DUP accept an Irish Language Act being passed at Stormont. This would be a legislative package designed to protect and promote the Irish language within Northern Ireland and would be modelled on similar laws elsewhere in the UK, including legislation to protect the Welsh language in Wales and Scots Gaelic in Scotland. However, the DUP insisted they could not accept any such act. They said they feared it could cost huge sums of public money as well as potentially resulting in Irish speakers getting an unfair advantage in society at the expense of their counterparts who speak only English.

At a micro-level, the debate was about the Irish language; however, as is almost invariably the case in Northern Ireland, the dispute was also about the much wider issue of whether the two 'sides' were truly equal. Technically speaking, the nature of power-sharing positioned the largest unionist party and the largest nationalist party as equals. Although the largest party's leader took the title of First Minister of Northern Ireland and the second largest took the title of Deputy First Minister of Northern Ireland, the hierarchy was purely linguistic: legally and politically speaking, the unionists and nationalists held equal power and responsibility. The implied hierarchy in the titles had been included to quell unionists' insecurities about being treated as equal to nationalists in power-sharing despite their greater electoral sway. The Northern Irish state had initially been founded on the basis of unionist suprema-cy, as boundaries were drawn to create a nation in which unionists would hold the majority. When the Good Friday Agreement was signed, therefore, although both nationalists and unionists were technically equal, a number of symbolic gestures were put in place to assuage unionist insecurity. This was not only limited to the titles of First Minister and Deputy First Minister, but was extended to a number of other symbols at Stormont. The Parliament building is in East Belfast, a staunchly unionist part of the city. It continues to fly not only one but often two Union flags, despite objections from nationalists that this is far from a neutral symbol. The Parliament also bears before it a statue of the unionist politician Edward Carson and inside it a statue of former unionist Prime Minister Lord Craigavon, who oversaw much discrimination against the nationalist/Catholic community. By contrast, there are few symbols or acknowledgements of the nationalist community's culture or traditions. Signs of Protestant/unionist culture also continue to be promoted much more than the nationalist culture in other areas of civic society. For instance, the two universities are named using unionist terminology – Queen's University Belfast (in tribute to the royal family, which many unionists consider themselves loyal subjects of, while nationalists do not identify with them) and Ulster University (using the loyalist term 'Ulster' for the region rather than the more neutral 'Northern Ireland' or even the nationalist term 'North of Ireland'). While, in 1998, many nationalists were still living in the shadow of unionist dominance and political supremacy and so accepted these symbols remaining, after two decades of power-sharing, political nationalism had begun to develop greater confidence and increasingly questioned whether they were in an equal partnership with unionists. The DUP have long held a negative view of the Irish language, but in the 2010s, this derision began to grate on the nationalist community, who were growing increasingly less apologetic about their culture and less tolerant of the DUP's attitude towards it. In November 2014, DUP politician Gregory Campbell stood up in the chamber at Stormont and mocked the Irish language. He began an address to the chamber by saying, 'Curry my yoghurt can coca coalyer' – a crude parody of the term 'Go raibh maith agat, Ceann Comhairle', which means 'Thank you, Speaker' and is often used by nationalist politicians as a term of courtesy during debates at Stormont. Mr Campbell refused to apologise for or accept the hurt that his parody caused. Then, in September 2016, after the DUP took over the agriculture ministry from Sinn Féin, the new DUP minister decided to rename a boat which had been given an Irish language name of Banríon Uladh ('Queen of Ulster') under the Sinn Féin ministry and use the English language translation instead.

In December 2016, another DUP politician made another controversial decision involving the Irish language when Paul Givan used his position as Minister for Communities to announce that he was scrapping a small scheme which gave bursaries for children from deprived areas to study the Irish language. The scheme cost the taxpayer around £50,000 per year, a relatively small sum in the grand scheme of Stormont's annual £10 billion budget. Amid outcry, Mr Givan eventually reversed his decision in early 2017, but for many in the nationalist community the damage was already done and it amounted to yet another deliberate attempt by the DUP to denigrate their culture.

How the DUP became so opposed to the Irish language and saw small advancements for Irish speakers as being such an existential threat to them is a complex issue; their position appears to have slowly escalated and hardened in recent years. The Irish language had always been a relatively fringe issue in Northern Ireland and did not feature significantly in the peace process or the Good Friday Agreement. However, it has always been symbolic to Republicanism. For the DUP, it appears to represent a threat to their sense of unionist identity, as it represents traditional Irish culture – which they fear could undermine what they consider to be Northern Ireland's Britishness. As a result, even small, incremental moves to support the Irish language were met with fierce opposition and dramatic statements that their Britishness was being fundamentally undermined and attacked. The feminist saying about backlash against gender equality might go some way in explaining it: 'When you have been accustomed to privilege for so long, equality feels like oppression.' Many hardline unionists were perhaps so used to seeing their experiences, customs and culture expressed in political and civic life in Northern Ireland as the dominant or even sole cultural expression that merely having to share a small part of that space with a different view seemed like a grave violation of their own rights.

In any event, their opposition to the Irish language ironically only strengthened the language's position in Northern Ireland society. Relatively few people in Northern Ireland's nationalist community spoke Irish prior to the stand-off between the DUP and Sinn Féin. However, following this series of perceived slights towards the Irish language from the DUP in the 2010s, the language experienced something of a boom. Classes teaching the language cropped up across the region and rallies of Irish language speakers were held on the steps at Stormont. Ironically, if the DUP had not attempted to undermine the Irish language, it would likely have remained a minority and relatively obscure issue of interest only to a few hardline linguists. However, through their extreme opposition to it, it became a live issue once more and a proxy war through which the nationalist community sought to reassert itself.

The DUP remained unrepentant, with DUP leader Arlene Foster stating in September 2017 that she felt Sinn Féin were using the language as a means to 'humiliate unionists'. In a later rally, a group of children who attend Irish language schools in Northern Ireland stood on the steps of Stormont under a large banner asking, 'Arlene, an náiríonn mo chearta thú?', meaning, 'Arlene, do my rights humiliate you?'

Sinn Féin politician Conor Murphy summarised the mood of many nationalists when he told the party's conference that year:

> They say giving Irish speakers basic rights would lead to cultural domination. I often reflect on that as I drive up to Stormont, as I cross Queen Victoria Bridge, travel along the Prince of Wales Avenue, past the statue of Carson and into a building with Britannia on the roof and on occasions not one but two union flags and then meet the statue of Craigavon at the top of the stairs.

He added sardonically: 'I think to myself, we really need to do more to reflect unionist political culture in this place.'

For many nationalists, therefore, the Irish Language Act became something of a TARDIS which contained within it a much broader collection of facets of the Catholic/nationalist community's culture. The DUP's opposition towards the language came to encapsulate the many different slights against nationalist culture which undermined the power-sharing principle of parity between the nationalist and unionist communities. In 1998, many nationalists had been content merely to have a seat at the table, but now it had grown to assert itself more and was questioning what power-sharing really meant. The Good Friday Agreement gave equal status to the British and Irish identities, and now the nationalist community was determined to see that principle followed through to the letter. Sinn Féin therefore insisted that the DUP agreeing to Northern Ireland having an Irish Language Act was now a red-line issue on which it would not be moved. Stormont, they said, could not return without it.

DEMOGRAPHIC SHIFTS

The wider backdrop to this political fallout comes in the form of demographic flux. The very formation of the northern state a century before had been decided on the basis of establishing a majority unionist region to ensure popular support for Northern Ireland remaining in the UK. Therefore, throughout the history of the state there has been a considerable focus on the demographic makeup of the region, with careful discussion of how many nationalists and unionists are born each year. For cultural reasons, Catholics tend to have larger families on average than Protestants do, resulting in a higher birth rate in Catholic areas of Northern Ireland. This has led to the crude expression in some nationalist areas that they will 'outbreed' the unionist community towards a united Ireland, as, if birth rates continue at their current rate, nationalists will outnumber unionists within a few generations.

As we saw at the 2017 Stormont election, unionism's once sizeable majority is shrinking. There is now just 0.2 per cent difference in the vote share between Sinn Féin and the DUP. It is not unthinkable that within the next decade Sinn Féin will be the largest party at Stormont, taking the First Minister title alongside a DUP politician as Deputy First Minister. That in and of itself should not be cause for concern for the unionist population, as the power-sharing Parliament will still in all political and legal aspects see them as equal, just as nationalists are now. However, over the course of the past decade, the DUP have hyped up the position of being the largest party as meaning they are far superior to the smaller grouping and so can use their position to dominate proceedings at Stormont. They have used this as an excuse to undertake a number of arguably petty swipes at Sinn Féin and play to their own supporters' desire to see the party humiliated and treated as lesser. Their behaviour as the largest party now will make it much harder for them to adapt to the secondary position they are likely to soon inhabit if the demographic changes continue. This may explain why the DUP have come to intensify some of their attacks on nationalist culture and insistence on the right of unionist culture to be dominant, as a kneejerk reaction to their increasing insecurity about unionism's position in Northern Ireland society.

DUP–CONSERVATIVE PACT

Against the backdrop of the power-sharing crisis at Stormont and repeated unsuccessful negotiations between the DUP and Sinn Féin, in April 2017, a surprise general election was announced across the Irish Sea as Prime Minister Theresa May sought to increase her small majority in the House of Commons. As she made the announcement, a triumph for the Tories seemed all but inevitable as her party looked set to issue a bruising defeat to a divided Labour Party still plagued by infighting under new leader Jeremy Corbyn. All May had to do was cobble together a convincing election campaign over the six-week election period and emerge victorious with a newly strengthened mandate, whereupon she could then enter Brexit talks with the EU.

As the history books show, what should have been a straightforward and almost pre-determined election turned out to be anything but. The election exposed May's leadership style as dithering and lacklustre in comparison to her quietly confident premiership, while pro-Corbyn grassroots groups such as Momentum, which had helped bolster his leadership bid, proved effective election campaigning machines. May's decision to hold an election she didn't necessarily need turned out to be one of the most hubristic political own-goals in modern memory.

On 8 June, I was at the Belfast election count when the 10 p.m. exit poll was announced. The poll is collated over the course of election day as voters exit the count centres and is kept top-secret until the polling stations have closed. In order not to influence the outcome of the vote, journalists are forbidden from transmitting the exit poll's predicted result until 10 p.m. The poll is seldom wrong and is almost always the strongest indicator of the result to come.

As the clock edged towards 10 p.m. in Belfast, election counters were milling around looking bored in front of their empty long wooden benches, waiting for boxes of ballot papers to arrive from the polling stations so their furious counting could begin. In the café, nervous election candidates and their aides had begun arriving in the hall and were queuing up for the first of the many coffees they would have as they braced themselves for an all-nighter. In the press section, journalists were hunkering down for another long night and grumbling about having to do it all again so soon after the March snap election to save power-sharing.

When the exit poll was announced, murmurs began to elicit a low hum across the centre as the news spread. The journalists were first to spot it and were soon pointing incredulously with wide eyes at their smartphones, beckoning each other over and shaking their heads in collective disbelief. Catching the mood in the room shift, the political aides soon began checking their phones too and urgently ushering over their candidates to brief them. According to the exit poll, Theresa May had not only failed to increase the Conservatives' majority: she had actually lost it. The poll could not accurately predict exactly by how much, but it appeared to be little more than a slither. A hung parliament was in the pipeline.

The outcome seemed so ironic that at this point in the evening few believed it. Election polls were always getting things wrong, a huddle of journalists concurred in the corner. Just look at how polls got the Brexit referendum outcome wrong and failed to predict Trump's election, they asserted.

But over the course of the night, as the results trickled in, it was clear that, on this occasion at least, the polls were bang on. By midnight, the naysayers could only look at their laptops in silent incredulity as the results from Britain trickled in. By the early hours of the morning, the Belfast count would normally be home only to hardened hacks and bleary-eyed politicians. But tonight, the place was electric with anticipation. The numbers being projected in Britain suggested that Theresa May's government was short by about a dozen or so MPs. The Liberal Democrats, still reeling from their bruising time in coalition with the Conservatives between 2010 and 2015, flatly ruled out the possibility of another coalition. That left only one realistic option for a coalition partner: Northern Ireland's DUP.

In the Belfast vote count centre, the DUP's politicians and aides could scarcely contain their glee as they appeared just a whisker away from power at Westminster. There were misty eyes, incredulous head shakes and grateful eyes rolled up to heaven in thanks. In the early hours, Arlene Foster arrived to a scene of nervous energy and triumph. The DUP had secured ten MPs, enough that if they pledged their support to the Conservatives, Theresa May could stay on as Prime Minister by bridging the gap that stood between her and a parliamentary majority.

Across the Irish Sea, however, this news was met with considerably less enthusiasm. Few journalists, never mind members of the public, had so much as heard of the DUP. Throughout the election campaign, as with every general election before it, Northern Ireland had not so much been an afterthought as not thought of at all. In analyses of polling data published by *The Times*, for instance, Northern Ireland did not receive its own party breakdown but was instead relegated to being eighteen 'other' MPs, a grey blob on the electoral map. Similarly, in televised debates, Northern Ireland did not receive a mention beyond attacks on Corbyn over the fact he was involved in talks with alleged IRA members during the peace process. This narrative meant many TV producers felt they had ticked the 'Northern Irish box' in their broadcasts by at least mentioning the region. However, it amounted to little more than an exercise of faux outrage on behalf of people in Northern Ireland and had no bearing on contemporary politics, focusing as it did on Corbyn's alleged links to Republicans some thirty years earlier.

On the ground, however, there was little interest in the claims against Corbyn, as people here with more awareness of the peace process know that English politicians from both the Conservatives and Labour engaged in talks with the IRA throughout the conflict. Northern Irish viewers therefore only saw the region mentioned in the context of right-wing English people expressing what many suspected was insincere outrage ostensibly on their behalf in order to play party politics. Meanwhile, issues of contemporary concern to people in Northern Ireland, which included the collapse of the peace process, ongoing higher rates of poverty, the ban on marriage equality and the recent arrests of women 'committing abortions', went unmentioned in the national media.

After decades of turning a blind eye to Northern Ireland, many in Britain now desperately searched online to find out the identity of this mysterious party who would now be at the centre of power. More often than not, they did not like what they saw. The DUP's previous homophobic comments and policies were circulated online, along with their support of Northern Ireland's abortion ban and the news that many of their politicians believe in Creationism. Confusion had been replaced with shock and now, for many British people, deep concern.

In England, a slight hysteria appeared to take hold as some politicians warned that the DUP could use their position in the new pact with the Conservatives to try to bring their policies to the rest of the UK. Former Northern Ireland Secretary and Conservative MP Owen Paterson told Radio 4 that it was possible the DUP would seek to now reduce abortion term limits in England. Scottish Conservative Ruth Davidson sought personal assurances from Theresa May that the DUP would not be allowed to enact homophobic policies in England, Scotland and Wales.

The deal had an odd and at times contradictory impact on the DUP's ego. On the one hand, the fluke scenario was a dream come true for the party. It thrust them into the centre of national government, thereby reminding the whole country that, legally and politically speaking, Belfast is just as British as Birmingham or Brighton. In particular, the nature of the hung parliament meant that the DUP were conscious that they were not only going into power in Westminster but doing so at a critical time to save the nation as a whole from uncertainty. This no doubt bolstered the DUP's sense of Britishness.

Yet, on the other hand, the deal with the Conservatives undercut the DUP's sense of Britishness in many ways. Prior to the pact with the Tories, politicians in the DUP will have been under little illusion that many in Britain knew who they were or what they stood for. However, many will have worked on the tacit assumption that if people in Britain had been familiar with them, they would have supported them and their cause. The party's British identity and desire to maintain and enhance Northern Ireland's links with Britain is at the core of their ethos and approach to politics. The clear revulsion with which many people in Britain responded to the sudden revelation of the DUP's policies must therefore have been rather bruising. The party became something of a national joke on panel shows and stand-up routines across the country, while social media flooded with memes mocking them, and newspaper cartoonists painted gruff ogres and thugs draped in Union flags and Orange Order sashes. It was clear that the DUP's British identity was not a form of Britishness recognised by many on 'the mainland' and indeed many sought to actively denounce and distance themselves from it. This exposed some of the tensions inherent within unionist/loyalist identity in Northern Ireland, where Britishness can be so highly performative that it becomes almost a parody of the national identity that exists elsewhere in the UK. Ironically, the more some loyalists aspire to perform Britishness, the more they achieve a high camp, almost burlesque form of it. While this tension has always existed at a low level in Northern Ireland, in the days immediately after the June 2017 election it became glaring obvious and may have caused considerable wounding to DUP politicians' sense of identity and self-esteem.

Although the DUP had already said they would enter a deal with the Conservatives to partner in a government together, the party was still shrewd enough to recognise that Theresa May's vulnerable position following her devastating election meant further opportunities could come to them if they played the game right. They coyly said they could not agree outright to the partnership but would need to get something in return. In true Northern Irish style, a period of intense negotiation followed. Many in the Conservative Party may have assumed that due to the DUP's perceived backward views they were somehow ignorant or daft politicians;

this was a profound error. As anyone in Northern Ireland could tell you, while many might criticise the DUP for holding views which mainstream society considers ignorant or backwards, the party are no one's fools, and comprise many highly intelligent and skilled negotiators. While many in England might have assumed they were dealing with provincial country bumpkins they could walk over, the party's politicians were in fact shrewd, smart and ruthless tacticians who had been raised on a diet of blunt negotiations. Unlike in the rest of the UK, such vigorous talks are the bread and butter of Northern Irish politics due to the unique nature of power-sharing. The ball was firmly in the DUP's court.

In the end, the DUP emerged with a deal to bring £1.5 billion to Northern Ireland. The extra cash would be spent on a range of projects including infrastructure, high-speed internet and the health system. In return, the DUP's ten MPs would use their ten votes to support May's government on a number of crucial votes and therefore ensure her minority government could limp on. May's government was keen to insist this was not a coalition government as had been conducted between the Conservatives and Lib Dems in 2010–15 but instead a confidence-and-supply arrangement. The difference was that the DUP would not receive ministries in the Cabinet or have a say in non-Northern Ireland affairs. Nevertheless, the DUP's ten politicians were triumphant and returned home to Northern Ireland to parade their success in bringing home the £1.5 billion cheque and what they saw as even greater British links.

However, the deal was less well received in Britain. The UK had been subjected to years of austerity as the Conservatives insisted the 2008 recession required public spending to be slashed. During the June 2017 election, Prime Minister Theresa May and Home Secretary Amber Rudd had uttered one of the most striking sound bites of the campaign when they told debate audiences: 'There is no magic money tree.' After years of building their economic policy around the logic of tight public spending and responsible finance, the same party were now handing a £1.5 billion cheque to the DUP to save their own skin. To many English voters, the hypocrisy was blatant. Attitudes towards the DUP risked hardening further, as many in Britain felt they had been fleeced by opportunists.

IMPACT ON POWER-SHARING NEGOTIATIONS

While the focus for much of June had been on London as the DUP–Conservative pact was hammered out, dust continued to gather on the empty pews in the Stormont chamber. While the DUP had apparently managed to walk all over the Conservatives in their negotiations, they had been unsuccessful in replicating the same manoeuvres with their considerably more seasoned sparring partners in Sinn Féin.

Indeed, one consequence of the election, which was considerably less dramatic than the DUP–Conservative pact but no less important, had been Northern Ireland's own results. The moderate political parties, the SDLP and the UUP, had been obliterated. The nationalist SDLP had lost every one of their three seats at Westminster, while the unionist UUP had lost their one seat. Northern Ireland's only independent MP, Lady Sylvia Hermon, had held on to her seat by the skin of her teeth as her previously healthy majority plummeted. As with the March 2017 snap election to save power-sharing, the voters had not been put off the DUP and Sinn Féin's obstinacy in refusing to return to partnership but had in fact rallied round them further. This no doubt emboldened both parties as they knew the stalemate at Stormont had, if anything, boosted their standing. The chances of either backing down now decreased dramatically. Neither party was being punished by their electorate for continuing to play hardball.

Furthermore, the DUP's deal in Westminster had to a certain extent reduced the importance of Stormont to them, as they wielded more political clout than ever before. Now they were at the heart of national government, the prospect of devolved government at Stormont dulled in comparison. The DUP's deal with the Conservatives would of course be merely temporary, lasting a few years at most, but while it was in place the DUP had considerably less of an incentive to reach a deal at Stormont. For them, the centre of power had shifted across the Irish Sea.

However, the pact did not only strengthen the DUP's hand but also that of Sinn Féin. Seeing the backlash and horror with which the DUP were met in Britain delighted many in Sinn Féin. It not only proved, in their eyes, many of their arguments about the DUP's out-of-step Britishness and their assertion that Northern Ireland was not as integral to the union as the DUP liked to think, but also won them many new allies. News bulletins and newspapers across the UK were full of anti-DUP stories, expressing horror and bewilderment that such a party could exist and hold such controversial views. Sinn Féin had spent the best part of the previous decade arguing as much, while seeing their assertions dismissed as sectarianism. In many ways, the backlash to the DUP throughout the month of June was priceless propaganda for Sinn Féin's cause. The UK's new introduction to the DUP brought a newfound sympathy for nationalists and their perspective.

Theresa May's unexpected general election and the fluke result appeared to have scuppered the already diminishing chances of a power-sharing deal. Both parties had found their egos massaged, for opposite reasons. Neither was now in the mood to compromise. Half-hearted talks continued at irregular intervals at Stormont but with no breakthrough.

NEGOTIATION

Further deadlines were set for the DUP and Sinn Féin to reach a deal to return to power-sharing in the autumn. To the surprise of few in Northern Ireland, these new deadlines came and went just as those before them had done. Throughout much of this period, I was based in the little press hub inside Stormont's basement. Initially, there were intense negotiations between Sinn Féin and the DUP which would take place in private behind closed doors, before a sudden media skirmish when they would give briefing updates in the Great Hall. After a while, though, the updates were the same: no Irish language agreement and no resolution. Soon, the time that would elapse between each briefing grew longer, before eventually the briefings dried up altogether.

Northern Ireland's Parliament buildings are an unusual place at the best of times. They are built in mock-Grecian grandeur, as, in the nation's early days, unionists sought to give the air that the fledgling state had existed much longer than it really had, in order to lend it a sense of authority and tradition. However, the effect was largely lost and the white marble building has never quite had the same gravitas as the Houses of Parliament in Westminster, being both newer and deprived of the same cultural position in public imagination. In the first few months of the power-sharing collapse, the corridors at Stormont were largely empty, with civil servants long dispatched on loan to other Parliaments and parliamentary aides reallocated to party offices. The building became eerily quiet. Where once more than a hundred politicians and their staff stalked the hallways, running to vote on bills, debate, legislate and hear pitches from charities and lobbyists, I now found myself capable of walking from the tip of one sprawling wing to the other, often not meeting a soul in the ten-minute stretch. In the canteen, chefs continued to cook dinners for politicians who did not turn up, and could only roll their eyes exasperatedly. The occasional sound of chatter would spark optimism, only to find on closer inspection that this was not a group of politicians turning up for work but tourists come to take selfies in the chamber. Security staff appeared startled when I would clock in each morning; often I was the only person they'd seen walk through the staff entrance for a while. I began to feel like a mad woman in a Victorian novel, rattling around an empty old estate utterly demented.

Civil servants were keeping departments running as well as possible. However, in the absence of any government ministers to make decisions or announce policies, they sought to carry out the spirit of the policies announced by the last post holder and avoided making decisions on any controversial issues. This naturally resulted in a serious democratic deficit, as none of the civil servants now running the government departments were elected, and they could not be held democratically accountable for any of their decisions. What was meant to be a temporary modus operandi soon became the norm and backlash was forthcoming. In September, civil servants at the Department for Infrastructure announced approval of a planning application for a controversial quarry to be built. The quarry had been rejected by many local residents, who had run a high-profile campaign against it, and the government minister responsible, Mark H. Durkan, had in 2015 announced he had rejected the proposal. Now, however, an anonymous press release announced after nine months without a minister that the department had decided to give it the green light after all. Mr Durkan said he was 'disappointed and angered' at the decision. Concern about who was running Northern Ireland grew, as many feared faceless civil servants were not appropriate gatekeepers for a democratic institution.

In November, as it was close to a year without a government sitting at Stormont and no politicians had been in place to pass a Budget, Northern Ireland began to run out of money. Education and healthcare funding was on the brink of drying up, sending the region into chaos as state services careened to a close, and civil society would soon risk breaking down. Finally, unable to move the goalposts once more to allow another deadline extension, James Brokenshire stood up in the House of Commons on 13 November and introduced a bill for the Budget to be passed in Westminster instead. This would stop society from descending into chaos and mean that hospitals and schools would still receive funding. However, he was keen to stress that 'this is not tantamount to direct rule'. London would pass the Budget but would not take over full running of Northern Ireland as it had during the Troubles and during the short-term blips in the first decade after the Good Friday Agreement. Technically, no one would be in charge of Northern Ireland, as Westminster would take over finances but nothing else, meaning no new laws could be passed on health, education or equality, which would have been possible if the London government had agreed to implement direct rule. This left Northern Ireland with something of a 'zombie Parliament', lingering on in a state between existence and non-existence, but most definitely veering towards the latter.

On that historic day, as Northern Ireland's Budget was presented to Westminster, the chamber was largely empty and the primarily vacant rows of green benches to which Brokenshire made his address were a jarring visual symbol of how far Northern Ireland had slipped down the UK's list of priorities.

HOPE FOR AN AGREEMENT

Suddenly, in February 2018, the mood at Stormont changed. Glimpses of Sinn Féin and DUP negotiators were spotted scuttling along once-empty corridors into various meeting rooms dotted around the Parliament building. In the evenings, where once Stormont was plunged into darkness as the security and canteen staff clocked off, upstairs meeting rooms were still flooded with light as negotiators worked into the night. Murmurings began that a deal may have been reached, or was on the cusp of being finally signed off on. Both sides were tight-lipped, refusing to respond to speculation and in so doing only fuelling it further. In January, a new Northern Ireland Secretary had been appointed following Brokenshire's resignation due to ill health. Karen Bradley was appointed to replace him, prompting hope that a fresh figure could help inject some energy into the stalemate.

On 8 February, the *Belfast Telegraph* published an article titled 'Stormont deal imminent', which reported that an agreement had been reached. A source involved in the talks had told the newspaper that 'the bones of a deal are definitely there', adding, 'We may not have an agreement within hours but we are potentially on the cusp of something within the week.' The *Belfast Telegraph* is a staunchly unionist and generally pro-DUP newspaper, making it likely that their source was the DUP, who appeared to have pre-emptively leaked the deal as a means of preparing their voters for an imminent announcement. The newspaper reported that the deal was based on:

- Arlene Foster returning as First Minister (representing a climb-down for Sinn Féin on their previous demands that she stand aside following the 'cash for ash' scandal);
- The DUP not having to agree to vote for same-sex marriage but symbolically accepting it would be likely to pass as they had lost the numbers they needed to block it using the Petition of Concern veto (representing a win for Sinn Féin, who support same-sex marriage);

- Creating a new mechanism to make it harder for one party to pull down power-sharing (representing a win for the DUP, who had argued that Sinn Féin had been wrong to pull down power-sharing and feared another collapse could happen in the future).

However, the article did not contain any details about the thorny issue of the Irish language and whether or not a compromise had been reached on it. The matter had been talked up for some time as a red-line issue for both parties, meaning any viable deal would have to address the issue.

Following the *Belfast Telegraph* report, the flurry of activity around Stormont continued to escalate. Satellite trucks rolled up Stormont's long drive and journalists poured back into the lobby of the Great Hall, keeping an eager eye on any sign of movement. News bulletins and talk shows were full of speculation about the likely deal. Tight-lipped negotiators on both sides refused to comment either way, but their increased presence late into the night for several days appeared to give credence to the growing speculation. That weekend, Sinn Féin were holding a special Ard Fheis (conference) for the official retirement of party president Gerry Adams. Mr Adams had been at the helm of the party for thirty-four years, making him one of the longest-serving politicians in the UK and Ireland. He was closely linked to Republicans throughout the Troubles and is widely understood in Northern Ireland to have been a member of the IRA, although he strongly denies the allegation. The 69-year-old had announced the previous November that he was to retire after four decades on the front line of Republicanism. His replacement, Mary Lou McDonald, was a marked difference from her predecessor and represented a considerable change of direction for the party. McDonald was the first woman to lead the party in its modern incarnation. In contrast to the party's working-class roots, she was brought up in a middle-class suburb of Dublin where she was educated at private school and Ireland's most prestigious university, Trinity College. McDonald was also a Southerner, in a party dominated by people from north of the border. Most crucially, she had no associations with the IRA and had not been involved in the Troubles conflict. As Adams officially handed over to McDonald at the Ard Fheis that Saturday, hopes for a deal increased further. Many of the DUP's core misgivings about Sinn Féin stem from the party's connections to the IRA and a particular reticence about Adams. By contrast, McDonald was seen by many as a much more acceptable face of Republicanism, prompting hope that the deadlock might finally be broken and an agreement could be reached to return to power-sharing. Similarly, within Sinn Féin there appeared to be greater focus on achieving a deal, perhaps as McDonald knew that reaching an agreement could be the first success of her leadership and bolster her position with the party.

The following Monday, 12 February, Theresa May visited Belfast to meet with the parties and Taoiseach Leo Varadkar. At that stage, it seemed the agreement was all but signed off on, as it was unlikely that the Prime Minister, who had taken an extremely hands-off approach to talks thus far, would make the trip unless a deal had been struck. As May and Varadkar posed for amicable photocalls and had press briefings on the Stormont estate, the familiar theatrics that tend to pre-empt an announcement in Northern Ireland politics were being put in motion.

Forty-eight hours later, the DUP stunned everyone as they announced the talks process had collapsed and the deal was off. In a statement, party leader Arlene Foster said: 'We have reached an impasse ... In our view there is no current prospect of these discussions leading to an executive being formed.' She went on to call for the London government to 'set a budget and start making policy decisions about our schools, hospitals and infrastructure'.

It is unclear and hotly disputed what happened in that intervening 48-hour period. Both the DUP and Sinn Féin have differing versions of events. It is possible that only the two parties will know for certain what occurred. A draft deal later leaked to journalists Eamonn Mallie and Brian Rowan stated that the DUP and Sinn Féin had reached an agreement. The leaked text stated that the parties had agreed to:

- an Irish (Respecting Languages and Diversity) Bill;
- an Ulster Scots (Respecting Languages and Diversity) Bill;
- a Respecting Languages and Diversity Bill;
- provisions that parties could not collapse power-sharing as easily again and would instead be required to enter a cooling-off and arbitration period;
- reform of the Petition of Concern, to make it harder for individual parties to veto or block single issues;
- the introduction of a committee to help the power-sharing parties to work together better, including a system to flag concerns before they escalated.

This draft agreement represented considerable concessions and successes for both parties. For Sinn Féin, the party had succeeded in achieving their beloved Irish Language Act, as well as reform of the Petition of Concern, making it more likely that same-sex marriage could be passed in the future. (Although the DUP have now lost the numbers they need to trigger the veto, a number of hardline UUP politicians opposed to marriage equality have said they will join them in any such vote to ensure it is still blocked.) By contrast, Sinn Féin had backed down on demanding money to fund legacy inquests into cold-case killings from the Troubles and appeared to have also accepted Foster returning as First Minister. They had also agreed to a mechanism which would make it much harder for them to pull out of power-sharing again.

On the DUP's side, the party had backed down on a major issue by agreeing to an Irish Language Act. However, they had secured provisions for the Ulster Scots language (another traditional language spoken by a small number of people in the unionist community), as well as a general 'respect and diversity' bill, which appeared to be little more than a smokescreen to hide their agreement to an Irish Language Act by allowing the DUP to claim it was really a general language bill (a small distinction, but one which would help the party save face with their electorate). The DUP had also succeeded by not having to agree to release legacy inquest funds, to agree to Foster standing down or to agree to passing same-sex marriage (although reform of the Petition of Concern meant it was likely their ability to veto the legislation would end in the future).

The document therefore appeared to be a reasonable text which did not amount to a triumph or a defeat for either side, but instead was based on some modest victories and concessions from both the DUP and Sinn Féin. It appears that this is the draft that was circulating in mid-February, as May and Varadkar posed smilingly within Stormont House. Why, then, did the DUP dramatically collapse the talks process on 14 February in their surprise Valentine's Day break-up with Sinn Féin?

It appears that after the DUP had agreed the draft text outlined above, they began their usual process of preparing their grassroots and party members for the deal before it was announced in order to ensure it received wider support. However, when they did so they were shocked by the intense outrage with which they were met. While the DUP's politicians were willing to accept the Irish language legislation, their voters and party members were not. Sam McBride, political editor of the unionist newspaper *The Newsletter* and one of the most respected authorities on political unionism in Northern Ireland, said in an article for the *i* newspaper that unionist sources had told him the Orange Order had gotten wind of the compromise and begun a campaign to make it clear they could support no such thing: 'The worshipful masters of several Orange lodges were using text messages to organise their members to lobby the DUP and ... DUP councillors' phones had been "red hot".' Indeed, in the intervening days, radio programmes and social media had been flooded by staunch loyalists expressing their horror at any prospect of an Irish Language Act. In light of grassroots unionism's clear objections to the prospect of the draft deal, it appears the DUP were spooked and suddenly pulled out of what they had preliminarily agreed with Sinn Féin, issuing Foster's 14 February statement saying talks had come to end without resolve.

For their part, the DUP have denied this. Their position is that the draft document that was leaked was one of a number of draft texts exchanged at the time but that just because something has been written down doesn't mean it has been signed off on. Sinn Féin have insisted the draft text was much more advanced and serious than that and claim the DUP had given them various assurances that they were about to sign off on it. Indeed, subsequent screenshots of emails between the two parties, also leaked to journalist Eamonn Mallie, appear to back up Sinn Féin's version of events, as they depict senior DUP figures discussing the agreement as being a draft text they had reached together.

So why were the DUP able to accept the deal but their party members were not? It appears that the DUP's leadership and senior politicians badly misjudged the strength of feeling against the Irish language among their own members. To a certain extent, it was a problem of their own making. For the previous year, the DUP had been justifying their hardline stance against Sinn Féin by making extreme and dramatic statements against the language. In repeated press conferences and media appearances, senior DUP figures had been seen stating that an Irish Language Act was completely unacceptable as it represented a real harm to Protestant/ unionist culture and would amount to a humiliation their community could never tolerate. When, after a year of talks, they came to realise a deal was dependent on them showing some compromise, party politicians such as Arlene Foster were able to stomach it, but the grassroots, who had been fed on a diet of fierce anti-Irish language rhetoric, were not. The DUP had simply talked themselves up to too high a point from which to stage a dignified climbdown.

This issue was further compounded by the DUP–Conservative pact, which had seriously undermined Foster's authority as party leader. As a result of the deal, the centre of power in her party had shifted away from her. Foster is an MLA, but not an MP. Normal political dynamics see Stormont as the centre of political power, meaning MLAs have greater authority than MPs in Northern Ireland. However, the unexpected 2017 general election result had elevated her ten MPs, giving them more power and influence than she did. This undermined her position within the party and may have made it more difficult for her to exercise discipline and control, in turn making it harder for her to insist that her party accept the terms of the draft deal.

After seeming on the cusp of reaching an agreement, a deal now seemed further away than ever before. Both parties have been bruised by the experience, with Sinn Féin now appearing to be leaking internal documents to the media and undermining the DUP's ability to trust them, while the DUP's internal party wrangling and power struggles have been exposed to the public in a raw and unflattering way.

IMPACT OF POWER-SHARING COLLAPSE

At the time of writing, Northern Ireland has just marked its first anniversary without a government. There is little reason at present to hold any optimism for its imminent return.

The Good Friday Agreement and power-sharing are inextricably linked. In many ways power-sharing is the foundation of the entire document, providing the stable base that makes all else, from passport rights to Anglo-Irish relations, possible. In November 2017, commenting on the power-sharing collapse, the Republic of Ireland's Foreign Affairs Minister Simon Coveney said that the Good Friday Agreement without a functioning Parliament at Stormont was 'like ripping the heart out of' the document.

For the generations who grew up after the ceasefire, power-sharing was a fact of life. Recent events suggest such confidence was unfounded. It would no more have occurred to my peers or I that power-sharing could simply stop any more than someone could just announce that the moon was being dismantled or the sea rolled up and taken away; implacable features of the landscape that we might not always notice but which provided the background landscape of our lives.

It is hard to identify the exact reasons for the demise of power-sharing. But, looking back, it seems that at the core was a growing resentment within the DUP at having to treat nationalists as true equals, as nationalist politicians grew less apologetic about demanding equal treatment. From the perspective of nationalists, it is perhaps the case that power-sharing never succeeded in cementing a true respect among 'both sides' but instead fostered a tactical tolerance which became unsustainable as the nationalists' power grew and hardline unionists panicked. Conversely, the unionist perspective would assert that their community had made many sacrifices to reach out to the nationalist community (not least by agreeing to go into political partnership with convicted terrorists), but these sacrifices had gone unappreciated by nationalists, who seemed to them to be hell-bent on constantly wanting more, edging them closer and closer to their ultimate goal of dismantling the state that unionists hold dear.

Ironically, it may be due to a growing confidence in the peace process that this collapse was possible. During the early days of power-sharing, such a meltdown would have brought with it the credible risk of a return to violence. However, violence has been gone from civil society in Northern Ireland for so long now that it is unlikely to return – at least not in the all-consuming way that caused a breakdown of everyday life during the Troubles. Whereas in 1998, the alternative to Stormont was a civil war, this 'incentive', to put it crudely, no longer exists. While a fallout between the political parties once brought with it the real chance that multiple lives could be lost in a backlash of violence beyond Stormont's walls, now the repercussion is having to hold an awkward press conference or missing out on getting to be a government minister. Such understated consequences are characteristic of most normal or non-conflict societies. Perhaps Northern Ireland's most tragic burden, that sense of constant gnawing dread, had been the invisible force propelling power-sharing forward all this time. Once the terror left, the momentum was gone.

In terms of political process, a limited number of options now lie ahead. The parties can continue to try to broker a deal. At present, it is hard to see how any such agreement can be found, as relations between the DUP and Sinn Féin lie in tatters following the February 2018 negotiating debacle. The Irish language issue has been talked up by both 'sides' to the point that it is too politically toxic for either side to make any compromise. Both parties have made direct and absolutist pronouncements that their return to power-sharing depends on an Irish language existing or not. A deal at this stage will require an embarrassing and politically damaging climbdown from one or both of them. However, it must be said that throughout Northern Ireland's political history the two 'sides' have both managed to bridge bigger gaps than those which lie between them at present. Not least of all in 1998, when both nationalists and unionists managed to make major sacrifices in order to broker the Good Friday Agreement deal. Politics in Northern Ireland has often stalled when politicians seem to have backed themselves irrevocably into corners, only for a daring escape to be managed.

In the absence of an agreement and a power-sharing government at Stormont, the British government has a statutory obligation to begin direct rule from Westminster. Thus far, No. 10 has declined to do so, with Secretaries of State Brokenshire and Bradley insisting they still hold faith that a deal can still be struck after more negotiations between the two parties. Their optimism is being shared by fewer and fewer people. At the time of writing, Westminster has stopped even setting deadlines for an agreement to be reached, after close to a dozen such dates have come and gone unheeded. In the meantime, Northern Ireland's budget continues to be set via MPs at Westminster and spent by faceless civil servants who are not democratically accountable to the electorate. In the absence of politicians to set laws, Northern Ireland falls further and further behind other parts of the world and is unable to respond to changing issues it faces. It is hard to see how much longer this vacuum can continue before Westminster has to accept a deal is not forthcoming and impose direct rule in order to give people a sense of stability.

However, Westminster's ability to rule Northern Ireland has been fundamentally compromised by the Conservatives' agreement with the DUP. The Good Friday Agreement commits the UK government to conducting itself on Northern Ireland matters with 'rigorous impartiality'. As Theresa May's minority government is currently dependent on the ongoing support of the DUP's ten MPs, claims to impartiality seem tenuous at best. Many people in Northern Ireland, particularly in the Catholic/nationalist community, would fear that direct rule from Westminster would not mean Conservative rule but effectively Conservative–DUP rule and would subsequently be far from impartial. Indeed, both Sinn Féin and the SDLP have demanded that rather than direct rule from Britain alone, they will only accept joint rule of Northern Ireland between the Republic and the UK. Similarly, this is a situation unionists cannot accept as they argue the Republic is a foreign country who cannot be allowed to have any say in internal UK matters.

Further issues are likely to make direct rule an unattractive option for Westminster. Not only are most civil servants and politicians focused on the all-consuming task of EU withdrawal, but direct rule would require them to act on a number of controversial and thankless issues which they are likely to want to avoid – namely, same-sex marriage and abortion. The UK government has long argued that it cannot intervene to legalise marriage equality or overturn the abortion ban as the matters are the responsibility of the devolved government. However, under direct rule, attention would likely turn to No. 10 to finally act. Many English politicians will be nervous of doing so, for fear of fundamentally altering the relationship between the devolved regions and central government, as well as causing social upheaval in Northern Ireland's conservative society. Furthermore, as the DUP are the strongest opponents in Northern Ireland to both abortion and same-sex marriage, it is possible that any such moves by the Conservatives could see them use their position in the pact to pull down the minority government in revolt. For these reasons, it is likely that London will want to put off imposing direct rule until it becomes utterly unavoidable.

In the meantime, Northern Ireland's claims to be a democracy grow more and more tenuous. Not only is there no government at Stormont, but great swathes of the population are no longer represented at Westminster either. While the June 2017 general election was most notable for the DUP–Conservative pact it produced, another shift in the political ground occurred which is likely to be just as seismic in the long run. The moderate nationalist party lost every single one of their three MPs, while Sinn Féin surged from four MPs to seven. Sinn Féin are therefore the only nationalist MPs elected to Westminster. Unlike the SDLP, who are moderate nationalists, Sinn Féin operate an abstentionist policy in Westminster. Due to their Republican ideology, they refuse to take their seats, in a rejection of what they consider to be a 'foreign' Parliament. As a result, following the June 2017 general election, nationalists are not represented in Westminster at all and only unionist MPs are present to advocate their perspective. This would be a concerning democratic deficit under most normal circumstances, but particularly so as it coincides with the power-sharing collapse. On previous occasions when Stormont has not been sitting, the argument could be made that Northern Ireland was receiving some democratic representation in Westminster. Now, however, that only applies to the Protestant/unionist community. Northern Ireland's relationship with democracy is currently unhealthy, to put it mildly.

With the local parties unable to reach agreement and the British government unable or unwilling to impose direct rule, it seems that an unexpected third option is emerging. It amounts to partial direct rule, a *via media* whereby the British government will not announce anything so dramatic or controversial as official direct rule, while it is also blatantly ruling directly. It has already begun setting budgets in Westminster and is coming under pressure to legislate in a number of other areas (such as passing a bill to release funding for survivors of institutional child abuse in Northern Ireland) and approve a pay increase for Northern Ireland police. The longer the vacuum at Stormont continues, the more likely it will be that politicians at Westminster feel compelled to act on a number of issues. It may decide to cherry-pick certain non-controversial policy areas on which to intervene. This would have the advantage of maintaining calm among the Northern Ireland population, as they can feel sensible adults are still in charge, without the political chill that could be caused by the official imposition of direct rule or the requirement on the British government to act on controversial policy issues.

Indeed, a strategic decision for the Westminster government may also be to pass Irish language legislation for Northern Ireland. This would take the most toxic political issue off the table at Stormont. It may be possible for Westminster to institute a bill that is tolerable to both sides by passing a watered-down version of Sinn Féin's proposals, with the DUP's proposals for Ulster Scots tied in. This would allow both sides to claim they had 'won' as Sinn Féin could tell their voters they fulfilled their pledge to secure the legislation and the DUP could tell their voters they stood firm on their promise not to vote for it, while also securing some sweeteners for the Ulster Scots-speaking community. This might create an environment in which the two parties could reconvene negotiations and gain momentum for a deal.

As has been outlined, none of the options for the future governance of Northern Ireland represents a clear or controversy-free solution to the current political crisis. Whichever steps are taken are likely to cause dissent locally. In February 2018, polling company Lucid Talk conducted a survey of Northern Ireland voters and what they wished to see happen next following the collapse of power-sharing negotiations. Unsurprisingly, the responses were divided on the traditional Orange and Green lines. Among respondents who described themselves as unionists, 83.3 per cent back direct rule being introduced, with 14.2 per cent backing further negotiations between the DUP and Sinn Féin and a mere 2.5 per cent backing the Republic and the UK ruling Northern Ireland jointly. Among respondents who described themselves as nationalists, the most popular option was the Republic and UK ruling Northern Ireland jointly, with 73.5 per cent support; 22.8 per cent backed more negotiations taking place and just 3.7 per cent backed direct rule from London.

*　*　*

Addressing the House of Commons in March 2018, just weeks ahead of the twentieth anniversary of the Good Friday Agreement, Northern Ireland Secretary Karen Bradley told MPs that the pending milestone would be a rather 'hollow celebration' due to the power-sharing collapse. Indeed, of all the present challenges faced by the Good Friday Agreement at this stage, the current political impasse is perhaps the most concerning. Many will be asking themselves what it says about the current state of the peace process that, twenty years on, the parties cannot agree to govern together. The collapse is a symptom of the ongoing volatility and vulnerability of political processes here, which have not managed to be fully normalised in the intervening two decades. The political issue continuing to divide the two parties – differing views on the status of the Irish language – is symptomatic of the wider ways in which fundamental issues between the two communities have not been truly resolved in Northern Ireland but instead appeared to be set aside with the signing of the Good Friday Agreement.

As Simon Coveney remarked, power-sharing was the 'heart of the Good Friday Agreement' and its greatest achievement as it forged a partnership and mutual understanding between the two communities necessary to bring about peace. However, the politicians have failed to embrace not only the Agreement's technical features but its ethos of inclusion and true partnership. The Agreement gave the parties a blueprint for working together in partnership but if the personalities involved lost the will to make it work, the document could not force them to do so. It was hoped that by requiring the parties to work in partnership, they would develop a mutual respect over time which would bring the peace process to a higher level. Sadly, the current collapse suggests that has not occurred. Rather than assert that the power-sharing collapse amounts to the Good Friday Agreement failing, it may be more accurate to say that the politicians in Northern Ireland have failed the Good Friday Agreement.

CONCLUSION

Twenty years on from the Good Friday Agreement, it is clear that the accord was a defining moment in Northern Ireland's history and a key factor in bringing peace to the region. The text's sophisticated and bold reframing of Northern Ireland's constitutional status was daring and highly imaginative, enabling the establishment of a new political environment that both communities could finally accept. Beyond the words in the text itself, the Agreement's success was bolstered by smart strategic choices, including the decision to hold a referendum soon after the political parties signed it, which meant it gathered unstoppable momentum and engaged not only politicians but the people whose lives it was to affect. As a result, it created an environment in which both communities felt a new and fairer future was possible. The bloodshed of the previous decades largely ceased and something resembling normality was established.

However, the success of the Good Friday Agreement lay in a number of strategic omissions. As we have seen throughout this book, the lack of a process to deal with cold-case murders continues to haunt Northern Ireland. A reductive and male-centred definition of violence also erased many instances of violence against women and ignored how such violence increased and worsened as an indirect result of the conflict. It is likely that if such issues had been addressed in the text of the Agreement, consensus would have been much harder if not impossible to reach, potentially putting the entire process at risk of collapse. Such omissions thus provided short-term successes, but at the expense of long-term stability. It may have been hoped that the Agreement would give Northern Ireland's politicians a basic initial foundation on which they could later build in passing years, once they developed the maturity and experience to make difficult political decisions such as what to do about cold-case murders. However, such a time has not yet come and this glaring omission continues to be a considerable source of pain to victims' families and risks undermining faith in the legal system.

Similarly, Northern Ireland continues to be torn over how to address social justice and equality issues such as LGBT rights and women's rights. As we have seen, the Petition of Concern, along with other protections put in place to protect minority groups, is currently being used as a means of oppression. This violates the spirit of the Good Friday Agreement, but it is made possible by its wording, as the text failed to consider oppression or discrimination on any other axis than traditional Protestant–Catholic lines. However, it is important to retain perspective on this issue, taking into account the historical environment in which the Agreement was signed. In 1998, LGBT rights and gender equality were even more marginalised issues than in the present day and the Agreement's signatories could not have known how the social importance of such issues would increase over the next generation. It is perhaps understandable, therefore, that the Good Friday Agreement did not consider discrimination and prejudice of this kind. However, it is undeniable that these issues are now causing considerable social unrest in Northern Ireland. Despite being a Parliament which is supposedly centred on human rights and equality, Stormont consistently denies rights to many groups which are most vulnerable and often, ironically, uses the Agreement to justify such oppression. The Good Friday Agreement has been outpaced by evolving social attitudes and limited by a failure to challenge discrimination beyond narrow sectarian terms.

Further afield, the Good Friday Agreement risks being overtaken by global politics as the UK embarks on the process of leaving the European Union. In 1998, the UK's membership of the EU was not in doubt, as Eurosceptic politics had yet to take root in popular public imagination in the way they did twenty years on. The Good Friday Agreement could not have anticipated such developments at the time of signature. At its heart is the premise of close cooperation and mutual respect between the two islands, granting the people of Northern Ireland numerous inalienable rights as a result. Insufficient information about what Brexit entails makes it difficult to know at this stage whether it violates the Agreement; however, it certainly risks unsettling the complex web of relations between the UK and the Republic of Ireland at the core of the Agreement. The fresh focus on the border and Northern Ireland's relationship with the Republic has reopened old wounds, particularly among border communities. If the letter of the text is not breached by Brexit, the spirit of it is certainly being tested to its limits throughout the process.

Finally, the power-sharing collapse which began in January 2017 is deeply concerning and poses a number of questions about how far Northern Ireland has come as a society in the twenty years since the Agreement's signing. As we have seen, the precise reasons for the DUP and Sinn Féin's fallout are complex, but its origins lie in the fundamental issue that Northern Ireland remains a deeply divided society. Although the violence has effectively stopped, true harmony or integration has not occurred between the two communities, which continue to live largely separate lives. It may be unfair to call this a failure of the Good Friday Agreement, as the accord could not force the two communities to reach true understanding and respect. The mechanisms put in place by the Agreement did everything possible to facilitate circumstances in which such integration could come about, most notably through mandatory power-sharing at Stormont, which many hoped would lead to such integration and respect developing naturally as the politicians worked alongside each other and their respective communities followed their leadership. However, this has not occurred. While the DUP and Sinn Féin refuse to co-govern, Northern Ireland cannot be said to be a truly normalised society. The Agreement could put the circumstances in place for such relationships to blossom, but no legal text could force the DUP or Sinn Féin to engage in sincere respect for each other. Indeed, in this case we might argue that this situation does not represent a failure of the Good Friday Agreement but instead illustrates how our politicians have failed the Agreement by failing to fully embrace its spirit. Northern Ireland remains a fundamentally divided society in the modern day, as ongoing segregated housing and education shows. Although sectarianism no longer has violent expression, it has in many cases evolved into more 'benign' or socially accepted means. While this is infinitely preferable to the dark days of the conflict, it cannot be said to be the mark of a truly healed society.

In conclusion, twenty years on from the Good Friday Agreement, a number of clear deficiencies in the accord have become apparent. It is a far from perfect text. However, it has proven a phenomenal success in doing what had previously been thought impossible by ending the horrors of the Troubles and giving new generations a chance to live their lives without the trauma and fear that crippled the region for decades. In this regard, the Agreement's success should not be downplayed. While the Agreement clearly has a number of failings, it has not in itself failed. If adequate and mature political leadership were in place at Stormont, along with an impartial government in London which prioritised the peace process, it would be possible to navigate challenges such as Brexit, to reform the Petition of Concern, and to make difficult decisions about cold-case killings. It might be possible to pass updates or reforms to the Agreement so that it becomes a flexible text capable of adapting to the changed society it has brought about. However, the current DUP–Sinn Féin fallout, the DUP–Conservative pact and Brexiters' disregard of Northern Ireland during EU withdrawal negotiations show the spirit of the Agreement has been violated and it risks being seriously undermined.

Despite this, the Agreement is likely to remain as the cornerstone of post-conflict Northern Ireland. Although it has its critics and detractors, none have been able to suggest a more workable alternative to the Agreement. Even if credible alternative models were suggested, it is difficult to imagine any circumstances in which they would be likely to receive the backing of the two groups in the singular way that the Agreement managed to capture public support. As dust once again gathers on the benches at Stormont, the spirit of compromise that was demonstrated by both sides on 10 April 1998 feels distant and unlikely to be replicated in the present day. Thus, the Agreement is likely to endure as the foundational text for Northern Ireland, imperfect as it is, in the absence of credible alternatives. The Agreement which has shaped this troubled place for the past twenty years will continue to guide Northern Ireland for the foreseeable future.

ABOUT THE AUTHOR

© Jess Lowe

Siobhán Fenton is a political adviser from Belfast. She has worked as a journalist reporting on British, Irish and Northern Irish politics for the UK and Irish media including as a correspondent for *The Independent* and a broadcast journalist for the BBC in Belfast.

INDEX

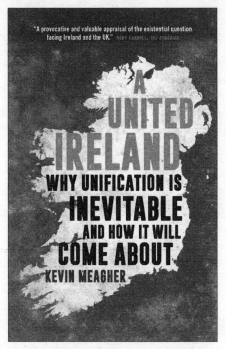